Formal Specification

Springer

London
Berlin
Heidelberg
New York
Barcelona
Hong Kong
Milan
Paris
Santa Clara
Singapore
Tokyo

Nimal Nissanke

Formal Specification

Techniques and Applications

 Springer

Nimal Nissanke, MSc, PhD
Department of Computing Science, University of Reading,
PO Box 225, Whiteknights, Reading RG6 6AY, UK

ISBN 1-85233-002-3 Springer-Verlag London Berlin Heidelberg

British Library Cataloguing in Publication Data
Nissanke, Nimal
    Formal specification : techniques and applications
    1.Software engineering   2.Computer software – Specifications
    1.Title
    005.1'2
ISBN 1852330023

Library of Congress Cataloging-in-Publication Data
A catalog record for this book is available from the Library of Congress

Typesetting: Camera ready by author
Printed and bound at the Athenæum Press Ltd., Gateshead, Tyne & Wear
34/3830-543210 Printed on acid-free paper SPIN 10658790

For Machiko

Preface

Formal specification is the application of mathematics to software specification, that is, for documenting customer requirements on software. The objective is to overcome the lack of precision and ambiguity inherent in informal specifications, arising primarily from the use of natural language as the medium of specification. Ill-specified customer requirements have long been identified as a root cause of many of the problems associated with software, including software not meeting requirements, delays in software delivery, high and unpredictable development costs and problems in maintenance. These are major concerns from the points of view of both the customer and the developer alike. The lack of formality has also been a major concern in the design and implementation phases of software development. As a result, mathematical (formal) methods of software development have been an active area of research, not only in developing approaches and making a case for such methods but also demonstrating, in the process, their viability in practical software engineering.

The above achievements, as well as their benefits to the industry, have been widely recognised by higher educational institutions. As a result, formal methods now form an important part of both undergraduate and postgraduate curricula. Despite the best endeavours of the higher educational institutions, however, the lack of professionals competent in formal methods, at least in sufficient numbers, continues to be a dominant factor in inhibiting the industrial use of formal methods. This situation is not helped by academic backgrounds of students entering higher education, making the successful delivery of formal methods courses a difficult task. As a result, many students are unable to profit from courses in the right manner, limiting their achievements in some cases to an awareness rather than a working knowledge. This book aims to alleviate these difficulties, by placing emphasis on the development of necessary mathematical skills in one particular area, namely formal specification, and at the same time giving the student a wider appreciation of the area. In this way, it is hoped, the book will facilitate greater industrial use of formal methods.

Being one of the first areas in software engineering to have been subjected to a mathematical treatment, formal specification is the most mature area of formal methods. This explains why this book concentrates on formal specification. Despite this, hopefully, the book will make a convincing case for a wider use of mathematics in software development.

A major part of this book is the result of a course given at the University of Reading, U.K. However, the book includes a significant amount of advanced material in order to cater for those wishing to acquire a deeper, and a more comprehensive, understanding. Therefore, the book is also suitable for the postgraduate student and the professional wishing to acquire a broad understanding of formal specification techniques.

Most specification languages consist of two easily identifiable ingredients: a branch of discrete mathematics with a standardised notation as the foundation of the language and an extended mathematical notation devised specially for structuring specifications. In the case of languages such as Z and VDM, the foundation mathematics consist of predicate logic and set theory.

The study of formal specification can be based on the above distinction between the branch of mathematics lying at the foundation of the specification language and the extended notation. This makes the study of standard mathematics and the study of formal specification two fairly distinct separate tasks, allowing a smooth progression from the former to the latter. In this context, most of the standard notation applicable to foundation mathematics can be found in many texts, including [4, 27, 28, 43, 45, 66]. The text [43] is a gentle introduction to the subject and motivates the study according to the needs of formal specification. Separating the two aspects of the specification language does not, however, imply their independence. Confidence in both is essential for developing the skills required in formal specification, both with respect to reading and writing specifications, as well as in mathematical reasoning about specifications, that is, in proof.

This text also deliberately exposes the reader to more than one popular specification formalism, primarily to make the point that, generally, the specifier will often have a choice at his disposal. As in everyday life, the tool must suit the task. The same applies to the language chosen for specification and, therefore, knowledge of other languages may help in making an informed choice. On the other hand, these formalisms are interesting from the mathematical point of view as well. Turning to the formalisms chosen for exposition here, the aim of covering VDM has been to broaden the experience. In the case of algebraic specification, the aim has been both to broaden the experience of specification approaches and deepen the knowledge of mathematics.

Chapter 1 is a general introduction to formal specification and its place in the wider context of software engineering. It is primarily intended as a motivation for the study but it also discusses some important issues concerning formal specification.

Chapters 2–7 are devoted to the specification language Z. Chapter 2 introduces its extended mathematical notation, namely the *Schema Language*, with equal emphasis on its role as a language and its use in specifying state based systems. It is an informal introduction to the language using small examples and follows the style of a reference source; this is because the material concerned is widely available (see the recommended literature). Chapter 3 is a specification case study of reasonable complexity and concerns an airline booking system. It places great emphasis on writing specifications and, in particular, on abstraction, modularisation and specification reuse. Chapter 4 is the first introduction to specification. It uses the party game *Musical Chairs* and the board game *Snakes and Ladders* as small case studies in order to illustrate some ideas in specification, in particular, the decomposition of systems for the purpose of specification. Chapter 5 is another case study, developed with the twin aims of specification and as a vehicle for discussion about proofs in the next chapter. Chapter 6 introduces the reader to different kinds of proofs encountered in formal methods. However, the material in this chapter is geared towards establishing logical implementability of specifications. Chapter 7 is another case study showing the application of a language like Z to a realistic computational task, namely the specification of a network protocol. It also shows how one may use Z as a design medium.

Although they continue to use specification constructs of Z, Chapters 8 and 9 are really aimed at widening our experience to other areas. Chapter 8 introduces an object oriented extension of Z and shows how specifications can be structured differently, namely around objects with a notion of an internal state. Object orientation enables the encapsulation of all the operations relevant to an object as part of its definition and offers other benefits such as the avoidance of information replication relying on inheritance. Chapter 9 illustrates the use of a language such as Z for specifying safety requirements in critical applications. The application of formal methods is seen as essential to the design of critical systems and this chapter shows the benefits to be gained, particularly in relation to the specification activity. However, it is to be noted that different languages offer different capabilities and, therefore, usage of any particular language in critical systems design may be limited to different aspects of the system under consideration or to different phases of the development process.

Chapter 10 is a brief introduction to the specification language VDM and relies on experience with Z. This is achieved primarily through a comparison of the two languages, but should be sufficient to demonstrate the similarities between the two languages and that VDM is within easy reach of anyone with some experience in Z.

Chapters 11 and 12 are devoted to algebraic specification. Chapter 11 introduces algebraic specification in general, dealing with different kinds of algebras, the relationship between algebraic specifications and associated algebras and the widely known initial and terminal algebras and their significance in specification. Chapter 12 is an introduction to a particular language, namely CLEAR, in order to illustrate algebraic specification. This is done using a case study on a filing system.

The text includes three appendices. The first two contain exercises which may be attempted any time after the coverage of the material in Chapter 2. Depending on the interest of the reader or the course of study, these exercises may also be used as exercises for Chapters 10 and 11. The exercises at the end of chapters, if given, concern only the chapter material itself. Appendix A provides two case studies and suggests another from a published reference for the purpose of improving specification reading skills. Appendix B, on the other hand, suggests a number of case studies for improving specification writing skills. Appendix C provides a brief summary of the mathematical notation used, mainly that of Z. Throughout the book the symbol $\heartsuit$, appearing near the right hand side margin, signifies the end of an example.

I am grateful to Ali Abdallah for suggestions, stimulating discussions and encouragement and to Simeon Veloudis for valuable comments on the manuscript. Certain aspects of the case study on clocks in Chapter 5, Figures 5.1, 5.2, 5.3 and 9.2, and a part of Appendix C also appear in [41]; I am grateful to Addison Wesley Longman for permission to reuse this material. I owe a special word of thanks to Rosie Kemp of Springer-Verlag (London) Ltd for for her patience and advice in bringing this book into existence. I owe my greatest debt to my family: Machiko, Samaya and Hikaru, for constant support, understanding and love.

Reading, U.K. 1999   *Nimal Nissanke*

Contents

"Suvorin had a rather solemn interest in intellectual problems. For example, he complains that in The Horse Thieves Chekhov had not taken sides and solved the problem. Chekhov replies:

> You confuse two things: *solving a problem* and *stating a problem correctly.* It is only the second that is obligatory for the artist. In Anna Karenina and Evgeny Onegin not a single problem is solved, but they satisfy you completely because all the problems are correctly stated in them.

Suvorin protests that this looks indifference to good and evil."

$\cdots$ the inner quotation by Anton Chekhov,
Suvorin being one of his closest friends.
in Chekhov - A Spirit Set Free by V. S. Pritchett,
Hodder & Stoughton, 1988.

1. Introduction

The advent of micro-processors, the recent advances in computer architectures and the emergence of the Internet as a 'universal communication
medium' have extended the horizon of computing beyond our imagination.
The scope of, and the challenges faced by, human computing endeavours are,
for all practical purposes, now limitless. Such endeavours aim at both material and intellectual enhancement of our life. Computers lie at the heart of
most of the equipment we use day to day. Computers control almost all vital
installations such as those in nuclear power and air traffic systems. Computers control and interpret the instruments which serve as our extended eyes
and ears, probing deep into outer space and the secrets of life and matter.

1.1 Specification and Correctness

Despite the undeniable benefits brought about by such computer systems,
the tasks handled by them are complex and costly, and often place both life
and property at danger. Unfortunately, it is not just a possibility: it happens
and the literature is full of evidence. In computer technology, something most
vulnerable to failure is software. But, what is a 'software failure'? It is essentially the practical outcome of an erroneous state of the computer brought
about by the execution of a faulty piece of code. Following the casual but
common practice, we are here indiscriminately associating the term 'software error' with software failures, errors, and faults. The primary objective
of formal methods is to eliminate design errors from software. The word 'design' is used here in a very loose sense; it encompasses the range activities
spanning from an initial problem description to code generation. The word
'formal' is used as a synonym for the word 'mathematical' but also carries
its usual meaning of 'adhering to rigid rules'. Although mathematics includes
it to an extent, adherence to rigid rules is an important principle in formal
software development, because it is the only way to manage with confidence
the complexity of very large systems. Software without errors means 'correct'
software and, therefore, in order to understand what software errors are; one
must understand what is meant by 'correctness'. As is often said, knowing
your enemy is half the battle.

It is crucially important to appreciate that 'correctness' is a mathematical notion. The word 'correctness' may not be used in the proper sense of the word without a *precise description* of the problem being addressed. '*Formal specification*' is the terminology being used in software engineering for such precise descriptions. However, precision alone is not sufficient. Formal specifications are also a means of communication and, therefore, they must be clear and concise and must employ an agreed language so that everyone uses and understands it in the same way. These are important features distinguishing formal specifications from descriptions conventionally produced and used by pure mathematicians. Pure mathematicians can afford to be liberal in terms of the notation and practice because after all they are dealing with abstract concepts and entities. An error could be just an embarrassment. By contrast, the formalists in software engineering do not enjoy this luxury because, firstly, they deal with complex problems that cannot be solved totally in abstract and, secondly, software development involves large teams of people working on such problems often in isolation and independently, but implicitly relying on a common understanding. The possible consequences of errors here include system malfunction and risks to safety. In this respect, formal methods form quite a unique branch of applied mathematics.

1.2 Specification as a Contract

Formal specification emerged as a response to the quest for approaches for developing correct software. The most important characteristic of formal specifications is that they share the overall objective of specifications in general. A specification is first and foremost a statement of what is required saying as little as possible, or preferably nothing at all, about how the task is to be accomplished. A formal specification is, in addition, a mathematical expression of what is required (a computational task) which may be subjected to mathematical scrutiny (reasoning or proof). The aim is to document precisely the customer's requirements of software, and then to validate both explicit and implicit requirements in the resulting document from the customer's point of view and in his language. Only once this task is accomplished to the customer's satisfaction is the software developer expected to proceed to other design tasks.

In summary, a specification is a document describing the function of a system. It answers WHAT the system does without saying HOW. It is foremost a contractual agreement between the developer and the customer, although it may serve other purposes such as design as discussed in Section 1.3.

Since this book is about formal specification, unless stated otherwise, the word 'specification' means hereafter 'formal specification'.

1.3 Specification as a Design Aid

From the developer's point of view, a precise statement in the form of a formal specification frees him, most importantly, from the uncertainty of requirements – a major source of alarming development costs. The developer also gains in another way. For him formal specification opens up a totally new possibility – a verifiable design process. If one views the design as the discovery of the actual system's internal structure by the gradual introduction of new features, the designer has now the possibility of mathematically verifying that with each new feature the design still retains its previously observable properties and behaviour. In other words, the newly introduced feature has not invalidated the blueprint which existed up to that point. If the whole process of design consists solely of verifiable individual design steps, the designer is then in the strong position to claim the correctness of the final product with respect to the initial specification by the mere fact the product has been built correctly. This is the basis of what is referred to as 'correctness of software by the method of construction'. Although the practical viability of this approach is still to be demonstrated, current achievements such as those of Morgan [40] have shown the possibility of developing software in this manner. Despite the novelty, Morgan's work represents a classic approach to program development – the development of programs by successive *refinement*. Leaving this debate aside, 'correctness by the method of construction' has another important contribution to the formal viewpoint, namely it gives the best possible insight into what is meant by software correctness. This appreciation is important in itself because understanding correctness helps us to do things correctly, and thus, to improve the quality of design from the point of view of correctness. Knowledge rears good practice.

1.4 Specification as a Human Endeavour

A frequent counter–argument against formal specification is that one can never establish the requirements completely and accurately in practice and, therefore, the cost of formal specification is not worth the effort. There is an element of truth in the premise of this argument. However, this drawback is a human limitation and, therefore, has to be addressed by other means. What is gained by using mathematics in the specification task is a framework which enables the production of a precise statement of customer requirements. Mathematics is another important tool in the armoury of the specifier. As with all tools, the success depends not on the tool itself but on the skill of its user.

The skill is what unites formal methods, and in particular formal specification, with many other human activities involving creativity. Skills cannot be taught; they have to be learned. They have to be learned by observing how others work and by constant practice. Skills have to be sharpened by creative experimentation. Here we may learn a great deal from other creative disciplines: painting, pottery, writing and so on. Knowing the colours and the techniques, knowing the object, knowing the purpose, knowing artistic 'abstraction', a painter succeeds in conveying an interpretation of the reality or thought. These are some of the key elements in determining his success. The same applies almost literally to formal specification. The success of a formal specifier depends largely on his knowledge of the mathematical concepts, on his skills in proofs, on his fluency in the mathematical language, on his understanding of the problem, on his appreciation of the purpose of the system being specified, on his ability to exercise mathematical abstraction and many other factors. Artistic solutions are not unique, neither are formal specifications and designs. Some solutions may be better than the others, or they may even be equally good. Formal specification is not a prescriptive application of mathematics; it is a highly creative activity relying greatly on intuition and discovery.

Understandably, the novice tends to experience difficulties in using mathematics as a language. This is a temporary difficulty and is usually indicative of lack of fluency in mathematics. Furthermore, the use of mathematics in tasks such as specification involves elevating ourselves to a new way of thinking. As with all languages, once fluent, the language of mathematics becomes a secondary issue, and one begins to enjoy a newfound freedom in thinking about problems. This freedom brings along a number of advantages. First of all, one will be free from the thoughts about low level issues (e.g. data structures and procedures in programming languages). Secondly, as a result, it will not be necessary to commit to any particular solutions unless one absolutely has to and, therefore, the designer can retain the greatest possible degree of flexibility at every stage until the very end. Thirdly, and most importantly, it allows the essence of a problem to be addressed at a much higher (abstract) level with a degree of precision and clarity unchallenged by any other alternative.

1.5 Specification as Abstraction

Any artifact can have a number of different views depending on the purpose. An architect views a building purely in terms of its geometry, a quantity surveyor views it in terms of a rough physical model alongside the geometrical model, and a structural engineer views it as a detailed physical model alongside a detailed geometrical model. Finally, a construction engineer perceives it with a method of its realisation as a real building. The architect initially plays the roles of the requirement analyst and the specifier. He establishes the requirements of the customer and produces an architectural drawing as a specification of customer requirements. How the building is to be built, or even whether it can be physically built at all, that is, in terms of available materials and technology, is not his concern. However, he is obliged to ensure that the building can be built 'logically', for example, from the point of view of the logic of space. The structural engineer's model, on the other hand, is a design model intended to satisfy the requirements expressed in the architect's model and give more information as to how the functionality of the building is to be achieved in terms of materials and structural components. The construction engineer's model is an implementation model giving more information on how the building is to be erected. Each of these models correspond to a different abstraction of the same thing but serve different purposes.

Similarly, there are several levels of 'abstraction' in software engineering. In fact, each phase in the software life cycle has a specific model of the software based on a different abstraction. Since our concern is specification, our task is close to that of the architect. As part of the specification, this involves the following:

1. Construction of an abstract computational model for describing customer requirements
2. Abstaining from attending to implementation issues of the computational task
3. Suppression of details irrelevant to customer requirements

In essence, the first forms the task of specification in its entirety. The second arises from the fact that we are dealing with specifications and that we are supposed to convey the object of specification without saying how its functionality is to be achieved. However, as the architect in our metaphor, the specifier may not be absolved from his responsibility for ensuring the logical implementability of the system, that is, that the system is implementable at least in theory. Note that a system may be un-implementable because of physical constraints.

The third notion of abstraction constitutes a deliberate choice of detail for describing the object of specification fully, or as completely as possible, but without unnecessary detail. Returning to the analogy with the building, it is obvious that no one deals with the building in its entire complexity. The molecular structure of materials, for example, is irrelevant in the engineering design stages and is of interest only to the materials scientist. The right amount of chosen detail is therefore important, and may only be achieved by questioning constantly the necessity of each and every detail, and by a thorough review of requirements. Too much detail, in other words, too low a level of abstraction, makes the specification task more difficult and confusing, and too little detail adversely affects the expressiveness.

When dealing with specifications, the first two notions above may not be localised to a particular stage of the specification task, and the specifier must bear them in mind as ongoing concerns right through his task. The activity wrapped up in the third notion, on the other hand, may be dealt with, to a substantial extent, as a part of the very few acts of the formalisation or, if not, may be localised. How this may be achieved will become clear later on in our case studies.

1.6 Modularity in Specifications

Abstraction concerns the extent of detail to be considered in the software as a whole. However, even in modest applications the resulting amount of information is so extensive that no realistic software may be constructed as one monolithic unit. Software development has to be approached as a problem–solving activity, where problem decomposition is seen as the main weapon against software complexity. Thus, it is important to identify subproblems in the software that may be solved, to a large extent, independently from each other. It is also important that these subproblems relate to each other in a well understood manner so that the solutions to subproblems may be easily composed in such a way that the assembled product exhibits the desired behaviour. The decomposition of software into manageable independent subproblems for subsequent independent development is often referred to as *modularisation*. Modularisation in modern software development acquire even greater importance for two major reasons, namely, the highly complex nature of applications and industrial software development employing independent teams of people.

Thus, modularisation generally addresses the organisational structure of software, and at the specification level, it addresses the organisational structure of the specification. Although modular specifications may suggest an immediate modular design, the purpose of a modular specification is different. Its purpose is to facilitate understanding of the specification by the reader and to make the task of constructing specifications easier.

Modularisation is a creative activity. If the system is already in existence in some form, then its structure may be taken as an initial scheme for modularisation. As strategies for modularisation, one may adopt the well known decomposition techniques in software engineering, namely functional decomposition and object oriented decomposition. Most software engineering texts give ample guidance on these techniques. Most specifications dealt with in this book are based on functional decomposition, although Chapter 8 illustrates an approach to specification based on object oriented decomposition.

1.7 Benefits Beyond Precision

The prevalent current practice in specification still uses informal and semiformal techniques. The informal techniques rely primarily on natural language, diagrams, charts, etc., and they result in an informal statement in natural language about a desired system existing in someone's mind. Any reasoning about the artifact is necessarily informal and is based on intuition, experience, etc. Although the requirements may be validated in later stages by prototyping, program reading and testing, there is no guarantee that software 'errors' can be totally eliminated by these means. Furthermore, we have to accept that not everything is testable. Unfortunately, these observations are not reassuring for users and the public at large alike.

Inadequacies in these informal techniques may sometimes be traced to the manifestation of ambiguity, context sensitivity and vagueness inherent in natural language in specifications. The informal techniques also usually result in incomplete and inconsistent specifications. These deficiencies may be attributed, in part, to the difference in 'culture' between the customer and the developer, that is, the difference between the domains of expertise of the customer and the developer, their professional background, their approaches to problem–solving and their aims. As discussed in Section 1.1, 'correctness' in the presence of such inadequacies becomes meaningless.

By contrast, a formal specification is a mathematical description of what is required, with any natural language playing a complementary role in order to make specifications more widely accessible. Formal specifications provide a basis for addressing the issue of 'program correctness', namely, by mathematically proving that the program satisfies its specification. This is fundamental to any discussion of other non-functional properties such as efficiency and reliability. The precision required in formal specifications helps to resolve ambiguities in requirements, as well as conceptual issues, early in the development process. Through mathematical reasoning about the consequences of formalised requirements, requirement validation may be conducted more rigorously than otherwise. Several major implementation concerns may be addressed in the form of reasoning about various properties of the specification. Furthermore, formal specification provides a common basis for communication during and after the development process, instead of each party working from unstated semantics.

The impossibility of getting a specification 'correct' and doubts about program proofs are sometimes cited as arguments against embracing formal specification. As pointed out in Section 1.4, the question about 'incorrectness' of specifications is not limited to formal specifications. It is not possible to give an absolute assurance against the likelihood of inaccuracies in any kind of specification, only to make the best effort, and to employ the best techniques and expertise available, in order to make sure that the specification expresses customer requirements fully and correctly. This assures what is termed 'relative correctness', namely the correctness of the rest of the phases of the software development with respect to the specification, thus drawing a clear line of responsibility between specification inaccuracies and inaccuracies in subsequent design phases. Mechanical proof checkers are promising to help eliminate human fallibility in proofs. 'Animation' or rapid prototyping in functional languages and theorem proving techniques for requirement validation and establishing the internal consistency are also being put forward ways of ensuring that specifications capture customer requirements correctly. These ideas offer hope and are promising, but their effectiveness in practice is yet to be seen.

1.8 Formal Specification as an Emerging Technology

Formal specification was a response to a conflicting state of affairs brought about by advances in computing technology. On one hand, computer hardware was offering hitherto unseen potential in terms of applications. On the other hand, in the early days these applications had to be developed on an imperfect infra-structure, compounded by the ever growing complexity of the applications themselves and their requirements. As a result, in addition to software not meeting requirements, problems such as frequent delays, unpredictable high costs, unreliability and unmanageable maintenance became common complaints in the industry.

The immediate response of the profession to this state was initially ad-hoc and inadequate, but in the medium term it resulted in improvements at the coding level and in high level languages and tools. A major positive outcome was the emergence of *software engineering* as a discipline, encompassing a range of highly specialised areas of knowledge and practice. Associated with it was the recognition of the *software life cycle*, namely that different phases of development require specialised expertise, techniques and tools and that the progress from one phase to another has to be managed in a disciplined manner.

From the point of view of our study, an important consequence is the recognition of the role of the early phases of the development process, namely requirement analysis, specification and high-level design. This is because, as with any specification, formal specification results from the requirement analysis and forms the basis for the subsequent design. These early phases acquire such importance, on the one hand, because of the progressively increasing costs of remedial work as the development process advances and, on the other, because of the highly error–prone nature of the activities involved in these phases. There is also the possibility that the importance of these phases will be underestimated by the developers and, as a result, they will receive low priority because of commercial pressures or the lack of trained specialists.

Despite the significant progress made since the early days, formal specification continues to experience difficulties. Some are symptoms of change and novelty. These concern the lack of awareness, appreciation and confidence, the lack of expertise and tools and the lack of legislative status. There are also symptoms of recent origin. Arguably, formal specification can not

fully address many practically relevant aspects of computing such as timing, performance and reliability issues, Human Computer Interaction (HCI)
and software maintainability. Furthermore, formal specification is perceived
by some as leading to increased development costs, in addition to requiring
long term investment in training and tools. Although some of these fears
may be allayed by actual data on commercial benefits, this is sometimes hin-
dered by the problems sharing experiences of real–life applications because
of commercial competition.

1.9 Specification Techniques

There are already a number of different established formalisms for software
specification. Some of these have specialised capabilities for dealing with
many computational features such as concurrency and real time. Our study is
restricted to the study of a few basic specification formalisms. Two dominant
approaches in this category are:

(i) Abstract model approach
(ii) Implicit definition approach

The abstract model approach relies on the construction of an abstract
model exhibiting the desired behaviour of the software. The model is constructed using objects, as well as associated operations, borrowed from some
mathematical domain such as set theory or graph theory. The approach works
well when the objects in abstraction have a 'natural' correspondence with
those in the application domain. Two exemplars of this approach are Z, a
language due to J-R Abrial developed at Oxford University, and the Vienna
Development Method (VDM), developed at the IBM laboratories in Vienna.
They are both based on set theory, propositional logic and predicate logic
and provide for a standardised and extended mathematical notation. Both
languages are intended for the specification of sequential state based systems. Some regard models in such languages as 'abstract implementations
and, therefore, the specifications contain extraneous detail. Despite this criticism, model based languages have proven to be effective on the tasks for
which they are intended.

The implicit definition approach, on the other hand, does not rely on a
model constructed using mathematical objects, such as sets, for conveying
the intended behaviour of software. A dominant technique in this category
is the algebraic approach, where the objects of the specification are defined
implicitly by first identifying operations permitted by the software and then
interrelating these operations in such a way that the properties of the objects
concerned are defined implicitly or indirectly.

2. Schema Language

This chapter introduces the extended mathematical language of Z known as the *schema language*. A rigorous introduction to schema language is beyond the scope of this text and the interested reader is referred to [57] and [56] for a full definition. What follows is an informal introduction to the language, mostly through small examples.

2.1 Introduction

Z is a formal language intended for the specification of systems. As a *formal language*, it has an agreed alphabet (a set of symbols), a precise syntax (a set of rules to form valid expressions from symbols), and a precise semantics (an agreed way to interpret such expressions).

In addition, Z is a *formal specification language* because of the nature of its intended use, that is, the precisely documentation of software requirements. As a formal language, Z allows abstract reasoning in the form of mathematical proofs, both about user requirements, i.e., in requirements validation, and about the final product, i.e., in system verification. As a specification language, its major concern is communication among professionals involved in a common computer systems project.

As a specification language, it differs from traditional mathematics by having:

- A standard notation for traditional mathematics, and
- An extended notation for structuring specifications.

A major difficulty in understanding mathematical theories, as expressed by mathematicians, is usually the use of different notations by different authors. This is unacceptable in the specification of large computer systems where the customer and a large number of different parties are trying to achieve the same objective in the development of a product. Communication is paramount in such endeavours, hence, the need for standardisation of the notation.

Turning to the extended notation, it is worth noting that a bottleneck of traditional mathematics in meeting the demands of software specification has been the extent of knowledge to be formalised about any software. In a typical application, it is no longer possible to present this knowledge in a few pages. On the other hand, the human capacity for comprehending and absorbing such knowledge also has limitations. This requires an intuitive organisation of specifications, so that they can be constructed, and understood, without too much difficulty. Specification languages provide special notational devices for this purpose. The schema language of Z is such a device.

Compared to other specification languages, Z has a number of attractions. Among them is its accessibility to a wide audience. The underlying mathematics of Z comprises set theory and logic – an area well covered in both popular and specialised literature. Furthermore, the mathematical text in specifications is usually supplemented by a narrative in natural language. This is done essentially to assist those with limited familiarity with the notation to read specifications. As a consequence, however, it becomes imperative to ensure that the narrative is consistent with the mathematical text.

Another attraction of Z is its facilities for specifying large systems in a systematic manner, enabling the modular and hierarchical construction of specifications. The basic unit of specification is the concept of a *schema* - a named body of mathematical texts devised especially for presenting mathematics.

The concept of the schema offers a number of advantages. Firstly, it facilitates abstraction (in constructing mathematical models), comprehension (thanks to its intuitive expressiveness), effectiveness in communication (thanks to precision, clarity and conciseness of schemas), and formal and informal reasoning. Schemas improve readability due to their inherent modularity and identifiability by name. Schemas may be used to highlight the shared, or the distinct, features and properties of a system. They allow the exploitation of genericity, parameterisation and specification libraries to create new specifications from old ones.

With the development of computerised tools for use in various tasks of the development process, particularly in relation to computer-assisted reasoning, Z is seen increasingly as a notation viable for use in the industrial setting. Furthermore, despite its common use in software specification, the language is also applicable to specification of all kinds of systems, both abstract and physical.

2.2 Type Definitions in Z

A document written in Z invariably relies on non-standard types of values. Types are *maximal* sets and, therefore, strictly speaking, a subset of a set can not be used as a type. The basic types may be introduced into a specification in several ways.

2.2.1 Generic Types

Generic types introduce the types of values relevant to a discussion without giving any formal definition. They are called *generic* since nothing prevents us from giving them different interpretations. However, it is good practice to indicate their intended use informally. Introduction of a generic (basic) type means that its further details are either not available or not important at the given stage.

EXAMPLE 2.1 We may introduce a set called NAME to be used as a type as follows.

[NAME]

Informally, NAME is supposed to consist of all possible names of interest in the given specification task. ♡

2.2.2 Free (Enumerated) Types

Each free type consists of a number of explicitly named distinct values. The names of such values are reserved for denoting those values only and, therefore, may not be used for any other purpose, even as elements of other free types. The simplest kind of free type introduces its values essentially by enumeration, but follows a specific style to emphasise that the names used for its values are not variables but are some constants.

EXAMPLE 2.2 The identifiers for four distinct banks may be introduced into our discourse as follows.

BANKS ::= NatWest | Barclays | TokyoBank | UnionBank

♡

Free types may be defined using elements of other sets. Such definitions have a more general form of syntax

$\langle free\text{-}type \rangle ::= \langle constant \rangle \mid \langle constructor \rangle \langle\!\langle\ \langle source\text{-}set \rangle\ \rangle\!\rangle$

where $\langle \ldots \rangle$ denotes a syntactic entity, whereas $\langle\!\langle \ldots \rangle\!\rangle$ the data, provided as a set, to be used in generating the values of the newly created free type. Mathematically, *constructor* is a total injective function from *source-set* to *free-type*. As indicated by the term *constant*, the free type can consist of other constants.

EXAMPLE 2.3 Consider that we require a representation for a decimal currency (monetary unit) such as the pound sterling or the dollar. In dealing with the former, we may introduce a type STERLING defined as

$\text{STERLING} ::= \pounds \langle\!\langle \{r : \mathbb{R};\ i, j : \mathbb{Z} \mid 0 \leqslant j \leqslant 99 \land r = i + j \div 100 \bullet r\} \rangle\!\rangle$

where it is assumed that the function symbols in the expression $i + j \div 100$ have been defined appropriately so that $i + j \div 100$ yields a real number. Thus, the real number 3.45 has a counterpart in STERLING, namely, £3.45 of type STERLING, whereas the real number 3.455 has no counterpart in STERLING.

The symbol £ in the above definition is a constructor and creates a distinct element in the free type STERLING for each and every element in the set given as data. Thus, £3.45 is a mathematical entity; informally speaking, it stands for £3 and 45 pence in sterling as used in ordinary language.

$\heartsuit$

NOTE: The above example uses sets such as $\mathbb{Z}$ and $\mathbb{R}$ for integers and real numbers respectively, which are assumed to have been defined elsewhere.

The form of syntax given above is also applicable to the recursive definition of free types. This is achieved by using the *free-type* itself in place of *source-set*, obviously, in conjunction with an appropriate constructor. Typical examples include the definition of natural numbers and data structures such as trees and sequences.

EXAMPLE 2.4 Natural numbers and a mathematical structure for binary trees may be defined as

$$nat \quad ::= \mathsf{zero} \mid \mathsf{succ}\langle\!\langle nat \rangle\!\rangle$$
$$b\text{-}tree ::= \mathsf{leaf}\langle\!\langle \mathbb{N} \rangle\!\rangle \mid \mathsf{node}\langle\!\langle b\text{-}tree \times b\text{-}tree \rangle\!\rangle$$

The above regards nat as different from $\mathbb{N}$ although, obviously, we expect them to have a certain similarity. The reader may find definitions of $\mathbb{N}$ elsewhere, including in [43]. The free type $b\text{-}tree$ for binary trees of numbers are constructed using two functions: a unary function $\mathsf{leaf} : \mathbb{N} \rightarrowtail b\text{-}tree$ (for introducing leaf nodes) and a binary function $\mathsf{node} : \mathbb{N} \times \mathbb{N} \rightarrowtail b\text{-}tree$ (for introducing interior nodes).

$\heartsuit$

2.2.3 Types Defined by Schemas

Types of values with any complex internal structure may be introduced by a *schema*, which is the subject of Section 2.6. Some obvious examples of such values are those representing dates, names, etc., with a number of internal components. In the case of the former, for example, these may cover attributes such as the year, the month, the day of the month, the day of the week, etc.

2.3 Mathematical Definitions in Z

A specification written in Z is a collection of mathematical definitions. The schema language offers a number of ways to present mathematical text so that such text can be subsequently referred to conveniently and, if necessary, manipulated when reused in a different context. The following is a brief discussion of different forms of such mathematical definitions.

2.3.1 Schema

Schemas are the most characteristic form of definition in Z. The rest of this chapter, beginning with Section 2.4, deals with schemas.

2.3.2 Axiomatic Definitions

Axiomatic definitions[1] use variable names to introduce global (free) variables and constants, or other symbols to be used as function symbols. The values of such axiomatically defined variables may not be changed within the scope of any given document. Therefore, one may regard the use of such variables as a way of parameterising a given specification. Free variables are effectively system parameters which are usually given by the customer. The definitions given below are some examples.

EXAMPLE 2.5 The following introduces a certain variable called *max-credit* of type STERLING. *max-credit* applies globally and since it is a parameter of the specification, its value may not be altered within the specification.

$$\begin{array}{|l}
\textit{max-credit} : \text{STERLING} \\
\hline
\textit{max-credit} \leqslant \text{£0.00}
\end{array}$$

Informally, *max-credit* denotes the amount of money that can be lent as credit. The predicate *max-credit* $\leqslant$ £0.00 constrains the values that *max-credit* can take.   ♡

As illustrated in the following example, axiomatic definitions may consist of just a declaration.

EXAMPLE 2.6 A global variable which we intend to use later is

$$\begin{array}{|l}
\textit{black-list} : \mathbb{F}\,\text{NAME}
\end{array}$$

It will be used as a record of the names of some 'black listed' people.   ♡

It is often the case that a free type such as STERLING, introduced in Section 2.2.2, requires other operations for manipulating its elements and for making various observations about them. Some examples are the operations for addition of monetary units, comparing them and so forth. Such operations can be introduced in axiomatic style. In this particular case, we can do so relying on standard operations on $\mathbb{R}$.

---

[1] The term 'axiomatic definition' is somewhat misleading, as it is generally used in mathematics to mean the definition of mathematical objects with a set of axioms, that is, using a set of formulae the truth of which is not questioned within the theory defining such objects.

EXAMPLE 2.7 Below is an illustration of how to define a binary function +
on STERLING for adding two amounts of money.

$$+ : \text{STERLING} \times \text{STERLING} \rightarrow \text{STERLING}$$

$$\forall\, m_1, m_2 : \text{STERLING} \mid \exists\, \bar{m}_1, \bar{m}_2 : \mathbb{R} \bullet m_1 = \pounds\bar{m}_1 \wedge m_2 = \pounds\bar{m}_2 \bullet$$
$$m_1 +_{\text{STERLING}} m_2 = \pounds(\bar{m}_1 +_{\mathbb{R}} \bar{m}_2)$$

where the subscripts in $+_{\text{STERLING}}$ and $+_{\mathbb{R}}$ underline the fact the symbol + in
the syntax definition is overloaded[2], that is, its meaning is to be interpreted
differently in the two domains. Likewise, other functions and relations such
as $-, \leqslant, \geqslant$ may be defined on STERLING; see Exercise 2.1   ♡

2.3.3 Generic Definitions

These introduce fixed definitions, typically, functions and operators that can
take as their arguments, and return as their results, values of different types.
Such definitions are applicable globally within any document and, in contrast
with the axiomatic definitions mentioned above, are usually introduced by
the specifier.

EXAMPLE 2.8 A unary predicate *currency-val* on $\mathbb{R}$, which identifies whether
its argument matches with a monetary unit of a decimal currency, can be
defined as

$$currency\text{-}val : \mathbb{P}\,\mathbb{R}$$

$$\forall\, r : \mathbb{R} \bullet currency\text{-}val(r) \Leftrightarrow \exists\, i, j : \mathbb{Z} \bullet 0 \leqslant j \leqslant 99 \wedge r = i + j \div 100$$

where, relying on the connection between logic and set theory, we use
currency-val(r) as an alternative to $r \in$ *currency-val*. The above is a fixed
definition applicable globally in a given specification, but is not generic since
it is restricted to $\mathbb{R}$. A more general definition involving generic types is the
following, illustrating a typical generic definition given in the reference source
[57] on Z.

♡

EXAMPLE 2.9 A function 'dom', returning the domain of a relation from a
set X to a set Y, may be defined as

$$[X, Y]$$
$$\text{dom} : (X \leftrightarrow Y) \rightarrow \mathbb{P}\,X$$

$$\forall\, R : (X \leftrightarrow Y) \bullet$$

$$\text{dom}\; R = \{x : X \mid \exists\, y : Y \bullet (x, y) \in R\}$$

---

[2] An operator is said to be *overloaded* if it has several context dependent meanings.

The above introduces an operator (a function) which takes a relation from X to Y as the argument and returns the set of values of X where the relation is defined. The sets X and Y represent two arbitrary types and are generic parameters local to the definition. Strictly speaking, the definition must be instantiated with the appropriate sets before use, for example, as in

$dom\_\mathbb{N} == dom[\mathbb{N}, \mathbb{N}]$

for establishing the domain of relations on natural numbers, $\mathbb{N}$. However, this is not always done, especially when there is no room for ambiguity.   ♡

NOTE: An alternative notation for $==$ is $\widehat{=}$. Both mean the equality by definition or the syntactic equality.

2.4 Presentation of Schemas

Each schema consists of a triple, namely:

- **Schema name**
  Naming a schema introduces a syntactic equality (equality by definition) of the schema name with the mathematical text involved. If necessary, the schema name may be replaced with the content of the schema, and vice versa.
- **Signature part**
  The signature part introduces components (identifiers) and declares their types using mathematical data structures such as sets, relations, functions and sequences.
- **Predicate part**
  The predicate part introduces constraints on the values that the components in the signature may take. The predicate as a whole is referred to as a data invariant in data abstraction, or as a state invariant in system specification.

In visual presentations, schemas are presented in two forms, namely

- Vertical layout
  This takes the form of a box subdivided by a horizontal line.

EXAMPLE 2.10 A specification for a basic bank account may be presented as below.

$\_\_BasicAccount\_\_$
$name : \text{NAME}$
$balance, credit\text{-}limit : \text{STERLING}$ } .... Signature Part
_____
$credit\text{-}limit \leqslant £0.00$
$balance \geqslant credit\text{-}limit$ } .... Predicate Part

♡

where *BasicAccount* is the name of the above schema.

Even the simplest schema represents a specification. For example, the schema *BasicAccount* given above may be seen as the specification of the state of an account, which must always be satisfied by its state variables *name*, *balance* and *credit -limit.*

In this layout several conventions apply, namely

− type declarations may be broken at a semicolon dropping the semicolon,
− a lengthy predicate may be broken at a conjunction dropping the connective, and
− a lengthy predicate may be continued on successive lines with an appropriate indentation.

• Horizontal layout

In horizontal layout of a schema, the mathematical text is enclosed in square brackets with an intervening bar subdividing the schema into signature and predicate parts.

EXAMPLE 2.11 A simple specification for a basic bank account is

$$\underbrace{VeryBasicAccount}_{\text{schema name}} \mathrel{\widehat{=}} [\underbrace{name : \text{NAME}; \ balance : \mathbb{R}}_{\text{signature part}} \quad \underbrace{|}_{\text{separator}}$$

$$\underbrace{currency\text{-}val(balance)}_{\text{predicate part}}]$$

♡

NOTE: As mentioned in Section 2.3.3, the symbol $\widehat{=}$ denotes the equality by definition, in other words, the syntactic equality of the schema name with the body of mathematics on its right hand side.

2.5 Schema Manipulation

A guiding principle in the construction of large and complex specifications is to handle the complexity of the task by 'specification in small' first, and then by composing the whole in a desired fashion. Thus, the construction of large specifications requires additional machinery to build more complex schemas from simpler ones, as well as to manipulate them. This section introduces some of the schema operators intended for this purpose.

In the description of these operators, the term 'utility' addresses the question 'What for?' and refers to the purpose of the operator from the point of view of specification as a task. The term 'usage', on the other hand, addresses the question 'How to use?' and explains the correct and effective use of the operator from a linguistic point of view. In some cases, however, the concrete syntax is given instead of, or in addition to, usage.

2.5.1 Schema Extension

We consider here three ways to extend a schema, namely by adding a new component to the signature, by adding a new predicate to the predicate part or by both.

Adding components

UTILITY: To add new state variables into a specification
USAGE: To extend the signature with one or more additional components
SYNTAX: $\langle schema \rangle$; $\langle new\text{-}declaration \rangle$

EXAMPLE 2.12

$\quad IntermediateAccount \mathrel{\widehat{=}} BasicAccount;\ max\text{-}withdrawal :$ STERLING

The above is equivalent to the following.

$$
\begin{array}{|l}
\underline{\ IntermediateAccount\ } \\
\quad name :\text{NAME} \\
\quad balance, credit\text{-}limit, max\text{-}withdrawal :\text{STERLING} \\
\hline
\quad credit\text{-}limit \leqslant \pounds0.00 \\
\quad balance \geqslant credit\text{-}limit \\
\end{array}
$$

$\heartsuit$

Adding predicates

UTILITY: To constrain a specification further
USAGE: To extend the predicate part with an additional conjunct
SYNTAX: $\langle schema \rangle \mid \langle new\text{-}predicate \rangle$

EXAMPLE 2.13

$\quad Account \mathrel{\widehat{=}} IntermediateAccount \mid credit\text{-}limit \geqslant max\text{-}credit\ \wedge$
$\qquad\qquad \pounds0.00 \leqslant max\text{-}withdrawal \leqslant balance - credit\text{-}limit$

The expanded version of the above is

$$
\begin{array}{|l}
\underline{\ Account\ } \\
\quad name :\text{NAME} \\
\quad balance, credit\text{-}limit, max\text{-}withdrawal :\text{STERLING} \\
\hline
\quad credit\text{-}limit \leqslant \pounds0.00 \\
\quad balance \geqslant credit\text{-}limit \\
\quad credit\text{-}limit \geqslant max\text{-}credit \\
\quad \pounds0.00 \leqslant max\text{-}withdrawal \leqslant balance - credit\text{-}limit \\
\end{array}
$$

♡

Schema inclusion

The schema inclusion permits the addition of new components and predicates in a single definition.

UTILITY: To add new state variables and new constraints into specifications

USAGE: The term 'schema inclusion' is frequently used in the context of presentation of schemas. Inclusion of the name of a schema in another schema has the following effects:

- The new definition inherits the signature declarations and predicates of the included schema. This means that the specifier is free to refer to the component names of the included schema in writing new predicates.
- The signatures of the included schema are added to the existing signature. Components with the same name 'collapse' into a single component, provided that they are type compatible. Type incompatibility of such components is not permissible.
- The predicates of the included schema are conjoined with the newly inserted predicates.

EXAMPLE 2.14 An alternative way for defining the schema *Account* is to include *BasicAccount* in its definition and then to extend it both in signature and with predicates as desired.

$$
\begin{array}{|l}
\hline
\quad Account \underline{} \\
\; BasicAccount \\
\\
\; max\text{-}withdrawal : \text{STERLING} \\
\hline
\; credit\text{-}limit \geqslant max\text{-}credit \\
\; £0.00 \leqslant max\text{-}withdrawal \leqslant balance - credit\text{-}limit \\
\hline
\end{array}
$$

The expanded version is identical to the version of the schema *Account* presented earlier.   ♡

2.5.2 Merging Schemas

Here we outline some binary schema operations. These operations are inspired by propositional connectives in logic and are intended for merging mathematical text in accordance with the corresponding logical rules. The utility of these operators and the notations used are given in Table 2.1. Each operation has the effect of:

- Merging the signature declarations of operand schemas. Components with the same name collapse into a single component, as mentioned under the schema inclusion earlier.
- Joining the predicates of operand schemas through the corresponding logical connective. Obviously, it is essential to exercise care here to ensure that the resulting schema is consistent, that is, it is free of any contradiction.

Table 2.1. Utility of binary schema operators

Operator	Notation	Utility
All		Composition of specifications with an appropriate joining of constraints. Utilities are various. Some frequently used specialised utilities are given below.
Schema Conjunction	$\wedge$	Defining the state of the system using specifications of subsystems.
Schema Disjunction	$\vee$	Defining the operations on the system using the specifications of primary operations and some exception handling operations.
Schema Implication	$\Rightarrow$	Mostly, in reasoning about specifications.
Schema Equivalence	$\Leftrightarrow$	As above.

It is the convention to use a larger symbol in order to distinguish it from the corresponding logical connective. In the case of schema conjunction, an alternative is to use the schema inclusion. The use of these operators is illustrated in the example below.

EXAMPLE 2.15 Consider the following schemas as operands.

```
┌─ ApprovedCustomer ──────────────────────────────
│  name : NAME
│ ─────────────────────────────────────────────────
│  name ∉ black-list
└───────────────────────────────────────────────────
```

```
┌─ CreditControl ────────────────────────────────────────────
│ balance, credit-limit, max-withdrawal : STERLING
│ ──────────────────────────────────────────────
│ credit-limit ⩽ £0.00
│
│ balance ⩾ credit-limit
│
│ credit-limit ⩾ max-credit
│
│ £0.00 ⩽ max-withdrawal ⩽ balance − credit-limit
└─────────────────────────────────────────────────────────────
```

The schema *ApprovedCustomer* is supposed to represent a record of approved customers, and *CreditControl* the rules on customer credit control. Consider now the following schemas formed by merging the above two schemas using different schema operators; for brevity only three of them have been expanded. The comments that accompany each operation explain user requirements on accounts as expressed in the resulting new specification.

The first schema operation is illustrated by introducing a schema *ControlledAccount* defined as

$$ControlledAccount \mathrel{\hat=} ApprovedCustomer \wedge CreditControl \mathrel{\hat=}$$

```
┌─ ControlledAccount ────────────────────────────────────────
│ name : NAME
│ balance, credit-limit, max-withdrawal : STERLING
│ ──────────────────────────────────────────────
│ name ∉ black-list
│
│ credit-limit ⩽ £0.00
│
│ balance ⩾ credit-limit
│
│ credit-limit ⩾ max-credit
│
│ £0.00 ⩽ max-withdrawal ⩽ balance − credit-limit
└─────────────────────────────────────────────────────────────
```

according to which, every account holder must be an approved customer (one who is not black-listed) and must satisfy the credit control requirements.

Schema disjunction is illustrated by defining a schema *FreeAccount* as

$$FreeAccount \mathrel{\hat=} ApprovedCustomer \vee CreditControl \mathrel{\hat=}$$

$$\boxed{\begin{array}{l} FreeAccount \\ \hline name : \text{NAME} \\ balance,\ credit\text{-}limit,\ max\text{-}withdrawal : \text{STERLING} \\ \hline name \notin black\text{-}list \lor \\ \quad (credit\text{-}limit \leqslant \pounds 0.00 \\ \quad balance \geqslant credit\text{-}limit \\ \quad credit\text{-}limit \geqslant max\text{-}credit \\ \quad \pounds 0.00 \leqslant max\text{-}withdrawal \leqslant balance - credit\text{-}limit) \end{array}}$$

The above allows a more liberal application of customer approval and credit control requirements, requiring as a minimum the observation of only one of these aspects. Customers who do not appear in the black-list may or may not be subject to credit control, but black-listed customers are subject to credit control without exception.

On the other hand, the schema *UnreasonableAccount* defined below

$$UnreasonableAccount \mathrel{\widehat{=}} ApprovedCustomer \Rightarrow CreditControl \mathrel{\widehat{=}}$$

$$\boxed{\begin{array}{l} UnreasonableAccount \\ \hline name : \text{NAME} \\ balance,\ credit\text{-}limit,\ max\text{-}withdrawal : \text{STERLING} \\ \hline name \notin black\text{-}list \Rightarrow \\ \quad (credit\text{-}limit \leqslant \pounds 0.00 \\ \quad balance \geqslant credit\text{-}limit \\ \quad credit\text{-}limit \geqslant max\text{-}credit \\ \quad \pounds 0.00 \leqslant max\text{-}withdrawal \leqslant balance - credit\text{-}limit) \end{array}}$$

imposes a somewhat unreasonable situation on all approved customers by subjecting them compulsorily to credit control but by giving the bank a free hand with respect to black-listed customers. Reverse schema implication, on the other hand

$$ConfusingAccount \mathrel{\widehat{=}} CreditControl \Rightarrow ApprovedCustomer$$

ensures that credit control applies exclusively to approved customers, although some of them may be exempt from it. All non-approved customers are exempt from the credit control measures defined in *CreditControl*.

Turning to schema equivalence, we have a specification

$$StandardAccount \,\widehat{=}\, ApprovedCustomer \Leftrightarrow CreditControl$$

according to which credit control applies exclusively and without exemption to approved customers. All non-approved customers are to be treated differently.

♡

2.5.3 Schema Negation

It follows from the above schema merging operations that there must be a unary schema operation which corresponds to the logical negation. Its functionality is as follows.

UTILITY: Various

USAGE: The operation has the effect of creating a new schema by the negation of the predicate of the operand schema. The signature is unaffected.

EXAMPLE 2.16

$$PrivilegedAccount \,\widehat{=}\, \neg\; UnreasonableAccount \,\widehat{=}\,$$

__ *PrivilegedAccount* _____

$name$: NAME

$balance, credit\text{-}limit, max\text{-}withdrawal$: STERLING

$name \notin black\text{-}list$

$\neg\,(credit\text{-}limit \leqslant £0.00$

$\qquad balance \geqslant credit\text{-}limit$

$\qquad credit\text{-}limit \geqslant max\text{-}credit$

$\qquad £0.00 \leqslant max\text{-}withdrawal \leqslant balance - credit\text{-}limit)$

The above limits the use of *PrivilegedAccount* to approved customers and introduces more favourable conditions on them by mandatory partial or full relaxation of the credit control requirements.

♡

Thus, the five ways of merging the two schemas *ApprovedCustomer* and *CreditControl*, namely using the four binary schema operators and the schema negation, result in different types of bank account, each with an entirely different set of user requirements.

2.6 Significance of Schemas

The examples in the previous section have illustrated the use of schemas as a kind of specification. Generally speaking, what do the schemas signify or represent? The answer to this question is "Various things!". As will become evident later, schemas are used primarily for defining systems. However, there are a range of other uses, which are the subject of this section.

2.6.1 Schemas Instead of Declarations

One of the uses of schemas is as an abbreviation for a lengthy declaration with, possibly, an additional constraint. It is a convention based on the way schemas were defined in Section 2.4, whereby a schema name can be substituted for the mathematical text it represents, and vice versa. Examples of this usage in different contexts will follow in Sections 2.6.4–2.6.7.

2.6.2 Schemas and Mathematical Relations

It is instructive to compare the schema *VeryBasicAccount*

$$
\begin{array}{|l|}
\hline
\text{\textit{VeryBasicAccount}} \\
\hline
\textit{name} \quad : \text{NAME} \\
\textit{balance} : \mathbb{R} \\
\hline
\textit{currency-val}(\textit{balance}) \\
\hline
\end{array}
$$

introduced in Example 2.11, with the relation defined below

$$RelAccount : \text{NAME} \leftrightarrow \mathbb{R}$$

$$RelAccount = \{x : \text{NAME};\ v : \mathbb{R} \mid \textit{currency-val}(v) \bullet (x, v)\}$$

where *currency-val* is a predicate defined in Example 2.8. Both *RelAccount* and *VeryBasicAccount* represent two sets of pairs, with one element of each pair being a name and the other a 'currency number'. In *RelAccount* the two elements in each pair are distinguished by the order, whereas in *VeryBasicAccount* this is achieved by the use of the names *name* and *balance*. Also, there is no such order of elements in schemas. Although it would be possible to use the same names in *RelAccount*, they would have had no significance other than as 'local' (bound) variables defining the set (of pairs) concerned.

A schema name enclosed in set braces

$$\{\,\textit{VeryBasicAccount}\,\}$$

is not quite a set. Its expansion would appear like

$$\{\textit{name} : \text{NAME};\ \textit{balance} : \mathbb{R} \mid \textit{currency-val}(\textit{balance})\}$$

and, obviously, is not a set properly written out, that is, it is not syntactically correct. In order to make the above a proper definition of a set, we should include a term as shown below

$$\{name : \text{NAME}; \ balance : \mathbb{R} \mid currency\text{-}val(balance) \bullet (name, balance)\}$$

but then, by definition, the set concerned is a set of pairs and the order of elements in each pair matters. However, these observations are made purely from a set theoretic point of view. As will be seen below in Section 2.6.4, from the point of view of Z, *VeryBasicAccount* can be viewed as a set, as well as a type.

Thus, the order of elements in a tuple as understood in traditional mathematics is suppressed in schemas and, instead, the elements are given explicit names for identification. The advantages gained by this move are significant in the specification of systems consisting of a large number of distinct components.

2.6.3 Bindings

How can we then visualise an object satisfying *VeryBasicAccount*? For this purpose, the schema language uses the concept of *binding*, which in visual presentations is shown by the notation $\langle\!\langle \ldots \rangle\!\rangle$. Using this notation, an example of an object satisfying *VeryBasicAccount* is the binding

$$\langle\!\langle name \rightsquigarrow \textsf{JohnSmith}, balance \rightsquigarrow \text{-23.56}\rangle\!\rangle$$

meaning, in an appropriate context, that the component *name* is *bound* to the value, or the object, JohnSmith and the component *balance* to the value -23.56. Note also that the order of individual bindings of variables to their values does not matter in expressions such as the above.

2.6.4 Schemas as Sets

The concept of binding allows a more meaningful treatment of a schema representing a structured object as a set. In fact, it is now possible to define the set represented by the schema *VeryBasicAccount* using set comprehension, namely as

$$\{name : \text{NAME}; \ balance : \mathbb{R} \mid currency\text{-}val(v) \bullet$$
$$\langle\!\langle name \rightsquigarrow name, balance \rightsquigarrow balance\rangle\!\rangle\}$$

or, alternatively

$$\{\textit{VeryBasicAccount} \bullet \langle\!\langle name \rightsquigarrow name, balance \rightsquigarrow balance\rangle\!\rangle\}$$

where, as mentioned in Section 2.6.1, we have used the convention that a schema name may be used where a declaration is expected. As a result, the above can be seen as a *set of bindings*. In the above two set comprehensions, the expression $\langle\!\langle name \rightsquigarrow name, balance \rightsquigarrow balance\rangle\!\rangle$, appearing in the place of the term defining the form of elements in the set, is called the *characteristic binding.* Note that the characteristic binding consists of two different occurrences of each component name with different meanings. For example, with reference to a symbol such as *name* in a binding of the form $\langle name \rightsquigarrow name, \ldots \rangle$, the first occurrence of *name* stands for the component name in the true sense, and the second for a value that the variable *name* is permitted to take.

A notation used to denote the characteristic binding is θ, used as a prefix to the schema concerned. Thus, we have

$$\theta \, VeryBasicAccount = \langle name \rightsquigarrow name, balance \rightsquigarrow balance \rangle$$

and, as a result, an abbreviated notation for sets of objects defined by schemas is the following

$$\{ name : \text{NAME};\ balance : \mathbb{R} \mid currency\text{-}val(v) \bullet$$
$$\langle name \rightsquigarrow name, balance \rightsquigarrow balance \rangle \}$$
$$= \{ VeryBasicAccount \bullet \theta \, VeryBasicAccount \}$$

NOTE: The syntax of Z permits dropping the term when there is only one named component in the definition.

2.6.5 Schemas as Types

Since sets defined by schemas are maximal, in the sense mentioned in Section 2.2, schemas may also be used as types. When a schema is used as a type, it is unnecessary in Z to use the full syntax given by

$$\{ \langle schema\text{-}name \rangle \mid \theta \langle schema\text{-}name \rangle \}$$

for the underlying set of bindings and, instead, it is the convention to use the schema name on its own. Therefore, the type declaration of any relation, a function, the power set and the Cartesian product may also be done using schema names wherever a type name is expected.

EXAMPLE 2.17 A relation *same-privilege* on *BasicAccount* giving pairs of accounts, where the two accounts involved in any pair are related by *same-privilege* to each other by having the same credit limit, can be defined as

$$same\text{-}privilege : BasicAccount \leftrightarrow BasicAccount$$
$$same\text{-}privilege = \{ x, y : BasicAccount \mid$$
$$x.credit\text{-}limit = y.credit\text{-}limit \bullet (x, y) \}$$

In the above, the term *x.credit-limit*, a notation to be introduced in Section 2.7.3, denotes the value of the component *credit-limit* of the object referred to as *x*. ♡

The use of a schema name in the type declaration of a function may be found in the next section.

2.6.6 In Lambda Notation

λ notation[3] allows a kind of function abstraction that does not use function names. Such functions are often referred to as 'anonymous functions' and are also supported in certain programming languages, namely in functional and other declarative languages. Any detailed study of this topic is beyond the scope of this text. Mathematical specifications often use λ–functions where it is unnecessary to introduce function names, especially when a function is used on a one-off basis with no subsequent reference to it.

λ–functions have the following syntax:

$$\lambda \langle signature \rangle \mid \langle constraint \rangle \bullet \langle function\text{-}body \rangle$$

EXAMPLE 2.18 Below are some simple λ–functions.

$\lambda \; x : \mathbb{Z} \bullet x^2$ – a total function (the squaring function)

$\lambda \; x, y : \mathbb{Z} \mid x \neq y \bullet (x + x \times y)$ – a partial function

$\heartsuit$

Following the convention that schemas can be used in place of declarations, it is perfectly acceptable to define λ–functions in the style

$$max\text{-}debit : BasicAccount \rightarrow \text{STERLING}$$
$$max\text{-}debit = \lambda \, BasicAccount \bullet (balance - credit\text{-}limit)$$

In the above, the λ–function takes an object satisfying $BasicAccount$ as the argument and returns $(balance - credit\text{-}limit)$ as the result.

2.6.7 Schemas in Predicate Logic Formulae

The last example shows how a schema has been used as a type in a type definition. This usage may be extended to include the case of formulae in predicate logic. For example, in the sentence below $ControlledAccount$ appears where a signature declaration is expected, and $StandardAccount$ where a predicate is expected.

$$\forall \, ControlledAccount \bullet StandardAccount \hspace{4cm} \text{(A)}$$

The above may be expanded as follows

---

[3] λ notation is a concept used in λ calculus – a branch of mathematical logic.

$\forall\, name : \text{NAME};\; balance, credit\text{-}limit,$

$\quad max\text{-}withdrawal : \text{STERLING} \mid (name \notin black\text{-}list \wedge$

$\quad credit\text{-}limit \leqslant \pounds 0.00 \wedge$

$\quad balance \geqslant credit\text{-}limit \wedge$

$\quad credit\text{-}limit \geqslant max\text{-}credit \wedge$

$\quad \pounds 0.00 \leqslant max\text{-}withdrawal \leqslant balance - credit\text{-}limit) \bullet$

$\qquad (name \notin black\text{-}list) \Leftrightarrow$

$\qquad\quad credit\text{-}limit \leqslant \pounds 0.00 \wedge$

$\qquad\quad balance \geqslant credit\text{-}limit \wedge$

$\qquad\quad credit\text{-}limit \geqslant max\text{-}credit \wedge$

$\qquad\quad \pounds 0.00 \leqslant max\text{-}withdrawal \leqslant balance - credit\text{-}limit)$

which is a long sentence in predicate logic. The rules of predicate logic on variable binding remain applicable to formulae involving schemas and, therefore, it is necessary to exercise care in the use of variable names in schemas.

Schemas may appear where a predicate is expected but without an appropriate schema in the signature at all. In this case, the signature part of such schemas has no significance other than giving the type information, and simply drops out from the predicate part of the formula. Thus, the following is an implication in predicate form but with no quantification over the (state) variables concerned.

$$ControlledAccount \Rightarrow StandardAccount$$

NOTE: The above may also signify a schema and not a predicate, in which case the signature part remains in the definition.

Therefore, if a truth-valued sentence is required, one has to qualify the status of variables using the usual quantifiers $\forall$ and $\exists$. Thus, we may express the formula (A) above in the following alternative form.

$\forall\, name : \text{NAME};\; balance, credit\text{-}limit, max\text{-}withdrawal : \text{STERLING} \bullet$

$$ControlledAccount \Rightarrow StandardAccount$$

2.7 Some Naming Conventions

The adoption of names for components, instead of the order in relational tuples, has repercussions. These concern, for example, how to access components of an instance of a schema, and how to refer to the same component in different instances of a schema.

2.7.1 Schema Decoration

UTILITY: Various, but mostly for referring to the 'after state' in operation specifications (to be discussed later).

USAGE: Schema decoration is a restricted global renaming facility. According to this convention, the application of a superscript, typically a single quote, to the schema has the effect that all its components are likewise superscribed everywhere within the schema. The decoration does not apply to variables outside the scope of the schema, for example, to free variables *black-list* and *max-credit* in the schema below. Furthermore, a decoration is immaterial in the case of any bound variable in a quantified formula appearing inside the schema.

EXAMPLE 2.19

$ControlledAccount' \triangleq$

$$
\begin{array}{|l}
\hline
\;\underline{\;\; ControlledAccount' \;}\underline{\hspace{6cm}} \\
\quad name' : \text{NAME} \\
\quad balance', credit\text{-}limit', max\text{-}withdrawal' : \text{STERLING} \\
\hline
\quad name' \notin black\text{-}list \\
\quad credit\text{-}limit' \leqslant \pounds 0.00 \\
\quad balance' \geqslant credit\text{-}limit' \\
\quad credit\text{-}limit' \geqslant max\text{-}credit \\
\quad \pounds 0.00 \leqslant max\text{-}withdrawal' \leqslant balance' - credit\text{-}limit' \\
\hline
\end{array}
$$

$\heartsuit$

2.7.2 Explicit Renaming of Components

UTILITY: To ensure matching names in operation specifications, message passing, etc., and generation of new specifications from existing ones.

USAGE: This facility allows the generation of new schemas by renaming individual components selectively. As with any substitution in mathematical expressions, inadvertent name clashing should be avoided. Note that renaming cannot be applied to types.

SYNTAX:

$\langle schema\text{-}name \rangle [\langle new\text{-}name_1 \rangle / \langle old\text{-}name_1 \rangle,$

$\langle new\text{-}name_2 \rangle / \langle old\text{-}name_2 \rangle, \ldots]$

EXAMPLE 2.20 The expanded version of

$$Invoice \mathrel{\widehat{=}} Account[customer/name, cash\text{-}payment/balance,$$
$$loan/credit\text{-}limit, payment\text{-}due/max\text{-}withdrawal]$$

is given by

┌─ *Invoice* ─────────────────────────────────────
│ $customer$: NAME
│
│ $cash\text{-}payment, loan, payment\text{-}due$: STERLING
├────────────────────
│ $loan \leqslant £0.00$
│
│ $cash\text{-}payment \geqslant loan$
│
│ $loan \geqslant max\text{-}credit$
│
│ $payment\text{-}due \leqslant cash\text{-}payment - loan$
└─────────────────────────────────────

$\heartsuit$

Thus, we have utilised an existing specification to generate a new one by a simple renaming of components. The two schemas are identical in structure and in mathematical significance, but differ in the intended use as specifications.

2.7.3 Dot Notation

UTILITY: For accessing (or referring) to components of an instance of a schema, that is, when the instance is introduced as an individual of the type defined by the relevant schema.
SYNTAX:

$\langle$*instance-name*$\rangle$.$\langle$*component-name*$\rangle$

given that the type has been declared as

$\langle$*instance-name*$\rangle$: $\langle$*schema-name*$\rangle$

EXAMPLE 2.21 Given that the identifier x has the type declaration

$x : Account$

the notation

$x.balance$

refers to the value of the component *balance* as defined in *Account*. For instance, we may state that the *balance* in the account of every black-listed customer is greater than zero as

$$\forall x : Account \bullet (x.name \in black\text{-}list \Rightarrow x.balance > £0.00)$$

$\heartsuit$

Using the λ notation, we may introduce a more formal definition for the dot notation as shown below

$$x.name \mathrel{\widehat{=}} (\lambda\ Account \bullet name)x$$

where the right hand side of $\widehat{=}$ shows the application of the function in parentheses to x, provided that $x : Account$.

2.8 Hiding and Projection of Components

UTILITY: To suppress one or more state variables from a specification
USAGE: Hiding suppresses the components mentioned explicitly as its parameters. Projection is the converse of hiding; it hides everything not mentioned and leaves those mentioned unaffected. The effect of these two operations is such that the components to be hidden are simply transferred from the signature part to the predicate part under existential quantification. Note that there is no facility in Z for complete elimination of components from a schema.
SYNTAX: Hiding

$\langle schema\text{-}name \rangle \backslash \langle component\text{-}name \rangle$, or

$\langle schema\text{-}name \rangle \backslash (\langle component\text{-}name_1 \rangle, \langle component\text{-}name_2 \rangle, \ldots)$

SYNTAX: Projection

$\langle schema\text{-}name \rangle \upharpoonright \langle component\text{-}name \rangle$, or

$\langle schema\text{-}name \rangle \upharpoonright (\langle component\text{-}name_1 \rangle, \langle component\text{-}name_2 \rangle, \ldots)$

EXAMPLE 2.22 Let us introduce the type

[ACC-ID]

for a type containing as elements some account identification numbers, and let

```
┌─ ProperAccount ─────────────────────────────────────────
│  Account
│
│  id : ACC-ID
│ ─────────────────────────────────────────
│  acc-name id = name
│
│  acc-balance id = balance
└─────────────────────────────────────────
```

where

$acc\text{-}balance$: ACC-ID $\nrightarrow$ STERLING

$acc\text{-}name$: ACC-ID $\nrightarrow$ NAME

and as their names suggest, they give respectively the balance and the customer name as recorded against a coded customer identification. Since such information is usually confidential, we would expect these functions to be defined outside the system specification given by this document.

We may provide a formal definition for confidential accounts where the customer name and the balance are hidden outside the definition in one of the following alternative forms:

$ConfidentialAccount$

$\qquad \widehat{=} \; ProperAccount \backslash (name, balance)$

$\qquad \widehat{=} \; ProperAccount \upharpoonright (id, credit\text{-}limit, max\text{-}withdrawal) \; \widehat{=}$

```
┌─ ConfidentialAccount ─────────────────────────────────────────
│  id : ACC-ID
│
│  credit-limit, max-withdrawal : STERLING
│ ─────────────────────────────────────────
│  ∃ name : NAME;  balance : STERLING •
│
│          ((acc-name id) = name ∧ (acc-balance id) = balance ∧
│
│          balance ⩾ credit-limit ∧
│
│          £0.00 ⩽ max-withdrawal ⩽ balance − credit-limit)
│
│  credit-limit ⩽ £0.00
│
│  credit-limit ⩾ max-credit
└─────────────────────────────────────────
```

$\heartsuit$

2.9 Notation for Specification of Systems

2.9.1 General

So far, our interest in the schema language has been limited to stating sentences in the language, and to expressing requirements common to all possible states of a given system. The state information, which is common to all possible states of the system, is referred to here as 'general state'. Obviously, the specification of the general state says very little about the evolution of a system. Full specification of the system requires the definition of several other aspects and generally consists of:

- The general state of the system
- Its initial and, where applicable, the terminal states
- State transformations under an agreed set of operations.

As indicated under the utilities of various schema operations, the notion of general state may be captured through a schema with the following understanding:

- Schema components represent the 'state variables'
- Schema predicates represent the 'state invariant'
- The above together represent the 'general state'.

However, in order to describe the system evolution properly, one has to deal with the operational aspects of the system. This requires some additional notation, which is discussed in Sections 2.9.3 and 2.9.4.

2.9.2 Types of Operations

Various operations applicable to a system may be classified in two ways. Firstly, they may be classified depending on the effect of the operations on the system state, namely as:

- *'Effective'* state transformations, that is, those which alter the state of the system
- *Query operations*, which do not affect the state of the system, but simply retrieve information about the state.

Secondly, operations may be classified from the user's point of view according to the expected behaviour:

(i) *Primary operations*
   These are the operations that describe the expected behaviour under normal circumstances, that is, under admissible inputs and states. Primary operations are supposed to fail if their preconditions are not met at the time of invocation.

(ii) *Exception handling operations*

These operations are designed to ensure an alternative 'user–friendly' outcome with some kind of error notification, and to prevent alterations to the system state in the event of failures of primary operations.

(iii) *Total operations*

These operations are guaranteed to succeed under all inputs and in all states. This is achieved by composing the primary operations with an appropriate set of exception handling operations which together ensure an identically true precondition.

NOTE: This text uses the same schema name for both the primary operation and its corresponding total version, but distinguishes the former from the latter by the subscript 0.

2.9.3 Naming Conventions

Among the notational devices intended for the specification of operations are the conventions given in Table 2.2.

Table 2.2. Conventions in schema usage in specification of operations

Utility	Convention
For identifying the <u>state before</u> the operation	Use the schema representing the given state in undecorated form. Let the undecorated schema components refer to the individual state variables of the <u>before state</u>.
For identifying the <u>state after</u> the operation	Decorate the schema representing the given state with a quote and use the quoted names for referring to <u>after state</u> variables.
For identifying the <u>initial state</u> (a unique operation with only an 'after state')	Use the schema name with the subscript '*init*' to identify the initial state and define the initialisation with the quoted schema name, quoted component names and, where applicable, any inputs.
For identifying the <u>terminal state</u>	Use the schema as in 'before state'.
For identifying the <u>inputs</u>	Postfix the identifier representing the input with a question mark '?'.
For identifying the <u>outputs</u>	Postfix the identifier representing the output with an exclamation mark '!'.

2.9.4 Some Common Abbreviations

Δ Notation

UTILITY: To identify two adjacent states of the system. The two states may in general be different, the difference signifying the expected transformation from one state to the other.

USAGE: The notation denotes the conjunction of the (undecorated) operand schema with its quoted version. Following the conventions given in the last subsection, the result is a schema allowing reference to a 'before state' at some appropriate time in the system history and its immediate 'after state'.

SYNTAX: Prefix Δ to the schema name.

For example, for a certain schema A

$$\Delta A \triangleq A \land A'$$

with A describing the before state of the system concerned, and A' its immediate after state.

Ξ Notation

UTILITY: To identify two adjacent states of the system, which are identical. Identical adjacent states are necessary for specification of query and exception (error) handling operations, where the system state is expected to remain unaffected.

USAGE: The notation denotes the conjunction of the (undecorated) operand schema with its quoted version, but with an added constraint requiring them to be equal. The result is a schema allowing reference to a 'before state' and its immediate 'after state'. However, no effective state transformation may take place.

SYNTAX: Prefix Ξ to the schema name.

For example, for the schema A used above

$$\Xi A \triangleq \Delta A \mid A = A' \triangleq A \land A' \mid A = A'$$

EXAMPLE 2.23 Bank Account

In order to illustrate the notation and the conventions outlined in this section, let us define two operations on *Account*: one for withdrawing money from the account and the other for querying the maximum permitted withdrawal from the account. Let us first define the primary operations.

In dealing with the exceptions, an enumerated type REPORT is used for a set of appropriate messages. Some of its values are as follows.

```
REPORT ::= 'Inappropriate credit limit!'
         | 'Customer name different!'
         | 'Debit amount is negative or exceeds the limit!'
         | 'Unknown account identifier!'
         | ······ etc.······
```

However, our first task is to define the initialisation of *Account*, which may be done as follows.

$$Account_{init} \; \widehat{=} \; [Account'; \; name? : \text{NAME};$$
$$credit\text{-}limit? : \text{STERLING} \mid$$
$$credit\text{-}limit? \geqslant max\text{-}credit \; \wedge$$
$$name = name? \; \wedge \; balance' = \pounds 0.00 \; \wedge$$
$$credit\text{-}limit' = credit\text{-}limit? \; \wedge$$
$$max\text{-}withdrawl' = \pounds 0.00] \; \vee$$
$$Excessive CreditLimit$$

where

$$Excessive CreditLimit \; \widehat{=} \; [credit\text{-}limit? : \text{STERLING};$$
$$rep! : \text{REPORT} \mid$$
$$credit\text{-}limit? < max\text{-}credit \; \wedge$$
$$rep! =' \text{ Inappropriate credit limit!'}]$$

Although the above two schemas are defined with no reference to an account, they use the notion of *precondition* for the first time. For example, the schema *Excessive CreditLimit* contains the formula

$$credit\text{-}limit? < max\text{-}credit$$

which checks whether the credit limit, input as part of this operation, is consistent with the maximum credit limit defined as a global constant. The preconditions appearing in operations such as $Debit_0$ given below are, perhaps, more meaningful since they are defined in the context of *Account*. A further discussion on this will follow in Section 2.11. Proceeding to the specification of these operations, we have:

$$
\begin{array}{|l}
\hline
\;\; Debit_0 \underline{\hspace{6cm}} \\
\;\; \Delta Account \\
\\
\;\; name? : \text{NAME} \\
\\
\;\; amount? : \text{STERLING} \\
\hline
\;\;\; \left. \begin{array}{l} name? = name \\ \pounds 0.00 < amount? \leqslant min(balance - credit\text{-}limit, \\ \qquad\qquad\qquad\qquad max\text{-}withdrawal) \end{array} \right\} \;\; \text{precondition} \\
\\
\;\;\; \left. \begin{array}{l} balance' = balance - amount? \\ name' = name \\ credit\text{-}limit' = credit\text{-}limit \\ max\text{-}withdrawal' = max\text{-}withdrawal \end{array} \right\} \cdots\cdots\cdots \text{ postcondition} \\
\hline
\end{array}
$$

where *min* is a function taking two numbers and returning the minimum of the two.

__ $QueryMaxWithdrawal_0$ _____

$\Xi Account$

$name?$: NAME

$amount!$: STERLING

$name? = name$ .... precondition

$amount! = min(max\text{-}withdrawal, balance-$

$\qquad credit\text{-}limit)$ .... the output
---

The operations $Debit_0$ and $QueryMaxWithdrawal_0$ are, in the terminology introduced earlier, primary operations. The behaviours not conforming to primary behaviour may be handled by the following exception handling operations:

__ $WrongCustomer$ _____

$\Xi Account$

$name?$: NAME

$rep!$: REPORT

$name? \neq name$

$rep! = $ 'Customer name different!'

__ $InappropriateAmount$ _____

$\Xi Account$

$amount?$: STERLING

$£0.00 \geqslant amount? \vee amount? > min(max\text{-}withdrawal,$

$\qquad\qquad\qquad balance - credit\text{-}limit)$

$rep! = $ 'Debit amount is negative or exceeds the limit!'

The total operations which combine both the primary behaviour and the exception handling behaviour may now be defined as

$$Debit \mathrel{\widehat=} Debit_0 \vee WrongCustomer \vee$$
$$InappropriateAmount$$
$$QueryMaxWithdrawal \mathrel{\widehat=} QueryMaxWithdrawal_0 \vee$$
$$WrongCustomer$$

$\heartsuit$

2.10 Schema Composition

UTILITY: This is the basic schema operator for sequential composition of sub-operations to form a more complex composite operation.

SYNTAX: $opA \, \mathbf{\mathring{}}\, opB$

both opA and opB being schemas defining operations. The above is to be read as 'opA followed by opB'.

USAGE: By convention, the after state of the operation defined by the schema opA automatically becomes the before state of the operation defined by the schema opB. Also, each matching inter-state variable is renamed into an appropriate third name and hidden. This has the effect of the before state of opA and the after state of opB defining, respectively, the before and after states of the composite operation. Furthermore, the inputs and the outputs of opA and opB become those of the composite operation.

Obviously, opA and opB cannot be two arbitrary operation schemas and must satisfy the following:

- The two operations must be compatible in terms of the states involved, that is, they must have the same state variables
- The after state of opA must satisfy the precondition of opB.

NOTE: The schema composition operator $\mathring{}$ is a mathematical relation on the set of system states. Therefore, one can speak of the iteration of the composition operator $\mathring{}$; see Section 4.2 (page 69) for an example.

EXAMPLE 2.24 Traffic Lights

This example concerns the specification of a single set of traffic lights. It is a simple example illustrating the specification of state based systems in Z, but we must acknowledge immediately that a language such as Z is not expressive enough to address the problem completely, in particular its timing aspects, which are ignored here as a simplification.

The lights may be represented mathematically in different ways, for example, as:

(a) a mapping from the positions in the frame to some representation of lights
(b) three distinct binary valued components
(c) a set of up to three colours

Our illustration is based on (c), the most abstract representation in the above list. Let us first introduce a free type called *Colour*

$Colour ::= \text{red} \mid \text{amber} \mid \text{green}$

The state of the set of lights may be captured then by the following schema

$$\begin{array}{|l}
\hline
\_\,Lights \,\_\rule{0pt}{0pt} \\
\quad display : \mathbb{F}\ Colour \\
\hline
\quad display \neq Colour \\
\quad display \neq \varnothing \\
\quad \{\mathsf{green, amber}\} \not\subseteq display \\
\quad \{\mathsf{green, red}\} \not\subseteq display \\
\hline
\end{array}$$

NOTE: Since *Colour* is a finite set, it is immaterial in the above whether *display* is of type $\mathbb{F}$ *Colour* or $\mathbb{P}$ *Colour*.

The changes taking place in the set of lights may be described in terms of two basic state transformations, namely, *Go* for changing the lights from red to green, and *Stop* for changing from green to red. *AmberRed* signifies a state where the display shows both amber and red simultaneously. These may in turn be decomposed further into state transformations as

$$Go \;\widehat{=}\; RedToAmberRed \,\mathbin{\raise.6ex\hbox{$\scriptscriptstyle\circ$}\mkern-4mu\lower.6ex\hbox{$\scriptscriptstyle\circ$}}\, AmberRedToGreen$$
$$Stop \;\widehat{=}\; GreenToAmber \,\mathbin{\raise.6ex\hbox{$\scriptscriptstyle\circ$}\mkern-4mu\lower.6ex\hbox{$\scriptscriptstyle\circ$}}\, AmberToRed$$

where we have used the schema composition operator $\mathbin{\raise.6ex\hbox{$\scriptscriptstyle\circ$}\mkern-4mu\lower.6ex\hbox{$\scriptscriptstyle\circ$}}$ to form the more complex state transformations from the simpler ones. The definition of these simpler transformations are straightforward. Below are just two of them.

$$\begin{array}{|ll}
\hline
\_\,RedToAmberRed \,\_\rule{0pt}{0pt} & \\
\quad \Delta Lights & \text{(i)} \\
\hline
\quad display = \{\mathsf{red}\} & \text{(ii)} \\
\quad display' = display \cup \{\mathsf{amber}\} & \text{(iii)} \\
\hline
\end{array}$$

The signature (i) illustrates the use of the Δ notation for introducing two adjacent states of the system described by *Lights*. The predicate (ii) is a precondition involving the before state and permitting the state transformation. The predicate (iii) states what should take place as a result of this state transformation. It illustrates the use of both quoted and unquoted components in specifying the state transformation, although there are other simpler ways of doing this.

In English, the above specification requires that the state of the lights should be transformed into displaying both red and amber by this operation, and that it should take place only if the display shows the red colour initially. Obviously, two further requirements implicit in the specification are the maintenance of the state invariant in the two states before and after the operation.

The second sub-transformation of *Go* is

$$
\begin{array}{|l}
\hline
\_AmberRedToGreen _____ \\
\Delta Lights \\
\hline
display = \{\mathsf{amber, red}\} \\
display' = Colour - display \\
\hline
\end{array}
$$

where the notation has been used in an identical manner to that in *Red-ToAmberRed*.

The two sub-transformations together define the final definition for *Go*. An outline of the fully expanded schema for *Go* may be revealing as to the amount of knowledge expressed in its specification.

$Go \mathrel{\widehat{=}}$

$$
\begin{array}{|l}
\hline
\_Go _____ \\
display, display' : \mathbb{F}\, Colour \\
\hline
\left.
\begin{array}{l}
display \neq Colour \\
display \neq \varnothing \\
\ldots
\end{array}
\right\} \ldots\ldots\ldots\ldots\ldots\ldots\ldots \text{ before state invariant} \\[6pt]
\left.
\begin{array}{l}
display' \neq Colour \\
display' \neq \varnothing \\
\ldots
\end{array}
\right\} \ldots\ldots\ldots\ldots\ldots\ldots\ldots \text{ after state invariant} \\[6pt]
display = \{\mathsf{red}\} \ldots\ldots\ldots\ldots\ldots\ldots\ldots\ldots\ldots \text{ precondition} \\[4pt]
\exists\, display'' : \mathbb{F}\, Colour \bullet \\
\qquad
\left.
\begin{array}{l}
display'' \neq Colour \\
display'' \neq \varnothing \\
\ldots\ldots
\end{array}
\right\} \ldots\ldots\ldots\ldots\ldots\ldots
\begin{array}{r}
\text{intermediate} \\
\text{state} \\
\text{invariant}
\end{array} \\[10pt]
\qquad
\left.
\begin{array}{l}
display'' = display \cup \{\mathsf{amber}\} \\
display'' = \{\mathsf{amber, red}\}
\end{array}
\right\}
\begin{array}{r}
\text{intermediate} \\
\text{state} \\
\text{transformation}
\end{array} \\[8pt]
display' = Colour - display'' \ldots\ldots\ldots\ldots\ldots \text{ after state} \\
\hline
\end{array}
$$

A comparison of the original expression for *Go* and the above expanded version demonstrates quite clearly the advantages offered by the schema language with respect to conciseness and clarity.   ♡

2.11 Pre and Post Conditions

Given the specification for an operation on a system, it is sometimes necessary to examine its pre and post conditions as expressed in the specification.

The schema language provides the following two schema operators for this purpose.

UTILITY: The operators 'pre' and 'post' enable the derivation of the pre and post conditions from operation specifications.

SYNTAX:

pre ⟨*operation-schema-name*⟩, or

post ⟨*operation-schema-name*⟩

USAGE: The operators are applicable to operation schemas involving two states. They have the following effect:

- the operator 'pre' hides the after state and outputs by existentially quantifying the relevant components in the predicate part.
- the operator 'post' hides the before state and inputs by existentially quantifying the relevant components in the predicate part. Also, the after state components are undecorated and the quantified components are appropriately renamed to prevent inadvertent name clashing.

EXAMPLE 2.25 Bank Account

The two operators yield the following when applied to $Debit_0$ defined in Section 2.23:

pre $Debit_0$ $\widehat{=}$

┌─ pre $Debit_0$ ─────────────────────────────────────
│ *Account*
│
│ *name?* : NAME
│
│ *amount?* : STERLING
│ ──
│ $name? = name$ ⎫
│ $£0.00 < amount? \leqslant min(balance - credit\text{-}limit,$ ⎬ pre
│ $max\text{-}withdrawal)$ ⎭ condition
│
│ $\exists\, Account' \bullet balance' = balance - amount?$ ⎫   hidden
│ $name' = name$ ⎬ ········· after
│ $credit\text{-}limit' = credit\text{-}limit$ ⎪   state &
│ $max\text{-}withdrawal' = max\text{-}withdrawal$ ⎭   inputs
└──

post $Debit_0$ $\widehat{=}$

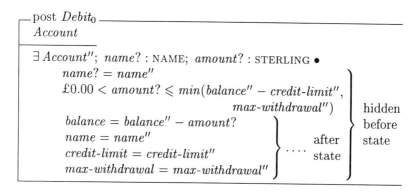

NOTE: The after state variables of $Debit_0$ are no longer quoted in the schema (post $Debit_0$).   ♡

EXAMPLE 2.26 Traffic Lights
Referring to Example 2.24 on traffic lights

pre $RedToAmberRed \cong$

```
┌─ pre RedToAmberRed ─────────────────────────────────────
│ Lights
│ ────────────────────────────────────────
│
│ display = {red} ..................................... precondition
│                                                          ⎫ hidden
│ ∃ Lights' • display' = display ∪ {amber} ...............  ⎬ after
│                                                          ⎭ state
└──────────────────────────────────────────────────────
```

post $RedToAmberRed \cong$

```
┌─ post RedToAmberRed ─────────────────────────────────────
│ Lights
│ ────────────────────────────────────────
│
│ ∃ Lights'' • display'' = {red} ∧                         ⎫ hidden
│      display = display'' ∪ {amber} ······ after state     ⎬ before
│                                                          ⎭ state
└──────────────────────────────────────────────────────
```

♡

2.12 Promotion

To integrate lower level subsystem specifications at a higher level system specification, this section introduces a technique called *promotion*. It may be used when the lower level subsystem definitions are treated effectively as *data types* at the higher level.

For example, if the definition of *Account*, introduced in Example 2.13, is to be used in defining the state of a bank operating, possibly, a large number of accounts, an appropriate mathematical representation would be the following schema:

$$
\begin{array}{|l}
\hline
\_Bank _____ \\
\quad accounts : \text{ACC-ID} \rightarrowtail\!\!\!\!\rightarrow Account \\
\hline
\end{array}
$$

consisting of an injective function from ACC-ID to *Account*. Note that the definition of *accounts*, and hence that of *Bank*, uses *Account* as a data type. In general, such higher level representations may require additional state variables and predicates, and not just one component as in the above.

If a choice of the above mathematical form is made, then it makes sense to use not only the definition of the state as defined by the schema *Account*, but also the operations defined on that state. This is the idea underlying the treatment of *Account* as a data type. In other words, the definition of *Account* is not just to be considered on its own, but in conjunction with its operations. Two such operations, namely *Debit* and *QueryMaxWithdrawal*, have already been defined in Example 2.23, but in order to model the functionality of a realistic bank, additional operations are obviously required. For the purpose here, however, let us assume that the definition of *Account* as a data type includes all such required operations on it.

The introduction of such lower level operations is usually motivated by various problem solving strategies, for example, from considerations such as how to decompose a problem, or how to specify a system in a hierarchical and modular manner. In this context, it is desirable that the definition of higher level *Bank* utilises the definition of lower level *Account* in defining the required operations at the level of *Bank*. A convenient way of doing this is as follows.

Given any particular account, sub-operations such as *Debit* affect only that account. Typically, the effect of such operations on individual accounts on the rest of the system is none or, if any, identical. Therefore, the effect can be either completely localised or, if there were to be a global effect, it is usually possible to identify a 'template' of any side–effect common to several lower level operations. Assuming that lower level operations have no effect on other parts of the system, it is therefore possible to 'factor out' the 'global effect' of any 'local operation'. In specification terms, this amounts to separating, as applicable, the higher level behaviour common to several lower level operations, and then reusing this partial specification repeatedly in producing the full specification of each of the higher level operations. Thus, the task turns out to be an integration of the lower level specifications with the above mentioned partial specification.

Returning to our example, elements common to all account operations at the higher level can be captured by the following subsidiary specification:

$$
\begin{array}{|l}
\_\,BankUpdate \underline{\hspace{5cm}} \\
\Delta Bank \\[4pt]
\Delta Account \\[4pt]
account\text{-}id? : \text{ACC-ID} \\
\hline
account\text{-}id? \in \mathrm{dom}\ accounts \\[4pt]
\theta Account = accounts\ account\text{-}id? \\[4pt]
\theta Account' = accounts'\ account\text{-}id? \\[4pt]
\{account\text{-}id?\} \lhd accounts' = \{account\text{-}id?\} \lhd accounts
\end{array}
$$

The above is a partial specification, specifying how the account system as a whole is to be updated in the event of any, yet undefined, operation on any account. With the above in place, it seems as possible to define the required operation of debiting a particular account at the level of the bank as:

$$BankDebit_{interim_1} \ \widehat{=}\ Debit \wedge BankUpdate$$

but the visualisation of its expanded version should indicate that this is not quite what is required. Indeed, its expanded form would consist of components such as *balance, credit-limit, max-withdrawal, balance*, etc., which are obviously superfluous at the level of the bank. Perhaps, the expanded form should be:

```
┌─ BankDebit_interim₂ ────────────────────────────────
│ accounts, accounts' : ACC-ID ⇸ Account
│
│ account-id? : ACC-ID
│
│ name? : NAME
│
│ amount? : STERLING
├────────────────────────────────────────────────────
│ account-id? ∈ dom accounts
│
│ ∃ Account, Account' •
│
│      θAccount = accounts account-id?
│
│      θAccount' = accounts' account-id?
│
│      accounts' = accounts ⊕ {account-id? ↦ Account'}
│
│      credit-limit ⩽ £0.00
│
│      balance ⩾ credit-limit
│
│      credit-limit ⩾ max-credit
│
│      £0.00 ⩽ max-withdrawal ⩽ balance − credit-limit
│
│      credit-limit' ⩽ £0.00
│
│      balance' ⩾ credit-limit'
│
│      credit-limit' ⩾ max-credit
│
│      £0.00 ⩽ max-withdrawal' ⩽ balance' − credit-limit'
│
│      name? = name
│
│      £0.00 < amount? ⩽ min(balance − credit-limit, max-withdrawal)
│
│              ⋮
└────────────────────────────────────────────────────
```

In short, the debit operation at the bank level should be of the form:

$$BankDebit_{interim_2} \mathrel{\widehat{=}} BankUpdate \wedge Debit \backslash (Account, Account')$$

The only improvement suggested in the above is to hide in the schema $BankDebit_{interim_1}$ the schemas $Account$ and $Account'$, appearing in the lower level operation $Debit$, as they are no longer necessary as part of the operation $BankDebit$ at the higher level.

The definition given above is still referred to as an interim specification. This is because, as it stands, the specification describes the behaviour of a *partial operation*; the operation can still fail should the inputs not satisfy the precondition. In order to make the operation a total one, we require an exception handling operation, dealing with unknown account identifiers provided as inputs. Let us define this exception handling operation as

```
┌─ UnknownAccountId ────────────────────────────────────
│  ΞBank
│
│  rep! : REPORT
│
│  account-id? : ACC-ID
├────────────────────────────────────────────────────────
│  account-id? ∉ dom accounts
│
│  rep! =' Unknown account identifier!'
└────────────────────────────────────────────────────────
```

The above exception handling operation should succeed in the event of *account-id?* not satisfying the precondition of $BankDebit_{interim_2}$. Thus, the total operation for debiting an account at the level of the bank is:

$$BankDebit \mathrel{\widehat{=}} ((BankUpdate \wedge Debit) \vee UnknownAccountId) \backslash$$
$$(Account, Account')$$

Analogously, the operation for querying the maximum amount of withdrawal from a particular account may be defined as:

$$BankQueryMaxWithdrawal \mathrel{\widehat{=}} ((BankUpdate \wedge QueryMaxWithdrawal) \vee$$
$$UnknownAccountId) \backslash (Account, Account')$$

Exercises

2.1 With reference to Examples 2.3 and 2.7, define predicates $\leqslant$ and $\geqslant$ for the comparison of monetary values as represented in STERLING, an operation for their subtraction and an operation for multiplying a monetary value by a number.

2.2 Because of its use as a running example, the specification of the bank developed in this chapter considers the formalisation of its various aspects without stating its requirements informally at the outset. Produce first an informal specification for a bank incorporating an appropriate subset of the requirements assumed in this formalisation, and then a better structured formal specification. Note that specifications in Z include a supplementary narrative, assisting those less familiar with the notation to understand the requirements expressed by the mathematical text.

2.3 Extend the informal specification produced in your answer to Exercise 2.2 by incorporating some additional requirements. For example, the reader may wish to consider additional types of accounts such as savings accounts and joint accounts and operations for adding interest or bank charges. Specify the functionality imposed by the additional requirements formally.

3. An Approach to Specification

This chapter is an account of the development process of a formal specification. Its purpose is to give the reader some guidance as to how a formal specification may be developed, in particular, to illustrate how to analyse a problem, how to put abstraction and modularisation into practice and how to construct a mathematical model of a system.

3.1 Introduction

In some ways, the task of formal specification may overwhelm a newcomer. This may be due to the lack of fluency in the mathematical language, but there are other important but less evident factors. These concern the creative aspects of formal specification. Intuition, discovery and abstraction all come into play in the process of specification. These were discussed in Chapter 1.

It is impossible, and inappropriate, to prescribe a general methodology for developing formal specifications. This is because problems vary in nature and any given problem may have a multitude of solutions. What follows is an illustration of a particular approach. With practice, the reader is likely to develop his own approach. It is important that he remains critical and alert for inspirations within. The reader is encouraged to seize the opportunity and pursue his own line of thought whenever he sees an alternative solution.

The problem we attempt is a simple airline seat booking system. It incorporates substantial simplifications in order to make the case study more amenable to our purpose. Below is an informal problem specification.

An Airline Booking System

An airline requires a simple software system for booking seats for its passengers and cancelling reservations. It operates flights along a number of different routes. At this stage, the major concern of the airline is to maintain an up to date record on seat availability on its different flights, including the flights in progress. The system must cater appropriately for any queries made by the operators on seat availability, and must be helpful to them when their requests can not be attended to for one reason or another. For simplicity, it has been decided not to consider other flight operational aspects, and to disregard problems with concurrent updates to the system.

3.2 An Initial Understanding

3.2.1 Identification of the Objects of Discourse and Operations

One of the first tasks of specification is to identify objects, physical or abstract, of interest to the task in hand, as well as the way that such objects are likely to be utilised by the users. Some of these objects may be directly evident in the original informal specification, while others may have to be discovered in the process of an extended requirements analysis. When appropriate, as in our exercise, the specifier may use his own understanding of the application to fill out any missing details. There is no specific method of identifying objects and operations of interest, other than by carefully examining the informal specification, and underlining or listing all items which appear to be important. Having surveyed the informal specification, supplement the list with any additional item which may appear to have been omitted. At this stage, there should not be any commitment to the items in the list, and the intention must be to ensure that nothing has been overlooked. The following is such an extended list of items of interest, the indentation indicating the different levels of detail.

Entities or objects

airline
    flights
        carriers
            seats
                capacity
                seat arrangements
                smoking areas
            last/current port on route
    routes
    personnel
        operators
            own operators
            agents
passengers
    name
    address
    telephone
    travel details
        port of travel origin
        port of travel destination

air ports
     city
     country
     name
     landing facilities

Operations (concerns only the maintenance of an up to date record on availability of seats)

booking
cancelling
queries on seat availability
        depending on flights
        depending on journeys
        vacancies

3.3 Abstraction and Modularisation

The above list gives a better idea of the task in hand but, at the same time, indicates a degree of complexity that was not evident in the informal specification. If we are to manage this complexity with ease, but without jeopardising the clarity and completeness, we must consciously follow the two most important principles in software engineering. These are:

- Abstraction
- Modularisation

and were discussed in Chapter 1.

3.3.1 Abstraction

First, let us attempt to put into practice the notion of abstraction. Recall that abstraction concerns the appropriate choice of detail. The list in Section 3.2.1 outlines the extent of detail currently envisaged. In general, some of these may be curtailed and others may have to be extended. The choice of detail may be guided by what we have been asked to do. Returning to our list, the specifier may question, for example, whether all passenger details are necessary, or whether we simply require their travel details. The informal specification mentions nothing about passenger queries, their travel details, airline personnel or travel agents except saying that the system is to be used by the 'operators'. It also does not deal with such matters as security. Had this been a real life application, it would have been prudent to clarify such matters, but let us ignore them since they are not mentioned in the informal specification. The only concern of the system appears to be the maintenance of a record of seat availability and, therefore, a simple passenger count will suffice and the maintenance of the accommodation layout of each carrier is unnecessary.

The above paragraph discusses what is necessary and what is unnecessary. Now, we will look at a slightly different aspect. Although the informal specification made no mention of the airport, we have decided to include it in our list and there is no difficulty in justifying it. However, we should question the number of airport details required in our representation. Do we really need to know airport names, country of location, facilities, and so forth? Such internal details are irrelevant at this stage. An appropriate decision is to defer the whole issue, or to refuse to be drawn into such detail. There always comes a time in any analysis when we should restrain our quest for detail, either by choice or due to the lack of relevant knowledge. Instead, we may appeal to an intuitive understanding of the objects concerned without giving a proper specification. Any set of objects whose internal structure has been ignored for one reason or another is referred to as *basic* or *generic type*; see Section 2.2.1. The way to introduce them is:

[*Airport*]

declaring effectively that *Airport* denotes a distinct set and is to be used as a type. Informally, *Airport* stands for the set of all such objects which we refer to as 'airport' in the ordinary language.

Looking back, we see a clear line of demarcation emerging between the details we feel are relevant to our work and those we may safely ignore. This line of demarcation also serves as the boundary between the formal and the informal worlds. The specification we intend to construct will still be founded on the informal understanding of certain objects. However, our specification will not be vulnerable to misinterpretation and inaccuracies, so long as the informal understanding is firm enough and is not likely to be disputed by the parties involved: the customer and the developer.

3.3.2 Modularisation

The second dimension of complexity in our task is the interdependencies between different aspects of the problem. For example, it is impossible to deal with accommodation aspects fully without knowing the carrier and the details of the route. However, in some cases, there may be a degree of independence between different aspects. Such aspects constitute sub-problems differing in nature, but exhibiting a limited number of clearly identifiable dependencies. Once such dependencies have been identified, it is initially possible to treat sub-problems in isolation and independently. For example, the accommodation issues and flight journey issues can be separated at a certain level. Certain aspects of flight accommodation may be handled with no reference to flight route, and vice versa. Obviously, at some stage the issues common to both must be addressed in conjunction. In the case of our example, we must make sure that the flight is not over-booked on any leg of the flight route and that bookings are made only for journeys served by the flight.

Thus, it is clear that we may treat:

- information on flight journey, and
- information on flight accommodation

separately. We adopt the above as a scheme for modularisation of our specification. When the specification is fully developed, the solutions to the sub-problems will take the form of subsystems of the more complex overall system. Section 3.4 concerns the definition of the subsystem dealing with the aspects of flight journey and Section 3.5 that dealing with accommodation issues. Section 3.6.1 brings these together by defining what is meant by a 'flight'.

It is clear from the above that if the system to be specified is already in existence in some form (a physical model, a real life application, or perhaps in some non-computerised form) the specifier may gain some inspiration as to how best to decompose the original problem into sub-problems. Clearly, such existing models reflect the organisational strategies based on experience and operational convenience.

3.4 Flight Journey

Let us consider first the sub-problem on flight journey, where we attempt to capture precisely the notion of a flight journey. It is clear that this notion should cover both flights yet to take place and those already in progress. These may be accounted for by considering the following two features:

- Flight route
- Next or last port of departure

From a computational point of view, we must begin to treat the above as certain attributes and, in this respect, let us use the following attribute names:

- *flightRoute* (flight route)
- *nextPort* (next port of departure)

Having introduced the attributes, we must be more explicit about the sort of information that should be gathered under these attributes. This may be done by examining the desired form (structure) of the relevant information, or the relationships these attributes are expected to express. The most concise way of stating this is by associating with each attribute a mathematical structure, such as a set, a relation, a function or whatever is appropriate. Dealing with the second item first, it is easily seen that *nextPort* must take a value from *Airport*. In other words:

$nextPort : Airport$

A mathematical representation of a route is slightly more complex. In fact, a route can be represented in a number of different ways. One representation that comes to mind immediately is a sequence of airports. An alternative would be a set of pairs of adjacent airports. The first alternative is discarded here in favour of the second, but is left as an exercise for the reader; see Exercise 3.2. Our justifications for this choice are as follows:

- The first alternative requires the imposition of a numerical ordering on a subset of *Airport*, which is, arguably, an unnecessary detail.
- It is also suggestive of certain obvious implementations, namely lists and arrays. We prefer not to prompt design decisions here, if it is at all possible.
- The second alternative is more interesting, mathematically, as a learning exercise.

Having made the choice of a relation on *Airport* for the attribute *flightRoute*, let us examine what kind of relation it is. The answer to this question lies in the requirements and, in particular, those on flight routes. Our informal specification says nothing about the matter, so it is up to us to develop our own understanding. In this respect, here are some points to consider:

- A flight is an unbroken non-circular journey between two airports.
- A flight visits any airport on its route only once.
- There are neither multiple ports of origin nor multiple ports of destination.
- There are no diverging (branching out) or merging (branching in) sub-routes within the flight route.
- There are no loops on the route, or away from it.

These together may be expressed in a slightly more mathematical language as:

- Existence of at least one pair of distinct elements in *flightRoute*.
- Absence of disjointed (fragmented) sub-graphs in the graph of *flightRoute*.
- Existence of ports of origin and destination (also, non-circularity of the graph of *flightRoute* and non-emptiness).
- Uniqueness of ports of origin and destination.
- Absence of loops.
- No diverging or merging arrows in the graph of *flightRoute*.

Some of these requirements may be captured neatly by specifying just the type of the relation *flightRoute*. For example, the choice of an injective function immediately satisfies the last requirement in the above list and, to an extent, the requirement on exclusion of internal loops and circularities. An exception to this is when *flightRoute* consists of a singleton made up from the same element. Thus, a signature such as the following:

$$flightRoute : Airport \rightarrowtail Airport$$

declares an appropriate mathematical structure for *flightRoute*. Let us now attend to the remaining requirements on flight routes. In order to satisfy ourselves that all the above requirements have been met, we need to be able to observe at some stage that the following statements hold.

(a) The relation *flightRoute* is not empty.

$$flightRoute \neq \varnothing$$

(b) There are no loops at nodes.

$$\text{id } Airport \cap flightRoute = \varnothing$$

(c) There are no circularities in the route.

$$\text{id } Airport \cap flightRoute^{+} = \varnothing$$

where *flightRoute*$^{+}$ denotes the irreflexive transitive closure of *flightRoute*.
(d) There is at least one port of origin and at least one port of destination.

$$\text{dom } flightRoute - \text{ran } flightRoute \neq \varnothing$$
$$\text{ran } flightRoute - \text{dom } flightRoute \neq \varnothing$$

(e) Ports of origin and destination are each unique.

$$\forall\, p, q : Airport \bullet$$
$$p, q \in (\text{dom } flightRoute - \text{ran } flightRoute) \Rightarrow p = q$$
$$p, q \in (\text{ran } flightRoute - \text{dom } flightRoute) \Rightarrow p = q$$

What we have above is a collection of mathematical statements. The assertion of such a collection amounts to a mathematical specification of requirements on flight routes. These statements are not all isolated facts and some are obviously related to one another. Therefore, is it necessary to assert each such statement individually? The answer is obviously 'no', because it is possible to treat our understanding of a flight route as a kind of a *scientific*, or a *mathematical, theory*, where we cite some of the statements as *axioms* and hope to deduce others as their consequences, that is, *theorems*. If we are to follow this route, we should make a choice in the above collection of statements, and assert an appropriate minimal set as our axioms. We have chosen the statements (c), (d) and (e), and hope to deduce the rest, as well as others, as theorems of this theory. Some interesting observations to be verified as such theorems are:

1. Absence of loops in *flightRoute*.

2. Reachability of the port of flight destination from that of flight origin by successively making n steps, n being the number of legs in the flight route.

3. The route is not disjointed; in other words, as a graph the flight route is compact.

The above analysis has enabled a better understanding of what is meant by a flight route, albeit limited to a specific purpose. However, even at this early stage, we begin to experience the large extent of possible mathematical statements in the formal description. From the writer's point of view, this poses a very serious difficulty in referring to any set of related mathematical statements serving, possibly, as a mathematical theory. From the reader's point of view, such a description may not be easy to read and comprehend.

This is a demonstration of the value of formalisms, such as the schema language of Z, intended for developing mathematical specifications. These benefits have been discussed elsewhere in this text; see Section 2.1. Relying on the concept of *schema*, Z allows us to express our present understanding of a flight route as:

$$
\begin{array}{l}
\underline{\quad Route \quad\quad\quad\quad\quad\quad\quad\quad\quad\quad\quad\quad\quad\quad\quad\quad\quad\quad\quad} \\
\quad flightRoute : Airport \rightarrowtail Airport \\
\underline{\quad\quad\quad\quad\quad\quad\quad\quad\quad\quad\quad\quad\quad\quad\quad\quad\quad\quad\quad\quad\quad} \\
\quad \mathrm{dom}\ flightRoute - \mathrm{ran}\ flightRoute \neq \varnothing \\
\quad \mathrm{ran}\ flightRoute - \mathrm{dom}\ flightRoute \neq \varnothing \\
\quad \forall\, p, q : Airport \bullet \\
\quad\quad\quad p, q \in (\mathrm{dom}\ flightRoute - \mathrm{ran}\ flightRoute) \Rightarrow p = q \\
\quad\quad\quad p, q \in (\mathrm{ran}\ flightRoute - \mathrm{dom}\ flightRoute) \Rightarrow p = q \\
\quad \mathrm{id}\ Airport \cap flightRoute^{+} = \varnothing
\end{array}
$$

The above is, in effect, a set theoretic treatment of graph theoretic properties of the route.

Having understood what a flight route means, it is time to examine the relationship between the route and the next port of departure, *nextPort*, introduced earlier. Obviously, the next port of departure must be a port from which the flight is scheduled to depart. Mathematically speaking, this amounts to:

$$nextPort \in \mathrm{dom}\ flightRoute$$

Incorporating the above and *Route* in one schema (using *schema extension*; see Section 2.5.1), we arrive at a definition for the flight en-route, containing, in addition to its route, the component *nextPort* as the means for keeping track of the current state of the flight.

$$Enroute \mathrel{\widehat{=}} [Route;\ nextPort : Airport \mid nextPort \in \mathrm{dom}\ flightRoute]$$

The informal specification has simplified our task by suggesting the operational aspects of flights are not addressed. This does not mean that we should not have addressed the aspects covered by *Enroute*, but that no operations are to be considered which involve changes to the components in *Enroute* or queries on them. This is an exception to the rule; subsystems typically involve some operations and, hence, require their specification.

3.5 Flight Accommodation

Let us now attend to the second subsystem, namely, the one dealing with the accommodation aspects on board the flight. Recall that actual layout of seats inside the cabin and seat numbering are not essential for addressing the task given. Maintenance of a passenger count, together with accommodation capacity, should be sufficient for responding to queries on seat availability. In this respect, the two attributes:

- *capacity* (passenger accommodation capacity on a given flight)
- *bookings* (the number of passengers already booked in)

should be sufficient. Addressing the question of mathematical structures to be associated with these, we note that *capacity* must be a strictly positive natural number, that is

$$capacity : \mathbb{N}_1$$

However, the mathematical structure to be associated with *bookings* is slightly more complex. This is because of the need to maintain the passenger count on each and every leg of the flight route. Bearing this in mind, consider the following:

$$bookings : Airport \times Airport \nrightarrow \mathbb{N}$$

Let us now consider the specific requirements on these components. The above already stipulates that only one count may be associated with each pair of airports. Now consider whether we need to impose further constraints on each component individually. As will be shown shortly, the pairs of airports in the domain of *bookings* cannot be arbitrary. Except for this, there does not appear to be any other independent constraint we may impose on each of the above components in isolation. Now consider whether we need to impose further constraints on pairs of components. In this respect, the two components together must always satisfy another constraint, namely that the passenger count on any flight leg should never exceed the accommodation capacity:

$$\forall\, n \in \mathrm{ran}\ bookings \bullet n \leqslant capacity$$

[Had there been more components in the given subsystem, we would have continued considering the relationships exhibited by triples of components and so forth.] The above understanding may be encapsulated by the schema:

__ *Accommodation* _____

$capacity : \mathbb{N}_1$

$bookings : Airport \times Airport \nrightarrow \mathbb{N}$

$\forall\, n \in \mathrm{ran}\ bookings \bullet n \leqslant capacity$

The above is a partial specification of accommodation on board the flight; other aspects are considered below.

3.6 Definition of Flight

3.6.1 Definition of Flight State

Sections 3.4 and 3.5 considered two different aspects of an arbitrary flight independently. The two resulting mathematical definitions correspond to specifications of two sub-modules, or subsystems, of what we may regard as a flight. The definition of a flight may be given as a composition of the definitions of these subsystems in an appropriate manner. Let us compose this new definition using *schema inclusion* (see Section 2.5.1) as:

__ *Flight* _____
Enroute

Accommodation

$\mathrm{dom}\ bookings = flightRoute$

The additional axiom in the predicate part ties the two subsystems together, by addressing an issue not covered in the definition of *Accomodation*. It ensures that bookings are to be made only on the set of pairs of airports served by the flight. It is an obvious consequence that this set of pairs of airports must also obey the same properties as *flightRoute* and that it must be possible to make bookings on each and every flight leg.

The above schema describes the notion of *general state* (see Section 2.9.1) of an arbitrary flight to be satisfied by all possible states of the flight. Thus, *Flight* is an abstraction of the state of affairs on board a flight, although limited to the consideration of only some aspects of its journey and passenger accommodation. The components declared, or inherited, in the signature play the role of *state variables*, and the predicates in the schema the role of the *state invariant*. Any change to this state, for example, an operation allocating space for a passenger during a booking, is a *state transformation*.

3.6.2 Initialisation of Flight State

A special kind of state transformation is the *initialisation* of a state, which is an essential part of the definition of states. In the given case, we do this as:

$$Flight_{init} \cong Enroute_{init} \wedge Accommodation_{init}$$

where $Enroute_{init}$ is assumed to be given, since operational aspects of the flight are being ignored here. $Accomodation_{init}$ may be defined by:

$$Accommodation_{init} \cong Accommodation'; \; capacity? : \mathbb{N}_1 \mid$$
$$capacity' = capacity? \wedge \mathrm{ran} \; bookings' = \{0\}$$

which initialises the capacity to the value given by the input *capacity?*, and the bookings on all flight legs to zero. As mentioned in Section 2.9.3, note a certain peculiarity with this definition, namely that there is only an *after state*.

3.7 Operations on Flight

The only operations we have been asked to consider are those for making or cancelling bookings, and querying the seat availability on board the aircraft.

3.7.1 Passenger Details

It is convenient to consider any common feature shared by two or more operations as an auxiliary definition. This applies especially to operations for making bookings and cancellations, since they both rely on passenger information.

Since no passenger list is maintained, it is unnecessary to identify passengers as individuals with names and other details. A suitable abstraction of a 'passenger' would be to consider the ports of origin and destination of the passenger's journey. Also, the passenger may have a particular route in mind, but such a route must exhibit exactly the same properties as a flight route. Fortunately, we do not have to repeat the exercise in Section 3.4 on flight routes in dealing with passenger routes, because the schema language provides a facility for generating this information in the required form by a simple *renaming of components*; see Section 2.7.2. The required information, that is, the ports of origin and destination and the travel route, may be considered as inputs and, since no passenger list is maintained, can be discarded after use. The schema *Passenger*, defined below, is an abstraction of a passenger in the above sense.

```
┌─ Passenger ──────────────────────────────────────────
│ Route[passengerRoute?/flightRoute]
│
│ origin?, destn? : Airport
├──────────────────────────────────────────────────────
│ passengerRoute?#passengerRoute? = {origin? ↦ destn?}
└──────────────────────────────────────────────────────
```

Thus, the passenger route comprises at least the ports of origin and destination of his travel, and these must be connected by an unbroken chain of ports lying along the route given by him.

3.7.2 An Auxiliary Definition

When dealing with a particular passenger request, it is necessary to make sure the request can be served on the flight under consideration, with respect to both space and time. In particular:

(a) the passenger route must be a sub-route of flight route, and
(b) the above sub-route must lie ahead of the next port of departure of the flight en-route.

Here is an auxiliary schema definition incorporating (a) and (b) above, introduced purely for convenience in formalising the booking and cancellation operations.

```
┌─ AcceptableJourney ──────────────────────────────────
│ Enroute
│
│ Passenger
├──────────────────────────────────────────────────────
│ passengerRoute? ⊆ flightRoute
│
│ (nextPort, origin?) ∈ flightRoute*
└──────────────────────────────────────────────────────
```

According to the first axiom in the above, the passenger route must be a sub-route of the flight route. Alternatively, we could have considered the following axiom instead:

$$passengerRoute? \subseteq flightRoute^+$$

thus relaxing the requirement that the passenger must specify all legs in his journey. The second axiom uses the reflexive transitive closure $flightRoute^*$ in order to ensure that the passenger route is yet to be served by the flight concerned. It allows for two possibilities:

• The passenger wishes to depart from the next port of flight departure. That is:

$$nextPort = origin?$$

- The passenger wishes to depart from a port yet to be served by the flight. In other words, the port of origin of the passenger journey is reachable from the next port of flight departure. Thus:

$$(nextPort, origin?) \in flightRoute^+$$

The above expresses a temporal state of affairs in predicate logic, which is not equipped with any logical notion of time.

3.7.3 Messages

The definition of operations must also be helpful to the user by outputting appropriate messages, indicating whether an operation has been successful or has failed. For this purpose, we introduce a new type, the values of which are messages; they cover a range of anticipated exceptional situations:

$Report ::= $ `'Operation successful!'` $|$
`'Unsuitable flight route!'` $|$
`'Flight has departed the starting port of journey!'` $|$
`'Some flight legs on journey fully booked!'` $|$
`'No bookings on some flight legs on journey!'` $|$
`'Seats Available!'` $|$
`'Successful flight identification!'` $|$
`'Unknown flight identification!'`

3.7.4 Operation of Booking a Seat

In defining operations, we follow the framework and the conventions proposed in Section 2.9.2. In particular, the subscript 0 in operation names distinguishes the primary operation from its total version. The primary operation $Booking_0$ should succeed only when:

(a) There is a vacancy in accommodation for the passenger over all relevant flight legs.
(b) All conditions stated in *AcceptableJourney* have been met.

Thus, the operation may be defined by incorporating *AcceptableJourney* using schema inclusion:

$$
\begin{array}{l}
\underline{\quad Booking_0 \quad\rule{6cm}{0pt}} \\
\Delta Flight \\[4pt]
AcceptableJourney \\[4pt]
\Xi Enroute \\
\hline
\forall leg \in passengerRoute? \bullet bookings\ leg < capacity \\[4pt]
bookings' = bookings \oplus \{leg : Airport \times Airport \mid \\[8pt]
\qquad\qquad leg \in passengerRoute? \bullet leg \mapsto succ(bookings\ leg)\}
\end{array}
$$

where *succ* and *pred* are the successor and predecessor functions on natural numbers; *pred* being a function to be used later.

The exceptions are to be defined by examining possible circumstances under which the precondition of $Booking_0$ is violated. For dealing with unsuitability of the flight on the grounds of passenger requirements, we define the schema:

InappropriateRoute
$\Xi Flight$

Passenger

rep! : *Report*

$(origin?, destn?) \notin flightRoute^+ \lor passengerRoute? \nsubseteq flightRoute$

$rep! = $ 'Unsuitable flight route!'

A situation where it is too late to accept a booking from the given starting port of journey may be handled by:

FlightDeparted
$\Xi Flight$

Passenger

rep! : *Report*

$(origin?, destn?) \in flightRoute^+$

$passengerRoute? \subseteq flightRoute$

$(nextPort, origin?) \notin flightRoute^*$

$rep! = $ 'Flight has departed the starting port of journey!'

Finally, the flight may be fully booked on some, or all, its legs over the passenger route; this situation may be handled by an exception handling operation:

FullyBooked
$\Xi Flight$

Passenger

rep! : *Report*

$\exists leg \in passengerRoute? \bullet bookings\ leg = capacity$

$rep! = $ 'Some flight legs on journey fully booked!'

The total operation may be defined by combining the primary operation with the above exceptions in the following manner:

$Booking \mathrel{\widehat{=}} (Booking_0 \wedge [rep! : Report \mid rep! =' \texttt{Operation successful!'}])$
$\vee \; InappropriateRoute \vee FlightDeparted \vee FullyBooked$

3.7.5 Operation of Cancelling a Booking

The primary operation $Cancellation_0$ should succeed only under the following circumstances:

(a) There are some bookings on every flight leg over the passenger route.
(b) All conditions covered in $AcceptableJourney$ are being met.

The successful primary operation is:

$Cancellation_0$

$\Delta Flight$

$AcceptableJourney$

$\Xi Enroute$

$\forall \, leg \in passengerRoute? \bullet (bookings \; leg) > 0$

$bookings' = bookings \oplus \{ leg : Airport \times Airport \mid$

$\qquad\qquad leg \in passengerRoute? \bullet leg \mapsto pred(bookings \; leg) \}$

The exceptions occur when $AcceptableJourney$ is not satisfied, or when no bookings are recorded to have been made on all, or some, legs over the passenger route. Thus, we can reuse some of the exception handling operations defined for $Booking$. The only other required exception handling operation is:

$NoBookingsMade$

$\Xi Flight$

$AcceptableJourney$

$rep! : Report$

$\exists \, leg \in passengerRoute? \bullet (bookings \; leg) = 0$

$rep! = \; '\texttt{No bookings on some flight legs on journey!'}$

The total operation may be defined as analogous to $Booking$

$Cancellation \mathrel{\widehat{=}} (Cancellation_0 \wedge$
$\qquad\qquad [rep! : Report \mid rep! = \; '\texttt{Operation successful!'}]) \vee$
$\qquad\qquad InappropriateRoute \vee FlightDeparted \vee$
$\qquad\qquad NoBookingsMade$

3.7.6 Query Operation on Seat Availability

As an illustration, we define here just one simple query operation. It is on seat availability and is defined using the exception handling operation *FullyBooked*, defined earlier, and the schema *SeatsAvailable* defined below:

$$
\begin{array}{|l}
\underline{\quad SeatsAvailable \quad\qquad\qquad\qquad\qquad\qquad\qquad}\\
\Xi\,Flight\\[4pt]
AcceptableJourney\\[4pt]
rep!: Report\\
\hline
\forall\, leg \in passengerRoute? \bullet bookings\ leg < capacity\\[4pt]
rep! =' \texttt{Seats Available!}'
\end{array}
$$

The seat query operation is defined as:

$$
SeatQuery \,\hat{=}\, SeatsAvailable \lor FullyBooked \lor InappropriateRoute \lor\\
FlightDeparted
$$

Thus, if the passenger route is acceptable according to the specification *AcceptableJourney* and the flight is not fully booked over the legs of the passenger route, the operation outputs the message '`Seats Available!`'. Otherwise, it outputs a message appropriate to the circumstances.

3.8 An Airline

3.8.1 Abstract Representation

So far we have been paying attention to individual flights. Since an airline operates a number of flights, it is essential to be able to refer to different flights, and to perform the operations formulated above in the global context of the airline. What is required is a way to move up to the next level in the hierarchy of the system, namely to the level of airline definition. The definition of the airline below uses the type:

$$[FlightId]$$

where we assume that the type *FlightId* is appropriately defined for identifying all flights operated by the airline. Again, this is used as a means to avoid dealing with details such as flight numbers, scheduled times, etc. At this level, an airline may be viewed in the rather simplified form of a partial function:

$$Airline \,\hat{=}\, [flights : FlightId \nrightarrow Flight]$$

3.8.2 Initialisation

The intention is to use the above as a definition of the state of the airline, so let us define its initial state as:

$$Airline_{init} \;\widehat{=}\; Airline'; \; ids? : \mathbb{P}\, FlightId \mid \mathrm{dom}\ flights = ids? \,\wedge$$
$$\mathrm{ran}\, flights \subseteq \{Flight \bullet \theta Flight_{init}\}$$

where we rely on $Flight_{init}$, introduced in Section 3.6.2. Obviously, there are other ways of initialisation, especially if the operational needs of introduction and withdrawals of flights are known.

3.8.3 Shared Auxiliary Specifications

The operations on bookings and cancellations in the global context are defined below as state transformations on *Airline*. Following the discussion in Section 2.12, our intention is to use the operations defined in Section 3.6 on *Flight*, which deals with individual flights considered in isolation, at the level of *Airline*. For this purpose, Section 2.12 introduced an approach called *promotion*. Thus, we introduce a common template called *AirlineOpContext*, which is shared by all operations under consideration on *Airline*.

```
┌─ AirlineOpContext ──────────────────────────
│ ΔAirline
│
│ ΔFlight
│
│ flightId? : FlightId
├─────────────────────────────────────────────
│ flightId? ∈ dom flights
│
│ θFlight = flights flightId?
│
│ flights' = flights ⊕ {flightId? ↦ θFlight'}
└─────────────────────────────────────────────
```

Thus, the 'before' and 'after' states of the particular flight are those defined by an appropriately specified flight identifier. No mention is made about the relationship between the two *Flight* states; this is left open for the time being and is to be filled by an appropriate lower level operation on *Flight*. The remaining flights remain unaffected.

Exception handling, as well as 'success handling', is also shared by all operations. Their definitions are straightforward, and can be introduced as:

```
┌─ UnknownFlight ──────────────────────────────────────────────
│ Ξ Airline
│
│ flightId? : FlightId
│
│ rep! : Report
├──────────────────────────────────────────────────────────────
│ flightId? ∉ dom flights
│
│ rep! = 'Unknown flight identification!'
└──────────────────────────────────────────────────────────────
```

```
┌─ OkFlight ───────────────────────────────────────────────────
│ Δ Airline
│
│ flightId? : FlightId
│
│ rep! : Report
├──────────────────────────────────────────────────────────────
│ flightId? ∈ dom flights
│
│ rep! = 'Successful flight identification!'
└──────────────────────────────────────────────────────────────
```

3.8.4 Airline Operations

With the above, it is quite simple to construct the total operations at the level of the airline for all cases. They are:

$$AirlineBooking \,\widehat{=}\, (AirlineOpContext \land Booking \land OkFlight) \lor$$
$$UnknownFlight$$
$$AirlineCancellation \,\widehat{=}\, (AirlineOpContext \land Cancellation \land OkFlight) \lor$$
$$UnknownFlight$$
$$AirlineSeatQuery \,\widehat{=}\, (AirlineOpContext \land SeatQuery \land OkFlight) \lor$$
$$UnknownFlight$$

The intended meanings of the operations are clear from the names being used.

Concluding Remarks

Thus, we have reached the end of the specification task. Its aim has been to show how to go about developing a mathematical specification. As mentioned in Chapter 1, there exists neither a unique solution nor a correct solution to a problem of this kind in the absolute sense. Construction of a mathematical specification does not end with the production of a specification to the specifier's satisfaction. Although the specifier may have spelled out his understanding of the problem mathematically correctly on paper, there is no guarantee that this understanding agrees with that of the user, or the customer. An allowance also has to be made for mathematical inaccuracies even in the case of competent specifiers, because the task of mathematical specification is, in general, a complex one. As a result, the specification must now be subjected to scrutiny by the specifier and by others. When this is conducted from the perspective of the user, this process is known as the *requirement validation*. Only subsequent to such a critical assessment, it is prudent to assume that the task has been accomplished successfully. Unfortunately, in the given case this cannot be undertaken properly, because of its limited scope as an exercise.

This chapter has emphasised the practical application of such concepts as abstraction, modularisation and hierarchical composition in developing a mathematical model from an informally stated problem specification. The underlying mathematical language is quite simple, but its effectiveness in addressing quite complex real life problems has been demonstrated. This has been especially evident in the study of the flight route.

Exercises

3.1 Extend the scope of the specification developed in this chapter, by defining operations for the introduction, withdrawal and modification of flights from an airline's operational point of view.

3.2 Using a sequence for the flight route, give an alternative definition for *Flight* and *Booking$_0$*. Compare and contrast the advantages to be gained by representing a flight route as a sequence of airports or as an injective function.

3.3 Section 3.4 explored certain properties we wish a flight route to possess, stated them as sentences (a)-(e) in predicate logic, and made the final choice of (c), (d) and (e) in defining *Route*. If the axiom (c) in *Route* was replaced by (b), would the new definition satisfy the requirement that the route contains no circularities? If so, prove it; otherwise provide a counter-example.

3.4 Although it is quite obvious from *Route* that *flightRoute* is never empty, provide a formal proof for it.

4. Specification for Fun

This chapter introduces two case studies, especially devised to make our study of formal specification more interesting. They also make the point that the inquisitive observer may find that mathematics is part of ordinary life. This awareness may encourage a positive attitude towards formal specification.

4.1 Games as Systems

Games are quite representative state based systems. The rules of any game define two major aspects: the features that must always be observed and how to play the game correctly. In the terminology used here with respect to formal specification, the former corresponds to the general state of the game, while the latter, since each move brings about a change in the state of the game, to state transformations. The rules governing a move may involve a precondition permitting the move, and a postcondition stating precisely how the state of the game is to be affected by the move. In addition, the game may require specific information about how a given move is to take place and, at the same time, may implicitly let the players know how their position has been affected. Such information corresponds, respectively, to inputs and outputs.

The mathematical description of such games must therefore include the specifications for the following:

(a) The state of the game in general as well as its initial and final states
(b) All the intermediate state transformations
(c) An appropriate composition of the above transformations showing the correct sequence of the game

4.2 Musical Chairs

4.2.1 The Problem Description

Recall the party game *musical chairs*. Let us express this game mathematically. The following is a brief informal description of the game.

The game starts off with a collection of chairs and a collection of players. There is always exactly one player more than the number of chairs. In every round of the game, the players first dance to some music played by a third party. In the middle of their dance, the music is terminated abruptly with no prior notice. The players must immediately occupy a chair. Before the next round, the person who happens to be without a chair is eliminated from the game, and so is one of the chairs. The winner is the person who managed to survive until the last round and to occupy the only remaining chair. Obviously, there are other rules which are taken for granted, for example, that any chair can accommodate only one person, that nobody is allowed to be seated while the music is being played and that the game is finitary (i.e. it does not go on forever).

4.2.2 A Mathematical Description

First, let us introduce the following types:

$[Player, Chair]$

denoting, respectively, the sets of all possible players and chairs.

In defining the general state of the game, we need to identify the required state variables. In this respect, we have identified three components: pl for the set of players taking part in the game in a given state, ch for the set of chairs, and $occupiers$ as a record of who is sitting where. The requirements of the game, which always apply, are expressed in the specification below.

$\quad$ _MusicalChairs_ _____

$\quad$ $pl : \mathbb{F}\, Player$

$\quad$ $ch : \mathbb{F}\, Chair$

$\quad$ $occupiers : Chair \rightarrowtail Player$

$\quad$ _____

$\quad$ $\#ch \geqslant 1$

$\quad$ $\#pl = \#ch + 1$

$\quad$ $\mathrm{dom}\ occupiers \subseteq ch$

$\quad$ $\mathrm{ran}\ occupiers \subseteq pl$

According to the above definition, pl and ch are both finite subsets of the appropriate type. Since a chair can accommodate one and only one person, $occupiers$ is represented as a partial injective function from $Chair$ to $Player$. The state invariant is such that there must at least be one chair and that there is always one more player than the number of chairs. Also, the occupiers of the chairs must be the players of the game and each may occupy only one chair out of those used in the game.

The game is initialised according to

$$MusicalChairs_{init} \;\widehat{=}\; MusicalChairs'; \; p? : \mathbb{F} \, Player; \; c? : \mathbb{F} \, Chair \;\mid$$
$$\#c? \geqslant 1 \;\wedge\; \#p? = \#c? + 1 \;\wedge$$
$$pl' = p? \;\wedge\; ch' = c?$$

where $p?$ and $c?$ are inputs giving the players and chairs at the time of initiation of the game.

Each round of the game involves the following events:

(a) Starting to play the music and the players taking to the floor
(b) Stopping the music and the players taking seats
(c) Eliminating the loser and setting the scene for the next round
(d) End of the game if there are not enough players for the next round

taking place in the order given. Needless to say that the game may be formalised by treating the above events as state transformations on *MusicalChairs*. Ignoring, for the time being, exception handling (see Exercise 4.1), these events are formalised as below

```
┌─ PlayMusic ─────────────────────────────────
│ ΔMusicalChairs
├─────────────────────────────────────────────
│ pl' = pl
│
│ ch' = ch
│
│ occupiers' = ∅
└─────────────────────────────────────────────
```

```
┌─ StopMusic ─────────────────────────────────
│ ΔMusicalChairs
│ out! : Player
├─────────────────────────────────────────────
│ ch' = ch
│
│ dom occupiers' = ch'
│
│ out! ∈ pl − ran occupiers'
└─────────────────────────────────────────────
```

```
┌─ EliminateLoser ────────────────────────────
│ ΔMusicalChairs
│ out? : Player
├─────────────────────────────────────────────
│ pl' = pl − {out?}
│ ∃ chair : Chair | chair ∈ ch • ch' = ch − {chair}
└─────────────────────────────────────────────
```

$GameFinish \stackrel{\frown}{=} MusicalChairs; \ winner! : Player \ |$

$$\#occupiers = 1 \ \wedge$$

$$winner! \in \mathrm{ran} \ occupiers$$

The above state transformations may be composed as below to show the order in which the above events take place and, hence, how the game is to be played:

$PlayMusicalChairs \stackrel{\frown}{=} MusicalChairs_{init} \,{}_9^{\circ}$
$\qquad\qquad (PlayMusic \,{}_9^{\circ}\, StopMusic \,{}_9^{\circ}$
$\qquad\qquad\qquad\qquad EliminateLoser[out!/out?])^n \,{}_9^{\circ}$
$\qquad\qquad GameFinish$
$\qquad\qquad\qquad Where \ n = \#c? - 1$

where the superscript n signifies the iterative composition of the schema enclosed within parentheses over itself n times. See the comment made in Section 2.10 on iteration of ${}_9^{\circ}$.

4.3 Snakes and Ladders

4.3.1 The Problem Description

The following is an informal description of *snakes and ladders* – a children's board game.

> The board consists of an equal number of rows and columns of numbered cells. A selected number of pairs of cells are connected by *snakes* and *ladders*. Each player has a uniquely identifiable, usually coloured, token occupying a cell on the board. The movement of tokens on the board is determined by the outcome of throwing a die. The players first throw the die to decide the order of starting. For example, the order of play may be determined by the order of the score (although, obviously, there are other ways for establishing it as well).
> The game may start by placing all tokens at the cell numbered unity or by keeping them all off the board. The game progresses by moving the tokens in the ascending order of cells by the number shown on the die as each player throws it. Any throw bringing a token to a cell with the foot of a ladder enables its player to move up to the cell at the top of the ladder. A throw bringing a token to a cell with a snake's head makes the token move down to the cell containing the tail of the snake. The player who reaches the cell numbered highest is the winner.

4.3.2 The Preliminaries

Let us first introduce a type to identify all possible players:

$[PlayerId]$

If the elements of *PlayerId* are already known, we could alternatively enumerate the elements of it as

$PlayerId ::= $ Red | Blue | Yellow | Green | White

which is a *free type* (see Section 2.2.2). Let us also define a global constant *Size* axiomatically (see Section 2.3.2) as:

$$\begin{array}{|l}
Size : \mathbb{N} \\
\hline
Size > 1
\end{array}$$

where *Size* denotes the number of columns, or rows, on the board. The cells may be defined as:

$Position == (1 .. Size) \times (1 .. Size)$

4.3.3 Some Notes on Decomposition

The strategy adopted here in decomposing the game is based on the view sketched below on its different aspects. This is not a recipe for decomposing any system; it is presented here to illustrate the different opportunities for modularisation of specifications.

- The general state
  - ◇ Permanent, or fixed, part of the system
    - ◇ Explicit features
      These may include, in this case, the geometrical features such as
      - ○ plain board
      - ○ 'start' and 'finish' positions
      - ○ snakes and ladders
    - ◇ Implicit features
      The features in this category are those not explicit in the physical structure of the system. For example, these include
      - ○ ordering of positions
      - ○ the manner of counting forward the moves of the markers
  - ◇ Dynamic, or variable, part of the system
    The variable part concerns the specification of constraints on features that vary over time. In this case, the features include
    - ○ positions of player markers
    - ○ set of players

◦ turn of playing order (the current player)
- State transformations
These correspond to the specific events that bring about changes in the system state. The complete list of such events are
  ⬦ Initialisation
  ⬦ Dice throw
     This event may be further decomposed into
       ◦ move the marker according to the dice outcome
       ◦ make a further move if there is a ladder or a snake
       ◦ eliminate the player if he reaches the 'finish' position
  ⬦ Game finish

4.3.4 A Simple Game

Let us first consider a simple game, without considering the snakes and ladders. We can specify this quite easily. First, the plain board!

┌─ *PlainBoard* ──────────────────────────────
│ *board* : $\mathbb{P}$ *Position*
│
│ *start*, *finish* : *Position*
├──
│ *board* = *Position*
└──

In order to describe the movement of markers belonging to different players, we introduce two functions:

- *enum* for totally ordering the positions on the grid, and
- *move* for moving a marker from one position to another after a dice throw.

┌─ *ImplicitPart* ────────────────────────────
│ *enum* : *Position* $\rightarrowtail$ $\mathbb{N}_1$
│
│ *move* : $\mathbb{N}$ $\rightarrow$ *Position* $\rightarrow$ *Position*
│
│ *finish* : *Position*
├──
│ $\exists\, m, n : \mathbb{N}_1 \mid n > m \wedge n - m + 1 = \#Position \;\bullet$
│
│   ran *enum* = $m \mathinner{\ldotp\ldotp} n$
│
│ $\forall\, s : Position;\; k : \mathbb{N} \;\bullet$
│
│ $(enum\ s) + k \leqslant enum\ finish \Rightarrow$
│
│ $enum(move\ k\ s) = (enum\ s) + k$
│
│ $(enum\ s) + k > enum\ finish \Rightarrow$
│
│ $enum(move\ k\ s) = enum\ finish$
└──

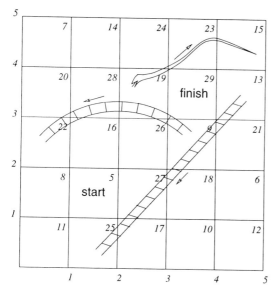

Fig. 4.1. Weird snakes and ladders

The first predicate in the above requires that the range of *enum* be a contiguous segment of natural numbers. The second specifies the function *move*. Note that no move takes a marker out of the board positions.

Now let us combine the above two definitions in defining the board without snakes and ladders.

```
┌─ SimpleBoard ────────────────────────────
│ PlainBoard
│ ImplicitPart
│ ──────────────────
│ ∀ x : Position •
│
│         enum start ⩽ enum x ⩽ enum finish
└───────────────────────────────────────────
```

The definition given below for *Players* ignores the disciplined order of playing the game by its players:

$$Players \,\widehat{=}\, [players : PlayerId \nrightarrow Position \mid players \neq \varnothing]$$

The state of this simplified game may be given as

$$SimpleGame \,\widehat{=}\, [SimpleBoard;\ Players \mid \mathrm{ran}\ players \subseteq board]$$

with the initialisation below

$$SimpleGame_{init} \,\widehat{=}\, [SimpleGame';\ players? : \mathbb{F}\ PlayerId \mid$$
$$players? \neq \varnothing \,\wedge$$
$$\mathrm{dom}\ players' = players? \wedge \mathrm{ran}\ players' = \{start\}]$$

Each turn of the play may be performed in two stages:

1. A straightforward move of player markers subsequent to a dice throw
2. Elimination of any winners immediately afterwards

These two sub-operations are defined below, but they are not composed together since our interest in this simple interim game lies solely in its strategic use.

$$
\begin{array}{|l}
\underline{\;PlaySimpleGame\;}\\
\Delta SimpleGame\\[4pt]
\Xi SimpleBoard\\[4pt]
who? : PlayerId\\[4pt]
dice? : \mathbb{N}_1\\
\hline
dice? \in 1 \mathinner{.\,.} 6\\[4pt]
who? \in \operatorname{dom}\ players\\[4pt]
players' = players \oplus \{who? \mapsto (move\ dice?\ (players\ who?))\}\\[4pt]
board' = board\\
\end{array}
$$

$$
\begin{array}{|l}
\underline{\;EliminateSimpleWinner\;}\\
\Delta SimpleGame\\[4pt]
\Xi SimpleBoard\\
\hline
players' = players \rhd \{finish\}\\
\end{array}
$$

4.3.5 The Full Game

Here we augment the simple game described above with the additional features, thus accounting for snakes and ladders. Let us consider them first in isolation.

$$
\begin{array}{|l}
\underline{\;SnakesAndLadders\;}\\
snk, lad \qquad : Position \nrightarrow Position\\
start, finish : Position\\
\hline
\forall s : Position \bullet s \in \operatorname{dom}\ snk \Rightarrow enum(snk\ s) < enum\ s \land\\
\qquad\qquad\qquad\quad s \in \operatorname{dom}\ lad \Rightarrow enum(lad\ s) > enum\ s\\
finish \notin \operatorname{dom}\ snk\\
start \notin \operatorname{dom}\ lad\\
\operatorname{dom}\ snk \cap \operatorname{dom}\ lad = \varnothing\\
\operatorname{dom}\ snk \cap \operatorname{ran}\ lad = \varnothing\\
\operatorname{ran}\ snk \cap \operatorname{dom}\ lad = \varnothing\\
\end{array}
$$

The appropriateness of the axioms in the above schema is the subject of Exercise 4.3.

Now we can combine the definitions *SimpleBoard* and *SnakesAndLadders* in order to define a board for the proper game:

$$ProperBoard \,\widehat{=}\, SimpleBoard \land SnakesAndLadders$$

and then the full game by incorporating *Players* as in:

┌─ *FullGame* ─────────────────────────────
│ *ProperBoard*
│
│ *Players*
├───────────────────────────────────────
│ *SimpleGame*
└───────────────────────────────────────

The initialisation follows from the earlier simple game:

$$FullGame_{init} \,\widehat{=}\, FullGame' \mid SimpleGame_{init}$$

The playing of the full game may be specified by describing three separate stages. The first and the last stages of this game are not greatly different from the two stages covered under the simple game. Simply, it is necessary to bear in mind that the stages corresponding to those in the simple game must take care of the additional features in the newly defined 'proper board'. That is:

┌─ *PlayIgnoringSnakes* ────────────────────
│ $\Delta FullGame$
│
│ $\Xi ProperBoard$
│
│ *PlaySimpleGame*
└───────────────────────────────────────

┌─ *EliminateWinner* ──────────────────────
│ $\Delta FullGame$
│
│ $\Xi ProperBoard$
├───────────────────────────────────────
│ *EliminateSimpleWinner*
└───────────────────────────────────────

However, the middle stage is new; it accounts for the additional moves of player markers, resulting from the application of functions that represent snakes and ladders, after the dice move.

┌─ *ClimbOrDescend* ───────────────────────
│ $\Delta FullGame$
│
│ $\Xi ProperBoard$
├───────────────────────────────────────
│ $players' = players \,\mathbin{\stackrel{\scriptscriptstyle 9}{\scriptscriptstyle 9}}\, ((\mathrm{id}\ Position) \oplus (snk \cup lad))$
└───────────────────────────────────────

Having defined the sub-operations related to the three intermediate stages, we can compose them in the following manner:

$$PlaySnakesAndLadders \,\hat{=}\, PlayIgnoringSnakes\,\raise{0.5ex}{\scriptstyle\circ}$$
$$ClimbOrDescend\,\raise{0.5ex}{\scriptstyle\circ}$$
$$EliminateWinner$$

describing, effectively, a sequence of possible outcomes following a dice throw. The full game comprises an indefinite sequence of state transformations of *PlaySnakesAndLadders* following $FullGame_{init}$. The game may no longer be played when the set *players* becomes empty.

4.3.6 An Illustration

The board is as shown in Figure 4.2. Let:

$players = \{(\mathsf{Green}, (2,5)), (\mathsf{Yellow}, (5,2))\}$

$who? = \mathsf{Green}$

$dice? = 3$

The function *enum* corresponding to the board shown in Figure 4.1 is:

$$enum = \{((1,1), 11), ((1,2), 25), ...((2,2), 5), (2,3), 27), ...$$
$$((5,4), 23), ((5,5), 15)\}$$

Then, according to *PlayIgnoringSnakes*:

$$
\begin{aligned}
players' &= players \oplus \{who? \mapsto (move\ dice?\ (players\ who?))\} \\
&= players \oplus \{\mathsf{Green} \mapsto (move\ 3\ (players\ \mathsf{Green}))\} \\
&= players \oplus \{\mathsf{Green} \mapsto (move\ 3\ (2,5))\} \\
&= players \oplus \{\mathsf{Green} \mapsto enum^{\sim} \circ enum(move\ 3\ (2,5))\} \\
&\qquad \text{composition (with the identity relation;} \\
&\qquad\qquad enum^{\sim}\ \text{being the inverse of } enum) \\
&= players \oplus \{\mathsf{Green} \mapsto enum^{\sim}\ (enum(move\ 3\ (2,5)))\} \\
&= players \oplus \{\mathsf{Green} \mapsto enum^{\sim}\ ((enum(2,5)) + 3)\} \\
&= players \oplus \{\mathsf{Green} \mapsto enum^{\sim}\ (6 + 3)\} \\
&= players \oplus \{\mathsf{Green} \mapsto enum^{\sim}\ 9\} \\
&= players \oplus \{\mathsf{Green} \mapsto (3,4)\} \\
&= \{(\mathsf{Green}, (3,4)), (\mathsf{Yellow}, (5,2))\}
\end{aligned}
$$

The above must be followed by *ClimbOrDescend*, assuming that:

$players = \{(\mathsf{Green}, (3,4)), (\mathsf{Yellow}, (5,2))\}$

and

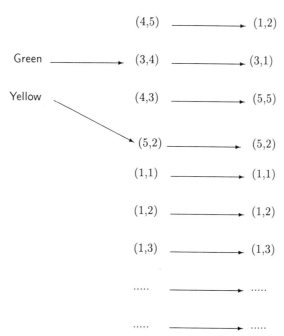

Fig. 4.2. Graph of function composition in example

$$players' = players \ \mathring{,} \ ((\text{id } Position) \oplus (snk \cup lad))$$

For convenience, let:

$$snk \cup lad = f$$

thus f represents the snakes and ladders as a single function. For the given layout of the board, f is defined by:

$$f = \{((3,4),(3,1)),((4,5),(1,2)),((4,3),(5,5))\}$$

and, therefore:

$$\text{id } Position \oplus f = \{((1,1),(1,1)),((1,2),(1,2)),....((5,5),(5,5))\} \oplus$$
$$\{((3,4),(3,1)),((4,5),(1,2)),((4,3),(5,5))\}$$

The above expression may be worked out using the graph shown in Figure 4.2. Therefore:

$$players' = players \ \mathring{,} \ ((\text{id } Position) \oplus f) = \{(\text{Green},(3,1)),(\text{Yellow},(5,2))\}$$

Exercises

4.1 With reference to musical chairs, first define the exception handling operations on various events, which were omitted in Section 4.2.2, and then the total versions of the relevant operations.

4.2 The definition given on page 75 for *Players* ignored the disciplined order of playing snakes and ladders by its participants. Incorporate such an order in this game.

4.3 With reference to the schema *SnakesAndLadders* in Section 4.3.5, representing snakes and ladders as functions *snk* and *lad* respectively, what are the consequences the following conjectures:

(a) $snk^\sim \cap lad = \varnothing$
(b) $snk \cap lad^\sim = \varnothing$
(c) $\mathrm{dom}\ (snk \cup lad) \cap \mathrm{ran}\ (snk \cup lad) = \varnothing$
(d) $\mathrm{ran}\ snk \cap \mathrm{ran}\ lad = \varnothing$
(e) $\mathrm{id}\ Position \cap snk = \varnothing$
(f) $\mathrm{id}\ Position \cap lad = \varnothing$
(g) $snk \cap lad = \varnothing$
(h) $snk \cap lad \neq \varnothing$

if any of them were to be true? Investigate their validity in the context of *SnakesAndLadders*. In each case, depending on your answer, provide either a formal proof of its validity or a counter-example demonstrating its invalidity.

4.4 A specification is required for a tournament of musical chairs, where the winners of all games participate in a final game. Stating clearly assumptions that deal with any missing details, extend the formalisation of musical chairs so that it describes how such a tournament may take place.

4.5 Consider the board games draughts, also known as checkers, and chess. Like the games considered in this chapter, the state of each game alters with every move of a piece on the board made by either of the two players. Using appropriate functions, relations and sets, formalise these two games.

5. A Specification for Clocks

This chapter attempts a specification of the functionality of clocks, with the intention of using it as a vehicle for a discussion of proofs in Chapter 6. It is an interesting case study, especially as it highlights the effectiveness of mathematics in unravelling intricacies which we otherwise hardly notice.

5.1 Representation of Time

5.1.1 Notions of Time

The problem we are attempting is the formalisation of a clock. As with any specification task, our interest here is really in the purpose of a clock, or what it does, and not in how it works. Clocks are so widespread in daily use that we hardly need an informal definition to start with. Even a child would say that "clocks tell us the time". This definition is more than satisfactory in our daily life, but is far from adequate if one thinks of clocks in advanced realtime systems.

This work distinguishes between the time in an objective sense, and the various representations of time on actual clocks. Such representations may cover different forms, from those on sundials through simple mechanical pendula and spring based clocks to advanced atomic clocks. The lack of such a distinction between time in an objective sense and its representations could be a source of confusion, especially in the mathematical treatment of time devices.

Let Θ denote the time in the objective sense, referred to here as *objective time* or *real time*, and $\mathbb{T}$ denote some desired representation of Θ on a clock, referred to here as *clock time*. We conceive both of them as sets of values, which the time in the objective sense, or the one of its representations, may assume.

Thus, both Θ and $\mathbb{T}$ are types. For obvious reasons, we expect both Θ and $\mathbb{T}$ to be totally ordered sets by some relation $\leqslant$, and with it, we take on board its other variant and extensions $<, >$, and $\geqslant$ inspired by number theory. Given two time values t_1 and t_2, $t_1 < t_2$ means that t_1 precedes t_2. One may infer the meanings of other relations accordingly. Let us also assume that these types are equipped with appropriate operators for addition $+$, subtraction $-$, etc.

5.1.2 Real Time

For assuring continuity of real time, it is essential that Θ is a denumerably dense set. For this reason, it is convenient to think of Θ in terms of the set of real numbers $\mathbb{R}$. This again is another representation of objective time, but differs from all other representations in that it can cope with our present intuitive demands, for example, the denumerability mentioned above, the absence of least and greatest elements and the total ordering of Θ. Thus, all other representations, and as such all other clocks, are approximations to the objective time.

In order to capture the notion of actual passage of time, let us introduce a certain global variable, NOW, of type Θ. Thus:

$$\text{NOW} : \Theta$$

denotes the current time in the objective sense. The nature of this variable is quite unique. Firstly, it never assumes a value it has assumed on a previous occasion and, secondly, no one has any control over it. The first feature agrees with our intuitive understanding of time as a continuously evolving process without repeating history in the absolute sense. Thus, NOW is a variable with a full awareness of its own history. Without the notion of a 'historical' trace, we cannot express this behaviour in our formal language, but let us be content with this informal, and nevertheless clear, understanding. The non-repeatability of values that NOW may assume poses a question as to the nature of the actual values of Θ. One way to think about NOW is in terms of a marker on an axis depicting the ordering of real numbers. The second feature characterises time as a free flowing process that may be observed but not influenced, and we may treat this aspect mathematically by letting NOW be a *free variable*.

For practical purposes, however, one needs to be able to record, and compare, values of NOW, and let us assume that NOW is made available to us by some means, for example, by means of a superior clock of acceptable quality. This 'superior' clock does not have to be a clock in the conventional sense, and how this is achieved should not concern us. For our purpose, it is sufficient to assume that the behaviour of NOW is independently specified and that it agrees with the informal description given above.

5.1.3 Points and Intervals of Time

The free variable NOW refers to points in a time axis. However, this treatment can sometimes be problematic when reasoning about time. A question it raises is about the instantaneity of time and, as a result, about our understanding of change, for example, whether instantaneity is a matter of perception or whether there are truly instantaneous events. An approach which avoids this question is to only consider events taking place over intervals of real time. In this connection, we use exclusively *right–open* (or *left–closed*) intervals of real time, a right–open interval being a contiguous stretch of time between two points of time including the starting point but excluding the end point. A common notation used for this purpose is $[t_1, t_2)$, t_1 and t_2 being, respectively, the start and end points of the intervals and $t_1 \leqslant t_2$. We return to a more detailed discussion of time intervals in Section 5.5.

NOTE: Using the square brackets to mean that the relevant end point is included in the interval, and parentheses to mean that the relevant end point is excluded, this notation can also be extended to other types of interval: (t_1, t_2) for *open* intervals, $(t_1, t_2]$ for *left-open* (right-closed) intervals, and $[t_1, t_2]$ for *closed* intervals.

5.1.4 Clock Time

Unlike real time, *clock time* is discretised. Its time values may be defined using the notion of *granularity*, denoted here by Δ. The granularity refers to a length of time between two elements in Θ and it defines the separation in real time between pairs of consecutive values in $\mathbb{T}$. This separation is calibrated on the clock using a constant ∇. Thus, ∇ is the counterpart of granularity Δ in $\mathbb{T}$ and is the unit of measurement for 'counting' time in $\mathbb{T}$. In other words, a clock measures the 'distances' between pairs of elements in $\mathbb{T}$ in integral multiples of ∇. We require that $\nabla \in \mathbb{R}^+$.

Every clock uses a distinguished element called *zero* in $\mathbb{T}$ as a datum for its measurements. Implicit in every clock is also an injective (one–to–one) function *next* on $\mathbb{T}$. The function *next* is analogous to the successor function *succ* on $\mathbb{N}$. Thus, *next*(t) returns the value immediately after t in $\mathbb{T}$. Values of $\mathbb{T}$ are thus of the form *zero*, *next*(*zero*), *next*^{2}(*zero*), *next*^{3}(*zero*), etc. Clearly, the relation $\leqslant$ may be inferred from *next*, and so are operators and relations such as $+$, $-$ and $\geqslant$. As shown in Figure 5.1, these ingredients establish how the two metrics Θ and $\mathbb{T}$ are related to each other.

It is clear that, whatever the representation of clock time values, $\mathbb{T}$ is closely related to $\mathbb{N}$. This relationship may be established by using a function *measure*:

$$measure : \mathbb{T} \to \mathbb{N}$$

defined recursively as:

$$measure(zero) = 0$$

and, for any $c \in \mathbb{T}$:

$$measure(next(c)) = 1 + measure(c)$$

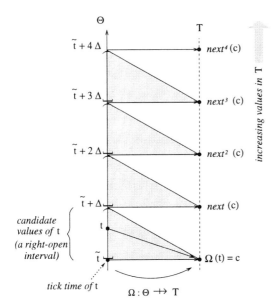

Fig. 5.1. Metrics of real time and clock time

It allows the calculation of the 'distance' between any pair of elements c_1 and c_2 in $\mathbb{T}$ as:

$$\| (c_1, c_2) \| = \nabla \times | \, measure(c_1) - measure(c_2) \, |$$

where $| \, n \, |$ denotes the absolute value of the number n.

The above provides us with a way of measuring time in the representation $\mathbb{T}$ in terms of numbers in $\mathbb{R}^+$. In order to relate $\mathbb{T}$ to Θ, what is required is the ability to relate Θ to $\mathbb{R}^+$, which can be achieved by relating Δ to $\mathbb{R}^+$. This is not difficult since, as mentioned earlier, $\mathbb{R}$ suits as an ideal representation of Θ.

5.2 A Mathematical Definition of Clocks

5.2.1 Clock Mechanism

Abstractly speaking, a clock 'works' by mapping real time to an appropriate representation. This can be modelled by representing it as a function from Θ to $\mathbb{T}$. Let this function be of the form:

$$\Omega \,:\, \Theta \,\nrightarrow\, \mathbb{T}$$

It is a partial function since clocks are, generally speaking, non-operable for certain time values. In addition to being a function, Ω possesses some further properties. These are as follows:

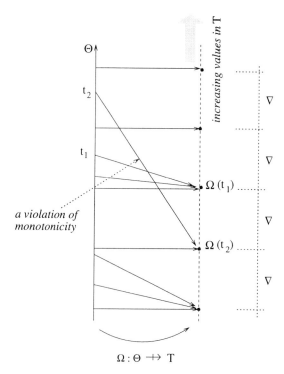

$$\Omega : \Theta \nrightarrow T$$

Fig. 5.2. On monotonicity

⬦ Representation of time must progress, or at least not regress, with time.

$$\forall t_1, t_2 : \Theta \bullet (t_2 > t_1 \Rightarrow \Omega t_2 \geqslant \Omega t_1) \wedge (\Omega t_2 > \Omega t_1 \Rightarrow t_2 > t_1)$$

where for any $t \in \Theta$, Ωt denotes the application of Ω to t, that is, $\Omega(t)$.

The above concerns the *monotonicity* of the representation. In other words, representation of any two distinct time values of real time must be in the same relation as the real times themselves, or at least, must be equal; see Figure 5.2.

⬦ Progression of temporal representation must be 'uniform' relative to real time.

$$\forall t_1, t_2, t_3, t_4 : \Theta \bullet t_2 - t_1 = t_4 - t_3 \Rightarrow$$
$$(\| (\Omega t_2, \Omega t_1) \| - \| (\Omega t_4, \Omega t_3) \|) \in \{-\nabla, 0, +\nabla\}$$

The above is the property of *uniformity*. However, this uniformity may be observed only to a certain accuracy; see Figure 5.3.

⬦ In order that clocks make progress with the passage of real time, let us require that:

$$\forall t : \Theta \bullet t \in \text{dom } \Omega \Rightarrow \Omega(t + \Delta) > \Omega(t)$$

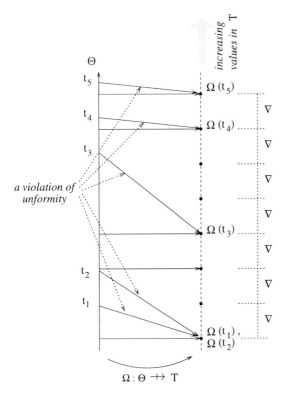

Fig. 5.3. On uniformity

It is clear that the above is a *liveness* property.

Let us summarise below our present understanding of the clock function Ω in the schema notation, where the mathematical text developed so far is identified with the schema name *EternalClock*. It is a partial specification of Ω. Also, note the parameterisation of the specification with respect to $\mathbb{T}$ so that the choice of a particular temporal representation is left for the future. When such a choice is made, the specification may be instantiated appropriately.

$$
\begin{array}{l}
\underline{\;EternalClock[\mathbb{T}]\;} \\
\Omega : \Theta \nrightarrow \mathbb{T} \\
\hline
\forall\, t_1, t_2 : \Theta \bullet (t_2 > t_1 \Rightarrow \Omega t_2 \geqslant \Omega t_1) \wedge (\Omega t_2 > \Omega t_1 \Rightarrow t_2 > t_1) \\
\forall\, t_1, t_2, t_3, t_4 : \Theta \ \bullet t_2 - t_1 = t_4 - t_3 \Rightarrow \\
\qquad (\| (\Omega t_2, \Omega t_1) \| - \| (\Omega t_4, \Omega t_3) \|) \in \{-\nabla, 0, +\nabla\} \\
\forall\, t : \Theta \bullet t \in \text{dom } \Omega \Rightarrow \Omega(t + \Delta) > \Omega(t)
\end{array}
$$

The predicates in the above schema axiomatise the requirements on the monotonicity, uniformity and liveness of clocks listed earlier. An additional property to be considered is:

⋄ All clocks have a certain life span.

Ignoring the time when a clock ceases to be a clock, the above notion of *partiality* of Ω may be expressed as in:

$$
\begin{array}{|l}
\underline{\ ClockWork[\mathbb{T}]\ } \\
\quad EternalClock \\
\hline
\quad \exists\, t_0 : \Theta \bullet \mathrm{dom}\ \Omega = \{t : \Theta \mid t \geqslant t_0\}
\end{array}
$$

The display of the clock showing the current time may now be modelled as:

$$
\begin{array}{|l}
\underline{\ IdealClock[\mathbb{T}]\ } \\
\quad ClockWork \\
\quad display\text{-}time : \mathbb{T} \\
\hline
\quad \mathrm{NOW} \in \mathrm{dom}\ \Omega \Rightarrow display\text{-}time = \Omega\ \mathrm{NOW}
\end{array}
$$

which includes the identifier *display-time*, denoting the current time in the chosen clock representation.

5.3 Clock Utilities

So far, we have been concentrating on clocks only as instruments for measuring time. In this section, let us consider clocks as an object of specification, that is, as a kind of system. Apart from the actual mechanism that enables measuring time, clocks have other utilities for the benefit of the user such as a facility providing some kind of display, an alarm and a timer. Let us consider the first two only and, for convenience, consider them separately from the 'clockwork'.

In formalising these aspects, let us first introduce a constant $\mathcal{N}$ to denote the number of multiples of ∇ the alarm bell continues to ring from the moment it starts. Thus:

$$\mathcal{N} : \mathbb{N}_1$$

We also introduce the binary valued free types:

SWITCH ::= On | Off	(for the alarm)
TONE ::= Ringing | Silent	(for the alarm)
TICK ::= Tick | betweenTicks	(for intermittent ticking)

for distinguishing between the possible states of individual components and the clock as a whole.

$$
\begin{array}{|l}
\hline
\;Display[\mathbb{T}]\\
\hline
\;display\text{-}time : \mathbb{T}\\
\hline
\end{array}
$$

$$
\begin{array}{|ll}
\hline
\;Alarm[\mathbb{T}]\\
\hline
\;alarm\text{-}time : \mathbb{T}\\
\;stop\text{-}time \quad : \mathbb{T}\\
\;setting \qquad : \text{SWITCH}\\
\;bell \qquad\quad : \text{TONE}\\
\hline
\end{array}
$$

We may define a 'clock shell' as:

$$
\begin{array}{|l}
\hline
\;ClockShell[\mathbb{T}]\\
\hline
\;Display\\
\\
\;Alarm\\
\hline
\;bell = \mathsf{Ringing} \Leftrightarrow\\
\\
\qquad alarm\text{-}time \leqslant display\text{-}time \leqslant alarm\text{-}time + \mathcal{N} \times \nabla \wedge\\
\\
\qquad setting = \mathsf{On}\\
\hline
\end{array}
$$

5.3.1 Idealised Clock with Utilities

We define a clock, which is equipped with the above utilities, by composing the schemas *ClockWork* and *ClockShell* as

$$
\begin{array}{|l}
\hline
\;Clock[\mathbb{T}]\\
\hline
\;ClockWork\\
\\
\;ClockShell\\
\hline
\;\text{NOW} \in \mathrm{dom}\;\;\Omega \Rightarrow display\text{-}time = \Omega\;\text{NOW}\\
\hline
\end{array}
$$

5.4 Operations and Transitions

5.4.1 Initialisation and Resetting

As a first step towards producing an initialisation specification, let us introduce an auxiliary schema *Create* containing a component Θ_0, which explicitly records the time of clock initialisation, that is, the time from which the mapping Ω is defined.

```
┌─ Create ─────────────────────────────────────────────
│ Clock'
│
│ display? : 𝕋
│
│ Θ'₀ : Θ
├──────────────────────────────────────────────────────
│ display-time' = display?
│
│ Θ'₀ = NOW
│
│ (Θ'₀, display?) ∈ Ω'
└──────────────────────────────────────────────────────
```

The initialisation specification of *Clock* may be defined now by hiding the variable Θ'_0 in *Create*. Thus:

$$Clock_{init} \mathrel{\widehat{=}} Create \setminus \Theta'_0$$

The resetting of the clock is similar, except that it also involves a 'before state'. Therefore, let us define an operation for resetting the clock display as:

$$Reset \mathrel{\widehat{=}} Clock \wedge Clock_{init}$$

5.4.2 Clock Advancement

The clock works by continuous internal transitions without any external intervention, that is, without any inputs. An underlying assumption is, however, that this takes place while the free variable NOW progresses thorough its evolution independently. Therefore, these transitions may take place as often as necessary so that the clock keeps up with the constant advancement of NOW but without violating the specification. Let us assume that these transitions are separated by an arbitrarily small but strictly 'positive' offset of ε real time. The nature of these transitions may then be described by:

```
┌─ ClockAdvance ───────────────────────────────────────
│ ΔClock
│
│ ΞClockWork
│
│ ΞAlarm
│
│ out! : TICK
├──────────────────────────────────────────────────────
│ display-time' = Ω(NOW + ε)
│
│ display-time ≠ display-time' ⇔ out! = Tick
│
│ Ω' = Ω
└──────────────────────────────────────────────────────
```

The above specification on the clock advancement stipulates that the display must show the right representation of time, and that the clock ticks only in transitions where the display is updated.

5.4.3 The Functioning of the Alarm

Setting the alarm is an externally performed operation and, therefore, it is input driven. It may be defined as:

$$
\begin{array}{|l}
\text{\textit{SetAlarm}} \\
\hline
\Delta\text{\textit{Clock}} \\
\Xi\text{\textit{ClockWork}} \\
\Xi\text{\textit{Display}} \\
\text{\textit{wakeupTime}?} : \mathbb{T} \\
\text{\textit{setting}?} : \text{SWITCH} \\
\hline
\text{\textit{bell}} \neq \text{Ringing} \\
\text{\textit{alarm-time}}' = \text{\textit{wakeupTime}}? \\
\text{\textit{setting}}' = \text{\textit{setting}}? \\
\text{\textit{bell}}' = \text{\textit{bell}}
\end{array}
$$

The precondition is to ensure that the alarm does not continue ringing up to the new setting, if the alarm is set whilst the bell is already ringing. However, the necessity of such a requirement may be disputed.

The ringing of the bell, and its termination after the expiry of allocated time, on the other hand, are internal transitions. This behaviour is formalised in the schema:

$$
\begin{array}{|l}
\text{\textit{ReleaseAlarm}} \\
\hline
\Delta\text{\textit{Clock}} \\
\Xi\text{\textit{ClockWork}}; \ \Xi\text{\textit{Display}} \\
\hline
\text{\textit{bell}} = \text{Silent} \\
\text{\textit{setting}} = \text{On} \\
\text{\textit{alarm-time}} = \text{\textit{display-time}} \\
\text{\textit{stop-time}}' = \text{\textit{display-time}} + \mathcal{N} \times \nabla \\
\text{\textit{bell}}' = \text{Ringing} \\
\text{\textit{setting}}' = \text{\textit{setting}} \\
\text{\textit{alarm-time}}' = \text{\textit{alarm-time}}
\end{array}
$$

$$
\begin{array}{|l}
\hline
\quad StopAlarm \underline{\hspace{9cm}} \\
\quad \Delta Clock \\
\\
\quad \Xi ClockWork; \quad \Xi Display \\
\hline
\quad bell = \mathsf{Ringing} \\
\\
\quad setting = \mathsf{On} \\
\\
\quad display\text{-}time = stop\text{-}time = stop\text{-}time' \\
\\
\quad setting' = \mathsf{Off} \\
\\
\quad bell' = \mathsf{Silent} \\
\hline
\end{array}
$$

$$
\begin{array}{|l}
\hline
\quad CancelAlarm \underline{\hspace{8.5cm}} \\
\quad \Delta Clock \\
\\
\quad \Xi ClockWork; \quad \Xi Display \\
\\
\quad setting? : \textsc{switch} \\
\hline
\quad setting? = \mathsf{Off} \\
\\
\quad alarm\text{-}time < display\text{-}time < stop\text{-}time \\
\\
\quad setting' = setting? \\
\\
\quad bell' = \mathsf{Silent} \\
\hline
\end{array}
$$

Note that the precondition in *CancelAlarm* may be too restrictive since the alarm may be turned off only when the display time is within a specific interval. The working of the alarm system, from the time when the alarm is activated until the alarm stops or it is interrupted, may be defined as:

$$RingAlarm \; \widehat{=} \; ReleaseAlarm \, \S \, (StopAlarm \vee CancelAlarm)$$

However, the rest of the clock, in particular, the display subsystem will continue to function independently. However, our notation is not expressive enough for an adequate description of this kind of behaviour.

5.5 Intervals in Real Time

Let us return to the topic raised in Section 5.1.3 and consider how to represent time intervals as sets of time values. In this connection, let us adopt $\mathbb{R}$ as a representation for real time values and define right–open intervals in this representation as:

$$[\,-\,,-\,) : \mathbb{P}\,\mathbb{R}$$
$$\forall\, t_1, t_2 : \mathbb{R} \mid t_1 \leqslant t_2 \bullet$$
$$[t_1,\ t_2) = \{t : \mathbb{R} \mid\ t_1 \leqslant t < t_2 \bullet t\}$$

with subsidiary functions:

$$left, right : \mathbb{P}\,\mathbb{R} \nrightarrow \mathbb{R}$$
$$length \qquad : \mathbb{P}\,\mathbb{R} \nrightarrow \mathbb{R}$$
$$\forall\, t_1, t_2 : \mathbb{R} \mid t_1 \leqslant t_2 \bullet$$
$$left\,[t_1,\ t_2) \quad = t_1$$
$$right\,[t_1,\ t_2) \quad = t_2$$
$$length\,[t_1,\ t_2) = t_2 - t_1$$

where the functions *left* and *right* refer, respectively, to the lower (left) and upper (right) ends of such an interval, and *length* for its length if $t_2 > t_1$ and zero otherwise. Furthermore, let Γ denote the set of all possible right–open intervals:

$$\Gamma : \mathbb{P}(\mathbb{P}\,\mathbb{R})$$
$$\Gamma = \{t_1,\ t_2 : \mathbb{R} \bullet [t_1,\ t_2)\}$$

Analogously, a set Γ_c may be defined to denote intervals measured with reference to clock time. The set of right–open intervals Γ in real time are related to the set of intervals Γ_c as:

$$\theta_c = \Omega(\!|\,\theta\,|\!)$$

which, effectively, specifies how an interval in real time θ is measured as an interval θ_c in a given clock representation. The precise relationship between pairs of θs and θ_cs is not obvious from the above and is not discussed here; the interested reader is referred to Nissanke [41].

There is a range of relationships between time intervals applicable to both metrics of time: real time and clock time. In practical terms, such relationships may be of interest because of the events taking place during the intervals concerned, or the states that prevail over them. In other words, formalisation of temporal aspects of the physical behaviour of a system over time may have to be expressed as relationships between the relevant time intervals. In this connection, there is a widely used set of temporal relationships between intervals, namely:

before, equal, meets, overlaps, during, starts, finishes $: \mathbb{P}\,\mathbb{R} \leftrightarrow \mathbb{P}\,\mathbb{R}$

Given any $\theta, \theta' : \mathbb{P}\,\mathbb{R}$ such that $\theta, \theta' \in \Gamma$:

$$\theta \ before \ \theta' \stackrel{def}{\Leftrightarrow} right(\theta) < left(\theta')$$
$$\theta \ equal \ \theta' \stackrel{def}{\Leftrightarrow} \theta = \theta'$$
$$\theta \ meets \ \theta' \stackrel{def}{\Leftrightarrow} right(\theta) = left(\theta')$$
$$\theta \ overlaps \ \theta' \stackrel{def}{\Leftrightarrow} left(\theta) < left(\theta') < right(\theta) < right(\theta') \ \lor$$
$$left(\theta') < left(\theta) < right(\theta') < right(\theta)$$
$$\theta \ during \ \theta' \stackrel{def}{\Leftrightarrow} left(\theta') < left(\theta) \land right(\theta) < right(\theta')$$
$$\theta \ starts \ \theta' \stackrel{def}{\Leftrightarrow} left(\theta) = left(\theta') \land right(\theta) < right(\theta')$$
$$\theta \ finishes \ \theta' \stackrel{def}{\Leftrightarrow} right(\theta) = right(\theta') \land left(\theta') < left(\theta)$$

A notation in common usage for *before* is:

$$\theta < \theta' \stackrel{def}{\Leftrightarrow} \theta \ before \ \theta'$$

It may be noted that:

$$\theta \ overlaps \ \theta' \Leftrightarrow \theta \cap \theta' \neq \emptyset \land \theta \neq \theta'$$

A non-primitive predicate is *in* defined by:

$$in : \mathbb{PR} \leftrightarrow \mathbb{PR}$$
$$\theta \ in \ \theta' \Leftrightarrow \theta \ during \ \theta' \lor \theta \ starts \ \theta' \lor \theta \ finishes \ \theta'$$

Concluding Remarks

A more detailed discussion on the behaviour of clocks, especially from the point of view of realtime systems, may be found in Nissanke [41]. The temporal relationships between intervals, discussed in Section 5.5, have their origins in a system of temporal logic due to Allen [3].

Exercises

5.1 Extend the specification to include a timer and a dual time representation (for example, to cater for regional variation of time). As usual, the features must be supported with operations for their setting, resetting and cancellation.

5.2 Propose a specific representation for $\mathbb{T}$ and the desired operations on $\mathbb{T}$, and explore how it may be incorporated into the specification as a refinement to the latter.

6. Reasoning About Specifications

This chapter is a discussion about certain kinds of reasoning about mathematical specifications. Such reasoning concerns the implementability of specifications. The discussion relies on the formalisation of clocks given in Chapter 5.

6.1 Introduction

A primary purpose of mathematical formalisation of software requirements is the attainment of precision and clarity. These two attributes are highly valued in pursuing better communication of software requirements. In addition, formalisation has two further purposes: reasoning about the object of specification as documented and reasoning about the specification itself as an artifact. These kinds of reasoning are conducted within a well established rigorous framework – the framework of mathematical reasoning or proof. In previous chapters, we have resorted to the expressive power of mathematics as a language, either from the point of view of reading formal specifications or writing them, relying, however, on our ordinary powers of reasoning in their understanding.

Naturally, this text places great emphasis on mathematical reasoning about software. However, it recognises the difficulties in practising it to the letter, whether due to the lack of mathematical expertise or the costs involved. As with any kind of problem solving, these difficulties often dictate striking a balance between the degree of formality and pragmatism. The following quotation makes this point lucidly:

> *Use theory to provide insight; use common sense and intuition where it is suitable, but fall back on the formal theory for support when difficulties and complexities arise.*
>
> David Gries [18], page 165

This comment is especially relevant to proofs. The burden of proof needs to be justified by the degree of criticality of the application, and a decision not to undertake a proof must be weighed against any adverse effect it might have on system attributes such as safety, security and reliability.

Generally speaking , the kind of mathematical reasoning in formal methods may be classified into three areas, namely:

(i) Reasoning about the consequences of requirements as expressed in a formal specification primarily from the user's perspective. In software engineering, this kind of reasoning is usually referred to as *requirement validation* or *external validation*, the latter term being especially apt in the context of (ii) below.

(ii) Reasoning about the internal consistency of a formal specification, conducted primarily from the software developer's perspective. This kind of reasoning is a recognition of the possibility of, and consequences thus arising from, ill-conceived problem specifications, especially when dealing with large and complex software. This kind of reasoning is generally referred to as *internal validation.*

(iii) Reasoning about the correctness of the design or the implementation. In software engineering, this kind of reasoning is referred to as *verification* of software with respect to precisely stated requirements or earlier design decisions. This is conducted entirely from the software developer's perspective.

Our discussion here concentrates on (ii), and to an extent on (iii), and it does not address the kind of reasoning in (i). The latter kind of proof involves proving, or refuting, conjectures on the basis of requirements which are either stated explicitly in the specification or follow logically from them. The proofs involved in (iii) are generally outside the scope of formal specification. More on this aspect may be found in Gries [18] and Morgan [40].

The kind of proof appearing in (ii) concerns reasoning about both desirable and undesirable properties of a given specification. Therefore, we will deliberately introduce, or substitute, features which are obviously inappropriate on different grounds. This is done purely for illustrative purposes. However, it is surprising how easily in real life similar, or worse, deficiencies slip into specifications.

6.2 Kinds of Internal Consistency

The objective of establishing internal consistency is to ensure the implementability of the specification from the logical point of view. The concern here is the external, or global, properties of the specification, rather than the consequences of its content from the user's point of view. Being a prerequisite for any physical/actual implementation of the specification, this activity has important practical implications. Although it may be performed within a mathematical framework, or by other means, our interest here is in the former and, in particular, in understanding the sources of inconsistencies and how to detect and demonstrate their existence or, preferably, absence. A thorough awareness of these issues will invariably make the specifier more alert to the problem, and thus to profit from elimination of potential inconsistencies early in the specification task.

An inconsistency in the specification may arise from:

- Ill–conceived problem specification resulting from the lack of understanding, or the misunderstanding, of the object of specification
- Incorrect formalisation
- Inadvertent side effects arising from specification construction, for example, following modular development.

These deficiencies may manifest themselves in different parts of the specification in different forms. If they exist, they may be traced back to the following types of specification entities:

(a) State specifications

Our concern here is the specification of the general state. An inconsistency may arise due to a contradiction in the state invariant.

(b) Initialisation specifications

The source of inconsistency is similar to the above, but may arise from the introduction of additional predicates expressing the initialisation requirements.

(c) Operation specifications

In this case, there are several possible sources of inconsistency, the most obvious being the violation of the state invariant and any inconsistency in input and output specifications. Inconsistencies in operation specifications concern the non-implementability of individual operations, but there is also the possibility of mutual non-implementability of a group of operations. The latter case deals with situations where, although each operation is implementable in isolation, implementation of one operation may in effect preclude the implementation of another.

A specification may be regarded consistent if, and only if, all its sub-specifications are consistent, whether they are state specifications, initialisation specifications or operation specifications. As in logic, the consistency is related to the existence of models, that is, knowing whether it is possible to find an assignment of abstract, or concrete, objects to state variables that satisfies the theory described by the particular specification. Thus, the consistency may be demonstrated by exhibiting at least one such model. In model oriented languages such as Z, this may be done within the set theory itself, using set theoretic objects such as sets, relations, functions and sequences, and appealing to various axioms of *axiomatic set theory*, which assures the existence of certain basic objects such as the empty set. Since these are not topics considered in this text, we often rely on informal reasoning in demonstrating the existence of such models.

6.3 Consistency of the General State

In order to illustrate the issues raised above, let us use the formal definition of clocks introduced in Chapter 5 as a running example.

Suppose that a specific representation is to be adopted in place of the parametric type $\mathbb{T}$ used in the definition of clocks given in Chapter 5. The representation proposed here for $\mathbb{T}$ is based on a 24 hour clock, each hour being measurable up to the accuracy of a minute. As far as the type Θ is concerned, let us use, as suggested in Chapter 5, the set of real numbers $\mathbb{R}$, but assume that the unit of measurement of real time is in minutes from some datum. Let Δ and ∇ be both equal to unity. Let us adopt a type $\mathbb{T}_1$ defined as:

$$\mathbb{T}_1 ::= hrs\text{-}min_1 \langle\!\langle 0 \ldots 23 \times 0 \ldots 59 \rangle\!\rangle$$

in place of the generic type $\mathbb{T}$ in *Clock*. Informally speaking, $hrs\text{-}min_1(13, 55)$ stands for 13:55 hours on a 24 hour clock, or 1:55 pm on a 12 hour clock. Furthermore, $\mathbb{T}_1$ is to be supplemented with other operators and relations[1], for example, $+$, $<$ and $\leqslant$ defined as:

$$
\begin{array}{|l}
\_ + \_ \qquad\qquad\quad : \mathbb{T}_1 \times \mathbb{T}_1 \to \mathbb{T}_1 \\
\_ < \_ \, , \, \_ \leqslant \_ \; : \mathbb{T}_1 \leftrightarrow \mathbb{T}_1 \\
\hline
\forall\, t_1, t_2 : \mathbb{T}_1 \bullet (\exists\, h_1, h_2, m_1, m_2 : \mathbb{N} \bullet t_1 = hrs\text{-}min_1(h_1, m_1) \,\wedge \\
\qquad\qquad\qquad\qquad\qquad\qquad\qquad\quad t_2 = hrs\text{-}min_1(h_2, m_2) \Rightarrow \\
\quad t_1 + t_2 = hrs\text{-}min_1(((h_1 + h_2 + (m_1 + m_2)\ \mathsf{div}\ 60)\ \mathsf{mod}\ 24), \\
\qquad\qquad\qquad\qquad\qquad\qquad\qquad\qquad (m_1 + m_2)\ \mathsf{mod}\ 60) \\
\quad t_1 < t_2 \Leftrightarrow h_1 < h_2 \vee (h_1 = h_2 \wedge m_1 < m_2) \\
\quad t_1 \leqslant t_2 \Leftrightarrow t_1 < t_2 \vee t_1 = t_2
\end{array}
$$

where div and mod are arithmetic operations[2].

With the above type, functions and relationships in place, and assigning a suitable value for the constant $\mathcal{N}$, let us define a simple clock as:

$$SimpleClock \mathrel{\widehat{=}} Clock[\mathbb{T}_1] \mid \Omega = \{t : \mathbb{R};\ i : \mathbb{Z} \mid i \leqslant t < i + 1 \bullet$$
$$(t, hrs\text{-}min_1(((i\ \mathsf{div}\ 60)\ \mathsf{mod}\ 24),\ i\ \mathsf{mod}\ 60))\}$$

The definition given for Ω in *SimpleClock* is a function and, thus, conforms to its signature in *Clock*. However, it may be easily seen that the axioms:

---

[1] Note the operator overloading of $+$, $<$ and $\leqslant$; see also the footnote on page 16.
[2] In $\mathbb{Z}$ properties of div and mod are such that:

$$0 \leqslant a\ \mathsf{mod}\ b < b$$
$$a = (a\ \mathsf{div}\ b) \times b + a\ \mathsf{mod}\ b$$

for $a, b \in \mathbb{Z}$ and $b > 0$.

$$\forall\, t_1, t_2 : \Theta \bullet (t_2 > t_1 \Rightarrow \Omega t_2 \geqslant \Omega t_1) \wedge (\Omega t_2 > \Omega t_1 \Rightarrow t_2 > t_1) \qquad \text{(i)}$$
$$\forall\, t : \Theta \bullet t \in \text{dom } \Omega \Rightarrow \Omega(t + \Delta) > \Omega(t) \qquad \text{(ii)}$$

in *Clock* are violated by the proposed instantiation. For example, consider the case:

$$t_1 = 1385$$
$$t_2 = 1530$$

for which:

$$\Omega t_1 = hrs\text{-}min_1(23, 5)$$
$$\Omega t_2 = hrs\text{-}min_1(1, 30)$$

but:

$$t_2 > t_1$$
$$\Omega t_2 < \Omega t_1$$

As a consequence, the instantiation $\mathbb{T}_1$ proposed above for $\mathbb{T}$ violates the axiom labelled (i) above. A similar example can be produced to show that the instantiation also violates the axiom (ii) and, as a result, the state invariant of the specification as a whole.

However, this has helped us to detect a deficiency in the original specification. It has arisen from the fact that a distinction was not made between the values of the representation adopted for $\mathbb{T}_1$ and the form in which such values are to be displayed. In this connection, an appropriate solution would be to introduce a new type $\mathbb{T}_2$:

$$\mathbb{T}_2 ::= hrs\text{-}min_2 \langle\!\langle \mathbb{Z} \times 0 \mathbin{..} 59 \rangle\!\rangle$$

redefine *SimpleClock* and Ω as given below:

$$SimpleClock \mathrel{\widehat{=}} Clock[\mathbb{T}_2] \mid \Omega = \{t : \mathbb{R};\ i : \mathbb{Z} \mid i \leqslant t < i + 1 \bullet$$
$$(t, hrs\text{-}min_2(i \text{ div } 60, i \text{ mod } 60))\}$$

and adopt only a subset of $\mathbb{T}_2$ for display purposes. The above changes, however, require redefinition of relations such as $<$, $\leqslant$, etc., on $\mathbb{T}_2$. The choice of a subset of $\mathbb{T}_2$ for display purposes also requires a similar choice of time for components such as *alarm-time* and *stop-time* in the *Alarm* subsystem. This requires the redefinition of several affected schemas. For example, the schema *Display* needs to be redefined as:

```
┌─ Display ────────────────────────────────────────────
│  display-time :  𝕋₂
├──────────────────────────────────────────────────────
│  display-time  ∈  {t : 𝕋₂;  h, m : ℤ | t = hrs-min₂(h, m) ∧
│
│                              0 ⩽ h < 24 ∧ 0 ⩽ m < 59 • t}
└──────────────────────────────────────────────────────
```

As indicated, the suggested modification has repercussions elsewhere in the specification, and further investigations are left as Exercise 6.1 for the reader.

So far, our concern has been to detect and eliminate inconsistencies. However, failure to detect them does not necessarily mean they are absent, i.e., that a given specification is consistent. Thus, the task of demonstrating the consistency remains to be addressed. As indicated earlier, this amounts to exhibiting at least one model satisfying the specification, namely producing instances of values for each and every component in the relevant specification which, taken together, satisfy its predicates. Returning to the case study of the clock, the expanded and revised outline specification given below lists these components:

$$
\begin{array}{|l}
\hline
\quad Clock \underline{\hspace{7cm}} \\
\quad \Omega \qquad\qquad\quad : \Theta \twoheadrightarrow \mathbb{T}_2 \\
\quad display\text{-}time : \mathbb{T}_2 \\
\quad alarm\text{-}time \;\; : \mathbb{T}_2 \\
\quad stop\text{-}time \quad\; : \mathbb{T}_2 \\
\quad setting \qquad\; : \text{SWITCH} \\
\quad bell \qquad\qquad : \text{TONE} \\
\hline
\quad \text{NOW} \in \text{dom } \Omega \Rightarrow display\text{-}time = hrs\text{-}min_2(h \bmod 24, m) \\
\qquad\qquad\qquad \text{given that } \Omega \text{ NOW} = hrs\text{-}min_2(h, m) \\
\quad \cdots (\text{and other predicates}) \cdots \\
\hline
\end{array}
$$

It may be seen that for $\Delta = \nabla = 1$, the following bindings would satisfy the specification:

$$
\langle\!\!\mid \Omega \rightsquigarrow \{t : \mathbb{R}; \; i : \mathbb{Z} \mid i \leqslant t < i + 1 \bullet (t, (i \text{ div } 60, i \bmod 60))\},
$$
$$
display\text{-}time \rightsquigarrow (((\text{NOW div } 60) \bmod 24), \text{NOW} \bmod 60),
$$
$$
setting \rightsquigarrow \text{Off}, bell \rightsquigarrow \text{Silent} \mid\!\!\rangle
$$

the bindings of other components being immaterial.

6.4 Initialisation Consistency

Inconsistencies in the initialisation specification are dealt with in a similar manner to the above. An initialisation specification differs from its associated state specification in its operational character. It consists of the state subsequent to initialisation and, if relevant, any inputs and outputs. Therefore, if the inputs and outputs are ignored for the time being, there are no differences in form between the two types of specification. Thus, our discussion above remains applicable to initialisation specifications. However, despite this similarity, it is important not to overlook their consistency.

As a simple example, consider the alternative specification given below for *Create*:

$$
\begin{array}{|l}
\hline
\text{\textemdash } \textit{Create-Alt} \text{\textemdash\textemdash\textemdash\textemdash\textemdash\textemdash\textemdash\textemdash\textemdash\textemdash\textemdash} \\
\quad Clock' \\
\\
\quad display? : \mathbb{T}_2 \\
\quad \Theta'_0 : \Theta \\
\hline
\quad display\text{-}time' = alarm\text{-}time' = display? \\
\quad \Theta'_0 = \text{NOW} \\
\quad (\Theta'_0, display?) \in \Omega' \\
\quad bell' = \text{Silent} \\
\quad setting' = \text{On} \\
\hline
\end{array}
$$

but keeping $Clock_{init}$ unchanged. It is obvious that the above contradicts an axiom in $Clock$ inherited through $ClockWork$, namely:

$$bell = \text{Ringing} \Leftrightarrow (alarm\text{-}time \leqslant display\text{-}time \leqslant alarm\text{-}time + \mathcal{N} \times \Delta \land$$
$$setting = \text{On})$$

The above defect has been introduced deliberately, but such defects can have different origins.

6.5 Consistency of Operations

6.5.1 Forms of Operation Inconsistency

Compared to other types of specification entity, operation specifications are perhaps constructed more often from sub-specifications. One reason for this is the common approach to specification of exception handling operations by decomposition. Obviously, decomposition requires subsequent composition – an activity prone to inconsistencies.

Demonstration of operational consistency addresses the following:

(i) Invariant preservation consequent to the operation
(ii) Satisfiability of predicates characterising the state transformation, inputs and outputs
(iii) Establishing the consequences of proposed preconditions of operations

The first two aspects concern the implementability of operations from an operational point of view, that is, in making sure that the operations concerned can actually take place. The third has a subtle difference; it also requires proofs substantiating the specifier's claims, in particular in relation to any precondition proposed by him. The two kinds of proof, or demonstration, involved are dealt with in separate sub-sections.

6.5.2 Proof of Operational Aspects

Aspect (i) listed above concerns the satisfaction of the state invariant both before and after the operation. The relevant checks may be conducted on the two states independently of each other, as well as other components involved in the operation. This kind of check is already familiar to us from our discussion in Section 6.3.

It is not always easy to separate aspects (i) and (ii). This is because the violation of the state invariant is often related to a shortcoming in the specification of the state transformation which, as a consequence, inhibits the the operation taking place. Thus, even though the first two aspects are listed separately, they are closely interrelated.

As an illustration, consider first the following trivial situation. Let a state specification A be made up from two sub-specifications P and Q. Thinking of them in terms of schemas, we may write:

$$
\begin{array}{|l}
\hline
\_A_____ \\
P \\[4pt]
Q \\
\hline
\cdots\text{(some predicates)}\cdots \\
\hline
\end{array}
$$

Let us also assume that the specification concerned consists of two operations on A defined as:

$$
\begin{array}{|l}
\hline
\_OpA_1_____ \\
\Delta P \\[4pt]
\Xi Q \\[4pt]
\ldots\ldots \\
\hline
\cdots\text{(additional predicates signifying a change in } P\text{, but not in } Q)\cdots \\
\hline
\end{array}
$$

$$
\begin{array}{|l}
\hline
\_OpA_2_____ \\
\Xi P \\[4pt]
\Delta Q \\[4pt]
\ldots\ldots \\
\hline
\cdots\text{(additional predicates signifying a change in } Q\text{, but not in } P)\cdots \\
\hline
\end{array}
$$

where we use the notation Δ and Ξ as suggested in Section 2.9.3.

Now, if there is a third operation OpA_3 defined as:

$$OpA_3 \;\widehat{=}\; OpA_1 \wedge OpA_2$$

it is clear that OpA_3 is not implementable even if the other two are. This kind of situation arises from specification building operations from simpler sub-specifications. Some of the specification building operators are not so straightforward, and require greater care in their usage. Note also the possible inadvertent binding of free variables by quantifiers in specifications when sub-specifications are composed together in the above manner.

Furthermore, in analysing a state transformation, it is important to bear in mind that there is no notion of 'time' in set theoretic specification languages. The operations should therefore be treated as taking place 'instantaneously'. As a result, any apparent 'temporary' violation of the state invariant, seen from an implementational point of view of sub-operations, should really be treated as a logical contradiction. Therefore, when addressing the consistency of an operation specification by demonstrating the existence of a model, it is necessary to show values for each component and its 'dashed' version, representing respectively the state before and the state after the execution of the operation.

6.5.3 Proofs Obligatory on Specification Grounds

This section deals with aspect (iii) listed in Section 6.5.1, namely establishing the appropriateness of any precondition proposed by the specifier in connection with an operation.

Our concern here is primarily the nature of the precondition, especially in the context of languages that allow the specification of preconditions separately. In general, a precondition may offer a range of options. A strong precondition narrows down the circumstances under which the operation is to take place, while a weak precondition widens the scope of possible implementations by allowing a larger number of possible 'before' states.

First, let us examine why a language may allow separate specification of preconditions. Usually, preconditions are stated as predicates in operation specifications themselves. However, a specifier may choose to supplement the precondition in the operation specification with additional clauses, for example, on the grounds of actual circumstances in which the system is to operate or heuristics expressing past experience, for system security, to introduce additional safeguards to maintain system integrity and so on. Alternatively, a specifier may choose to state the precondition completely separately, perhaps to highlight its various aspects explicitly to the reader of the specification. The possibility of separately specified preconditions raises an important issue, namely their relationship with the rest of the specification.

For the purpose of our discussion, let us view the components of a certain schema A in the form given below:

```
┌─ A ─────────────────────────────────────────────────────
│  ······    } sig       signature declarations of components
├─────────────────────────────────────────────────────────
│  ······    } inv       predicates (state invariant)
└─────────────────────────────────────────────────────────
```

Obviously, the above is intended as the specification of the general state of a system. Let us also introduce the schema OpA:

```
┌─ OpA ───────────────────────────────────────────────────
│  A         } sig       signature declarations for 'before' state
│  A'        } sig'      signature declarations for 'after' state
│  ······    } sig?      signature declarations for inputs
│  ······    } sig!      signature declarations for outputs
├─────────────────────────────────────────────────────────
│  ······    } inv       'before' state invariant
│  ······    } inv'      'after' state invariant
│  ······    } pre       predicates involving 'before' state and inputs
│  ······    } post      other predicates potentially involving all
│                                                          components
└─────────────────────────────────────────────────────────
```

as an associated operation.

Let us also consider a schema of the form:

$$pre\_OpA \mathrel{\widehat{=}} A;\ sig?\ |\ pre_{prop}$$
$$\mathrel{\widehat{=}} [\ sig;\ sig?\ |\ inv \wedge pre_{prop}\ ]$$

which will play the role of a 'proposed precondition'. For the time being, the schema pre_OpA represents a stand alone specification for which we have no operation in mind. The appearance of the script OpA in the schema name pre_OpA has nothing to do with the operation specification OpA itself. The schema pre_OpA is also not an operation specification, for it contains no 'after' state but just a single 'before' state and, possibly, some inputs. Note also that the predicate pre_{prop} may not necessarily be the same as pre in OpA given above.

As with all other specification entities, however, we must first apply the test of consistency to each proposed precondition, and in this case to pre_OpA, because we intend to use it shortly as a proposed precondition. In other words, pre_OpA must be 'meaningful' or satisfiable. Restricting the terminology to precondition specifications alone, let us call a precondition specification of the form pre_OpA as *viable* if and only if:

$$\exists\ sig;\ sig? : inv \wedge pre_{prop}$$

Obviously, we are using the term *viable* in a meta–theoretic context. Viability of *pre_OpA* in this sense is a statement about nothing but *pre_OpA* alone.

Let us now assume that *pre_OpA* is an independently specified precondition to be used in conjunction with the operation defined by *OpA*. However, the viability of *pre_OpA* says nothing about whether the operation *OpA* may actually take place, because the operation may fail on other grounds. The only way to guarantee that an operation backed up by a specially devised precondition can take place is to ensure the attainability of an after state characterised by the postcondition *post* together with the invariant *inv'*, provided that *inv* and pre_{prop} hold in the before state. In this connection, we introduce another meta-theoretic term, namely *effective*, in order to relate an independently specified precondition to an operation specification.

Before defining the term *effective* formally, let us first recall the usage of the schema operator 'pre', introduced in Section 2.11. The distinction between the operator 'pre' and the proposed preconditions is crucially important to our discussion. Note that 'pre' is an operator, which is used for calculating the precondition of a given operation specification. Application of 'pre' not only extracts the relevant state and the inputs but also hides the 'after' and the outputs in the result. Note that, according to the convention in Section 2.8, hiding means the existential quantification of the relevant components in the predicate part of the given schema.

NOTE: Analogous to 'pre', 'post' is meant for calculating the postcondition of an operation specification.

Returning to our previous discussion, we say that a precondition specification *pre_OpA* is *effective* in relation to an operation specification *OpA* if and only if:

$$\forall sig;\ sig? \bullet (inv \Rightarrow (pre_{prop} \Rightarrow (\exists sig';\ sig! \bullet (inv' \wedge post)))) \qquad (6.1)$$
$$\Leftrightarrow \forall sig;\ sig? \bullet (inv \wedge pre_{prop} \Rightarrow (\exists sig';\ sig! \bullet (inv' \wedge post))) \qquad (6.2)$$

Now, if it can be further shown that:

$$\forall sig;\ sig? \bullet (inv \wedge pre_{prop} \Rightarrow inv \wedge pre) \qquad (6.3)$$

then the formulae (6.1) and (6.2) are logically equivalent to:

$$\forall sig;\ sig? \bullet (inv \wedge pre_{prop} \Rightarrow$$
$$(inv \wedge pre \wedge (\exists sig';\ sig! \bullet (inv' \wedge post)))) \qquad (6.4)$$

Using schemas as predicates, the above may be paraphrased as:

$$\forall sig;\ sig? \bullet (pre\_OpA \Rightarrow pre\ OpA) \qquad (6.5)$$

In other words, *pre_OpA* is said to be *effective* in relation to *OpA* if and only if (6.5) holds true.

Note again the difference between the two preconditions, namely that:

pre_OpA   –   is a proposed precondition

pre OpA   –   is a precondition calculated using the operator 'pre'

Whether a proposed precondition is *effectively* applicable to a specific operation has to be validated only by verifying that the predicate (6.5) holds. In practical terms (6.5) amounts to 'implementability' of the given operation with respect to the proposed precondition. Any claim, or challenge, as to whether this is indeed the case has to be substantiated by proving the above as a 'theorem' of the theory described by the specification concerned. In Z this theorem is often referred to as the *precondition theorem*.

The proof of the precondition theorem is slightly different from other kinds of reasoning about specifications encountered in this chapter. This is because the concern of the latter has been to demonstrate the existence of models satisfying particular states. By contrast, what the precondition theorem asserts is not the existence of models of a state satisfying inv' and $post$, but the achievability of that state, whenever the proposed precondition is true. Given that the proposed precondition is true, then the satisfiability of a state with inv' and $post$ follows from this theorem.

Using the notation $\Gamma \vdash \phi$ to mean that ϕ is provable from a list of formulae Γ, we may express the precondition theorem in the following alternative forms:

$$\vdash pre\_OpA \Rightarrow \text{pre } OpA$$

$$pre\_OpA \vdash \text{pre } OpA$$

In summary, the proof obligations with respect to any given precondition are two fold, namely:

1. A proposed precondition must be satisfiable or viable (from the point of view of existence of models). That is:

$$\exists pre\_OpA \qquad\qquad (6.6)$$

2. A precondition must be effectively applicable to the operation for which it was intended (from the point of view of implementability of the operation). That is:

$$pre\_OpA \vdash \text{pre } OpA \qquad\qquad (6.7)$$

The above constitute the criteria for judging whether a precondition proposed in connection with an operation is meaningful or not.

6.5.4 An Illustration

This section demonstrates the use of the precondition theorem in specification. The example is based on an extension of our case study *Clock* in Chapter 5. The extension concerns a 'snooze function' – a facility for stopping a ringing alarm immediately and making it ring a little later.

We extend the *Clock* specification in the following manner. Firstly, we add a new mechanism for interrupting the alarm. It is essentially a device for generating an input to the clock through a channel, analogous to the way the channel *out!* is used in *ClockAdvance* to model the clock ticking. Since it is an input, we call it simply *in?* taking values from a certain binary valued type SNOOZE-ENTRY defined as:

SNOOZE-ENTRY ::= Delay | NoDelay

Obviously, the value Delay represents a request for delayed ringing of the alarm and NoDelay is a default value which means that there is no such request.

Secondly, we introduce a new constant M, such that $M > \mathcal{N}$, to denote the number of multiples of ∇ by which alarm is to be delayed. Thirdly, we add an extra operation *Snooze* defined as:

$$
\begin{array}{|l|}
\hline
\_\,Snooze\,\rule{6cm}{0pt}\_\, \\
\Delta Clock \\[4pt]
\Xi\,ClockWork; \quad \Xi\,Display \\[4pt]
in? : \text{SNOOZE-ENTRY} \\
\hline
in? = \text{Delay} \\[4pt]
bell = \text{Ringing} \\[4pt]
setting = \text{On} \\[4pt]
display\text{-}time \leqslant stop\text{-}time \\[4pt]
setting' = \text{On} \\[4pt]
bell' = \text{Silent} \\[4pt]
alarm\text{-}time' = alarm\text{-}time + M \times \nabla \\
\hline
\end{array}
$$

to enable the user to cancel the alarm immediately and delay its ringing.

NOTE: Although it is an aside, note that requirements in the operation specifications *StopAlarm* and *Snooze* could come into conflict with each other for certain values of components. These concern situations where *Snooze* happens to take place exactly when the display reaches the alarm stop time. This requires imposition of some order of preference between the two operations in the event both are permitted to occur by their preconditions. The specification of this ordering is left as an exercise for the reader. The last predicate is written in the given form deliberately in order to couple the before and after states; this may be justified by the fictitious nature of our requirement on alarm delay.

Let us now consider four schemas for potential use as proposed preconditions. Let us also name them in such a way that the reader does not unwittingly infer any relationships between them and the operations we will be dealing with. The proposed preconditions are:

$$
\begin{array}{|l}
\hline \_\, pre\_Cond_1 _____ \\
\;\; Clock \\[4pt]
\;\; in? : \text{SNOOZE-ENTRY} \\
\hline
\;\; in? = \mathsf{Delay} \\[4pt]
\;\; bell = \mathsf{Silent} \\[4pt]
\;\; setting = \mathsf{On} \\[4pt]
\;\; stop\text{-}time = display\text{-}time \\
\hline
\end{array}
$$

and

$$pre\_Cond_2 \,\hat{=}\, pre\_Cond\_Aux \mid display\text{-}time < stop\text{-}time$$
$$pre\_Cond_3 \,\hat{=}\, pre\_Cond\_Aux \mid display\text{-}time = stop\text{-}time$$
$$pre\_Cond_4 \,\hat{=}\, pre\_Cond\_Aux \mid display\text{-}time \geqslant stop\text{-}time$$

where:

$$
\begin{array}{|l}
\hline \_\, pre\_Cond\_Aux _____ \\
\;\; Clock \\[4pt]
\;\; in? : \text{SNOOZE-ENTRY} \\
\hline
\;\; in? = \mathsf{Delay} \\[4pt]
\;\; bell = \mathsf{Ringing} \\[4pt]
\;\; setting = \mathsf{On} \\
\hline
\end{array}
$$

Let us consider the viability of the above proposals, as well as their applicability with respect to operations *StopAlarm* and *Snooze*. The reader may easily verify that pre_Cond_1 is not viable since the explicitly stated predicates in its definition contradict the predicates inherited through *Clock*, namely the state invariant of the latter. Therefore, it is futile to consider it further as a potentially applicable precondition.

On the other hand, the other three proposals, pre_Cond_i for $i \in 2 \,..\, 4$, are viable and, as such, may be considered as candidate preconditions for whatever operations we have in mind.

Let us consider the applicability of pre_Cond_i, $i \in 2 \,..\, 4$, in turn in relation to the two operations. As it may be seen, the precondition pre_Cond_2 is not applicable to *StopAlarm*. However, it is applicable to *Snooze*, but with the tightening of the precondition as a consequence. This may be seen as a way of avoiding the conflict between *StopAlarm* and *Snooze* mentioned earlier. The third proposal is applicable to both the operations, although one might question the resulting strong requirement on *Snooze* that the alarm may be delayed only when its stop time is reached. Thus, the use of proposed preconditions may have repercussions on customer requirements. The fourth proposal is applicable to neither operations, despite its viability.

These statements on applicability of the proposed preconditions to the two operations have been made purely on an informal basis. Thus, they are conjectures. Let us provide a more formal argument substantiating one of them. It concerns the claim that pre_Cond_2 is effective in relation to the operation *Snooze*. In this respect, it is necessary to show that:

$$\vdash pre\_Cond_2 \Rightarrow \text{pre } Snooze$$

Justification of the above is given below as a proof outline.

Given that *Clock*; *in?* : SNOOZE-ENTRY

1. pre_Cond_2 – assumption
2. $Clock \wedge in? = \text{Delay} \wedge bell = \text{Ringing} \wedge$ – definition of pre_Cond_2
    $setting = \text{On} \wedge display\text{-}time < stop\text{-}time$
3. $display\text{-}time < stop\text{-}time$ – from 2; $\wedge$-Elim
4. $display\text{-}time \leqslant stop\text{-}time$ – from 3; $\vee$-Intro
5. $Clock \wedge in? = \text{Delay} \wedge bell = \text{Ringing} \wedge$ – from 2; $\wedge$-Elim
    $setting = \text{On}$
6. $Clock \wedge in? = \text{Delay} \wedge bell = \text{Ringing} \wedge$ – from 4 and 5; $\wedge$-Intro
    $setting = \text{On} \wedge display\text{-}time \leqslant stop\text{-}time$
7. $\exists alarm\text{-}time' : \mathbb{T} \bullet$ – def. of $+$ on $\mathbb{T}$
    $alarm\text{-}time' = alarm\text{-}time + M \times \nabla$
8. $\exists bell' : \text{TONE} \bullet bell' = \text{Silent}$ – type TONE being non-empty
9. $\exists setting' : \text{SWITCH} \bullet setting' = \text{On}$ – type SWITCH being non-empty
10. $\exists Clock' \bullet setting' = \text{On} \wedge$ – from 7-9 and existentially
    $bell' = \text{Silent} \wedge$ quantified equalities of display
    $alarm\text{-}time' = alarm\text{-}time + M \times \nabla \wedge$ time etc. through a series of
    $display\text{-}time' = display\text{-}time \wedge$ quantifier eliminations and
    $\Omega' = \Omega$ introductions
11. $Clock \wedge in? = \text{Delay} \wedge bell = \text{Ringing} \wedge$ – from 6 and 10; $\wedge$-Intro
    $setting = \text{On} \wedge display\text{-}time \leqslant stop\text{-}time \wedge$
    $\exists Clock'; \; \Xi Display; \; \Xi ClockWork \bullet$
    $(setting' = \text{On} \wedge bell' = \text{Silent} \wedge$
    $alarm\text{-}time' = alarm\text{-}time + M \times \nabla)$

12. pre *Snooze*   — from 11 and def. of *Snooze*

13. *pre_Cond$_2$* $\Rightarrow$ pre *Snooze*   — from 1 and 12; $\Rightarrow$-Intro

□

The above is presented as a proof outline because of the brevity of steps such
as (10) and (11).

Exercises

6.1 The discussion on page 99 suggested the adoption of $\mathbb{T}_2$ as a specific
type that can be used in place of the parametric type $\mathbb{T}$. Examine its appropriateness further. If it is appropriate, give the formal definition for the
relations such as $<$ and $\leqslant$ and the operator $+$.

6.2 Continuing the above exercise, complete the modifications required in
other schemas as a result of the adoption of a subset of $\mathbb{T}_2$ for display purposes
and the alarm.

6.3 Provide more rigorous arguments to substantiate, or to refute, the
claims made on page 109 regarding the viability of proposed preconditions *pre_Cond$_i$*, $i \in 2 .. 4$ and their effectiveness in relation to operations
StopAlarm and *Snooze*.

7. Specification of a Network Protocol

This chapter illustrates the use of Z in capturing certain aspects of the state information relevant to a network protocol. Its aim is both to illustrate the applicability of formal specification to realistic computer systems and to demonstrate the use of a formal framework for design. The description covers an abstract design of a network protocol, along the lines of the seven layer network protocol model proposed by the International Standards Organisation (ISO) for Open System Interconnection (OSI). The design is conducted by a kind of refinement, starting from a high level specification. An alternative way of looking at each refinement is as a different abstraction of the protocol. The chapter also shows the kind of proofs that may be required in such refinements and how these may be accomplished.

The reader is referred to Section 7.9 for additional information on the specification of network protocols.

7.1 Introduction

When dealing with communication networks, we are likely to encounter formalisms such as process algebras, Petri nets, finite–state models and certain kinds of temporal logic in describing their behaviour under different protocols. Most of these approaches aim to specify protocols in terms of their external behaviour, allowing the designer to concentrate on the desired functionality without becoming too involved with the structural composition of networks and protocols.

However, as the attention shifts towards implementation, it becomes necessary to focus on structural details. Obviously, the structure and behaviour are complementary to each other and an appropriate structure is a prerequisite for achieving the desired behaviour. Therefore, the amount of emphasis placed on external behaviour and that placed on structure is an issue dependent on the stage of design. With the growth of the structural complexity, relying solely on the above mentioned formalisms to describe design may not be an effective approach.

A natural ally in this respect are frameworks with a richer notion of state. These can serve as an effective complementary medium for expressing designs. Compared to conventional approaches such as finite state machines and pushdown automata, the more recent mathematical formalisms such as Z and VDM offer some advantages, particularly in terms of mathematical reasoning and expressiveness and, with the growing use of mathematics in software design, as languages for abstract design.

The given case study is a demonstration of how a state based formal framework can be used for designing communication protocols. The case study is related to the seven layer model proposed by the ISO for OSI. An outline of the OSI model is given in Section 7.2. For reasons of space, the chapter covers an outline definition and design of the top layers, namely, application, presentation, session and transport layers. Despite this limited scope, the description forms a clear demonstration of the feasibility of design in abstract, as well as its benefits. Designing in abstract means confining yourself to conceptual issues relevant to the current stage, and considering the bare minimum of detail needed at each stage. This allows moving to lower level design stages in a disciplined manner. This is possible only if the medium of expression of the design is high level, as otherwise, the low level constructs of the language tend to force the designer to work at a low level.

7.2 OSI Reference Model

Open Systems Interconnection is a reference model drawn up by the International Standards Organisation in order to provide a common structure so that it serves, one one hand, as a basis for developing communication software and, on the other, as a framework for cohabitation of proprietary network architectures produced by different manufacturers. The OSI reference model consists of seven different 'layers'. Each layer provides a different abstraction of the underlying communication network. From the user's perspective, each layer performs a specific function, but it does so relying solely on the services provided by the layer below. In the case of the top four layers, interaction between two users over the network takes place as if directly between them and purely within the corresponding two layers. In the case of the bottom three layers, interaction between two users is represented as an interaction involving several communicating computers.

An immediate benefit of this kind of approach is the hiding of software complexity, enabling a better understanding of the software. Another advantage is that it provides a practical way to isolate the more stable upper layers from the layers that lie below, which are more susceptible to frequent changes brought about by advances in technology. Therefore, both these have significant practical dividends in cost in the development, intermediate upgrading and maintenance of communication software.

The functionality of different OSI layers can be outlined as follows:

1. *Application layer*
   This layer provides its users with network wide distributed services such as file transfers between different hosts, remote transaction processing,

issuing control signals to equipment in an industrial plant, relaying to the user similar information passed by other users, and so on.

2. *Presentation layer*

The primary function of the presentation layer is to translate messages from the application layer to a common standard representation for the purpose of transfer, and vice versa. It may additionally perform such functions as data encryption and decryption of messages required for secure communication, as well as data compression for efficient transfer.

3. *Session layer*

The session layer enables the presentation layer to set up, and later close, a dialogue with another host computer, provides the means to synchronise the dialogue and, following a failure, facilitates recovery from a recent 'checkpoint' rather than from the beginning of the dialogue.

4. *Transport layer*

This layer packs the data into smaller units for transmission and, when receiving data from another source, unpacks and reassembles the data before passing them to the session layer. It enables the communication to take place as if between 'ports', a software–defined entity within each computer. Depending on the amount of data to be communicated, real-time constraints and the costs involved, the transport layer may resort to using more than one network connection per communication, or multiplex several communications into a single connection.

5. *Network layer*

The network layer is responsible for routing data from the source to the destination. Routes can be permanently fixed, set up at the beginning for the duration of the dialogue, set up independently for each packet depending on the current network load or for congestion control.

6. *Data link layer*

Being just above the lowest layer, the data link layer is responsible for the integrity of the communicated data. In order to achieve an error-free transmission from the network layer's perspective, it transmits the data in small 'data frames', verifies the receipt of each at the destination through an acknowledgement, retransmits the frame in the event of its loss, takes care of any duplicates resulting from loss of acknowledgements themselves, regulates traffic so that any mismatch between the rates of transmission of data and its receipt does not result in overflow of buffer capacity at nodes on the route, etc.

7. *Physical layer*

The main function of the physical layer is to interface with the underlying physical medium and to transmit the information passed to it as binary digits (bits) of 0s and 1s in the form of two kinds of electrical pulse, each with a precise voltage and for a precise duration.

The above is a brief description of the OSI reference model with many simplifications. Despite this, the model is still too large for a formal treatment here. Therefore, we adopt a model with a similar structure to the OSI model but with further simplifications. As a result, the formalisation attempted in this chapter addresses only one aspect of an OSI-type model, namely, how the messages originated by user requests are transformed into different forms as they pass from the application layer down to the transport layer, and vice versa.

Knowledge of the OSI model in full detail is not absolutely essential for understanding the formal definition given below but, if required, more details can be found in many standard texts such as Coulouris [13], Halsall [22] and Tanenbaum [59].

7.3 Some Preliminaries

Since this is an exercise in design, let us first describe how it will be conducted. Each design stage progresses through a number of smaller steps. In this respect, we advocate the following phases or steps:

(i) The design process begins with as concise and abstract as possible a statement about the primary function of the system being envisaged.

(ii) Each subsequent stage chooses a particular aspect of the current design for further development, and then identifies the objects most relevant or essential for representing it. In practical terms, this amounts to introducing new (set-theoretic) objects, constants and parameters which are absolutely necessary for the earmarked development. Their introduction is to be motivated only by the additional functionality to be achieved, or by the need for making the previous design more concrete on the grounds of such factors as accessible technology.

(iii) These new items are then integrated into the existing design of the general system state. In the abstract representation, this amounts to additional state variables in the signature, additional predicates to describe the state so extended, or both. These predicates may address the role of newly introduced state variables, as well as the extended, or the revised, role of the existing state variables.

(iv) This is to be followed by the introduction of any additional functionality being sought. This may involve the extension or modification of existing operation specifications, including that of the initialisation, or the introduction of completely new operations.

(v) Finally, both the integration of the new objects and the extended functionality are to be verified in terms of their consequences in relation to original requirements, the requirements of the previous layer or the specific objectives of the current design stage. Undoubtedly, the most effective form of verification is the mathematical proof.

A major difference between step (i) and the rest is the absence of a previous step for extension. However, we advocate subjecting all phases of the design process to the same criteria of conciseness and abstractness as in (i), but to a different extent because of the increasing number of issues addressed by the lower level design steps.

The importance of proof required under (v) is not to be seen solely from the standpoint of verification of requirements. Proof is an integral part of the design process and gives a unique insight into design, often exposing flaws which may not be detected otherwise, or at least early enough. This is especially true of formal proofs, where nothing is taken for granted. Some of the proofs which were found to be particularly useful in the design process are included in Section 7.8.

In addition to the limitations mentioned in Section 7.2, the description given here is incomplete in another sense, namely in that it covers only the normal behaviour in each stage. Thus, we depart from the normal specification practice by not defining here the exception handling facilities and the initial states. Exception handling is an important aspect of network protocol, and the fact that it is omitted here should not be interpreted as an underestimation of its significance. In principle, their incorporation in the full design is not different from the way it is done in other system specifications.

Since the system and its subsystems display a different view of the network at each stage, we distinguish different views by attaching an appropriate subscript to each of their specifications. The subscripts a, p, s, t stand for application, presentation, session and transport layers respectively. The use of subscripts in this manner is simply a device for referring to specification entities relevant to a particular layer. Omission of these subscripts may be taken as a reference to the most recent definition. In addition to relying on inheritance of a schema decoration by a superscript by its components, where necessary, we also extend this convention to subscripts such as a, p, etc., and other numerical subscripts.

7.4 Application Layer

At the highest level, the system can be viewed as a set of host computers each supporting a collection of processes executing one or more application programs. The primary function of the system is to enable these processes to exchange various kinds of information in the form of messages. Of course, there may be other tasks associated with local communications, but they are of no relevance here.

In order to describe the network behaviour, let us first introduce certain non-empty sets as types. The type *Application* stands for all possible user programs. Such programs generate various kinds of requests to other programs, including those providing distributed system services. These requests are conveyed as messages. Let *Message* denote the set of all possible messages that may be exchanged over the network. *ProcId* and *HostId* denote two sets of names for identifying, respectively, the computational processes and hosts.

Although, as a part of the design process, we will return in the next section to a more detailed discussion about *Message*, for the time being let:

$$[Application, Message, ProcId, HostId]$$

all be some generic types.

In respect of *Message*, however, it is possible to characterise certain important properties that its elements must exhibit. For example, some elements of *Message* may denote the same message in terms of meaning, although their actual representations may be different. On the other hand, even the different messages may have some attributes in common, in particular the language of their expression.

With the above in mind we introduce two relations on *Message*. One of them is an equivalence relation ≈ meaning that, for any messages a, b, $a \approx b$ is true if and only if a and b have the same message content or, in other words, they are identical in meaning. The intention is to allow different hosts the freedom to have potentially different representations of the same message. This may be justified on different grounds, for example, physical needs such as formatting or security needs such as data encryption. The second relation on *Message* is also an equivalence relation and is denoted by ≃ . Given that a, b are two messages, $a \simeq b$ is true if and only if a and b are messages expressed in the same language.

It may be desirable that each host has a unique script, or a unique representation, for any given message and communicates only in one language. Therefore, we define below a set of scripts:

$$Script_a\ Message == \{ mes : \mathbb{P}\ Message \mid mes \in (Message/ \simeq) \wedge$$
$$\forall\, a, b : Message \bullet \{a, b\} \subseteq mes \wedge$$
$$\{a, b\} \subseteq [a]_\approx \Rightarrow a = b\}$$

where $[a]_\approx$ denotes the equivalence class of a induced by ≈ and $Message/ \simeq$ the quotient of *Message* by ≃ . Thus, each element in the above set is a set of messages expressed in some given language, with each message having a unique meaning.

NOTES:

1. Given an equivalence relation R on a set A, associated with each element a of the set A is a set:

   $$[a] == \{x \mid x \in A \wedge (a, x) \in R\}$$

   The set $[a]$ is called the equivalence class of a.
2. The notation $[a]$ is also used in literature to denote the singleton sequence containing the element a.
3. Given an equivalence relation R on a set A, the quotient of A by R is denoted by A/R and is defined as the set of equivalence classes of all elements in A. That is:

   $$A/R == \{[a] \mid a \in A\}$$

Every host computer is restricted to communicating with the external world in a fixed language. Let us record these languages of communication in the function *tongues*:

$$tongues : HostId \nrightarrow Script$$

For later use, let us also introduce two auxiliary functions *host* and *proc*, defined as:

$$host : HostId \times ProcId \rightarrow HostId$$

$$proc : HostId \times ProcId \rightarrow ProcId$$

$$\forall h : HostId;\ p : ProcId \bullet host(h, p) = h \wedge proc(h, p) = p$$

In defining processes, we come across a deficiency in state based approaches to specification, namely, how to describe a 'pattern' of change of a given entity, such as a process undergoing continuous changes. For our purpose, however, we may adequately capture the notion of a process as follows. Our concern here is not how each process evolves over time, but its relationship with the external communications and, in particular, with the incoming communications. The component *mail* below refers to the incoming communications only and all messages are communicated in a single 'script', that is, in the form of messages in one language but with each message written in a unique form.

$$
\begin{array}{|l}
\hline
\ Process_a[Message] \underline{\hspace{5cm}} \\
\ pid : ProcId \\[4pt]
\ prgm : Application \\[4pt]
\ mail : \text{bag } Message \\
\hline
\ \exists\, scr : Script \bullet \text{dom } mail \subseteq scr \\
\hline
\end{array}
$$

The above allows *mail* to contain replicates of a message. However, without much loss of generality, an ordinary set may have been equally suitable for *mail*, especially if *prgm* relies only on one instance of a message or if all the messages are time-stamped in order to make sure that each message is different from the others. Another possible representation for *mail* is a sequence, which would be suitable if *prgm* relies on the order of receipt of messages, possibly with replicates. The symbol *pid* denotes the process identifier.

Process requires two obvious operations, one to generate a message and the other to receive a message from another process. How messages are generated and used by a process depends on its program, but our task does not require this knowledge. The two operations required at the process level are:

___ New-Request[Message] _____
| $\Xi Process_a$
|
| $mes! : Message$
|
| $from!, to! : HostId \times ProcId$
|_____
| $proc(from!) = pid$
|
| $proc(to!) \neq pid$
|_____

___ Get-Reply[Message] _____
| $\Delta Process_a$
|
| $mes? : Message$
|
| $from?, to? : HostId \times ProcId$
|_____
| $proc(to?) = pid$
|
| $proc(from?) \neq pid$
|
| $mail' = mail \uplus [\![mes?]\!]$
|
| $prgm' = prgm$
|
| $pid' = pid$
|_____

where each of *from!* and *to!*, as well as *from?* and *to?*, denotes a pair, consisting of the host identifier and the process identifier of the process concerned. Furthermore, according to these operations, no process exchanges any message with itself and processes only issue messages with their own identification and accept messages if the messages are meant for them.

A host computer may then be viewed as a finite collection of such processes, which is restricted to communicating with the external world in its own 'native tongue'.

___ Host_a[Message] _____
| $hid : HostId$
|
| $processes : \mathbb{F}\, Process$
|
| $native\text{-}tongue : Script$
|_____
| $hid \in \text{dom } tongues$
|
| $native\text{-}tongue = tongues(hid)$
|
| $\forall\, p_1, p_2 \in processes \bullet p_1.pid = p_2.pid \Leftrightarrow p_1 = p_2$
|
| $(\bigcup_{p \in processes} \text{dom } p.mail) \subseteq native\text{-}tongue$
|_____

In order to define the effect of generation, or of receipt, of a message by a process on a host computer, let us separate what is common to both these operations at the level of the host. This is given in the schema below:

```
┌─ Host-Update[Message] ─────────────────────────────
│ ΔHost
│
│ ΔProcess
│
│ mes : Message
│
│ p : Process
│
│ venue : HostId × ProcId
├─────────────────────────────────────────────────────
│ mes ∈ native-tongue
│
│ host(venue) = hid
│
│ proc(venue) = p.pid
│
│ p ∈ processes
│
│ p = θProcess
│
│ processes' = (processes − {θProcess}) ∪ {θProcess'}
│
│ hid' = hid
│
│ native-tongue' = native-tongue
└─────────────────────────────────────────────────────
```

where *mes* denotes the message being input or output, *p* the particular process affected by it and *venue* a pair giving, respectively, the identifier of the host where the operation concerned takes place and the identifier of process *p*.

Using the above, the task of sending and receiving messages is presented below purely as a local affair within the host computer. Note that, as an implication of the renaming of the component *mes*, the message being transmitted, or received, has to be in the native tongue of the host. Thus:

```
┌─ Send_a[Message] ──────────────────────────────────
│ Host-Update[mes!/mes, from!/venue]
│
│ New-Request
└─────────────────────────────────────────────────────
```

```
┌─ Receive_a[Message] ───────────────────────────────
│ Host-Update[mes?/mes, to?/venue]
│
│ Get-Reply
└─────────────────────────────────────────────────────
```

According to the above, sending a message should not affect the host at all, but receiving a message does affect it as a result of updating the mail bag of the recipient process.

As was mentioned earlier, due to the lack of appropriate constructs the evolution of a process affected by any of the above operations cannot be fully expressed in Z. We also ignore here other potential internal events in host computers.

The network at the application level may be viewed as a finite set of host computers maintaining some 'virtual' interconnections between their processes for the purpose of communication. The following formalises the general state of the network in this sense. Its requirements are fairly obvious, namely that the hosts engaged in the virtual sessions (*v-sessions*) are those in the network and the processes involved in these sessions are those being executed on the host computers.

$$
\begin{array}{l}
\hline
Net_a[Message] \\
\hline
hosts : \mathbb{F}\ Host \\
v\text{-}sessions : (HostId \times ProcId) \leftrightarrow (HostId \times ProcId) \\
\hline
\forall\, h_1, h_2 \in hosts \bullet h_1.hid = h_2.hid \Leftrightarrow h_1 = h_2 \\
\{hst : Host;\ h : HostId;\ p : ProcId \mid \\
\qquad (h, p) \in \text{fld } v\text{-}sessions \wedge hst.hid = h \bullet hst\} \subseteq hosts \\
\{prs : Process;\ h : HostId;\ p : ProcId \mid (h, p) \in \text{fld } v\text{-}sessions \wedge \\
\qquad prs.pid = p \bullet prs\} \subseteq \bigcup_{h \in hosts} h.processes \\
\hline
\end{array}
$$

where 'fld' of a relation denotes its field, that is, the union of its domain and range.

We require here only one operation on the state defined by *Net*, namely a definition of how it is affected as two processes exchange a message. For this purpose, continuing the style of promotion used elsewhere, let us define a 'template' on two adjacent states of *Net* in order to make the aspects which will be affected by this operation explicit.

$$
\begin{array}{l}
\rule{0pt}{0pt}\text{—}\,\textit{Net-Update}[\textit{Message}]\,\text{———————————————}\\
\quad \Delta Net\\[4pt]
\quad \Delta Host_1;\ \ \Delta Host_2\\[4pt]
\quad from, to : HostId \times ProcId\\[4pt]
\quad h_1, h_2 : Host\\[4pt]
\quad p_1, p_2 : Process\\
\quad\rule{6cm}{0.4pt}\\
\quad host(from) = h_1.hid\\[4pt]
\quad host(to) = h_2.hid\\[4pt]
\quad h_1 = \theta Host_1\\[4pt]
\quad h_2 = \theta Host_2\\[4pt]
\quad proc(from) = p_1.pid\\[4pt]
\quad proc(to) = p_2.pid\\[4pt]
\quad hosts' = (hosts - \{\theta Host_1, \theta Host_2\}) \cup \{\theta Host_1', \theta Host_2'\}
\end{array}
$$

where, as was noted in Section 7.3, the subscripts 1 and 2 are to be applied consistently to all components declared in the respective schemas.

The transmission of a message from one host to another may then be seen as a state transformation on the global network, affecting the ones engaged in the given communication only. The establishment of the required virtual session is of no concern at this level.

$$
\begin{array}{l}
\rule{0pt}{0pt}\text{—}\,\textit{Transmit-aux}_a[\textit{Message}]\,\text{———————————————}\\
\quad Net\text{-}Update\\[4pt]
\quad Send_a[Host_1/Host, Host_1'/Host', p_1/p, from/from!, to/to!]\\[4pt]
\quad Receive_a[Host_2/Host, Host_2'/Host', p_2/p, from/from?, to/to?]\\
\quad\rule{6cm}{0.4pt}\\
\quad (from, to) \in v\text{-}sessions\\[4pt]
\quad mes! \approx mes?
\end{array}
$$

$$
Transmit_a[\textit{Message}] \ \widehat{=}\ Transmit\text{-}aux_a[\textit{Message}] \setminus h_1, h_2, p_1, p_2
$$

According to the above, $Host_1$ sends a message $mes!$ written in its native tongue to $Host_2$, which receives an equivalent message $mes?$, in the sense of $\approx$, in its native tongue, updating simultaneously its $mail$. This particular state transformation to the network is somewhat unrealistic since it does not take into account the temporal order of any given pair of $Send$ and $Receive$

events. This is an instance where the relevant realtime issues need to be taken into account. However, in situations where they can be ignored, the description adequately captures how the state of the network is affected at the application level by the two events.

7.5 Presentation Layer

7.5.1 Refinement of the Data Type *Message*

In formalising communications at the level of the application layer, the type *Message* was treated as an arbitrary set with the requirements limited to those imposed by the relations $\approx_a$ and $\simeq$ on it. However, since the primary function of the network is to transfer messages, we must now examine *Message* more closely. From the perspective of the presentation layer at a given node, because of the costs involved, it is impractical to transmit messages in all kinds of languages. Furthermore, it will become apparent later that messages cannot also be transmitted in full and without interruption. This is because, under fluctuations in the workload as well as in the capacity of the medium, the nodes often face conflicting demands and, as a result, preempt ongoing transmissions for various reasons, including newly requested higher priority transmissions. As a consequence, the messages have to be constructed from simpler forms of data so that a message can be decomposed, if necessary, into several smaller messages.

In other words, it is necessary first of all to restrict the way that the presentation layer handles messages. In order to address this new requirement, we need, on the one hand, identification of some internal structure within objects belonging to *Message* and, on the other, a type of object which is more primitive than *Message*. With this in mind, let us introduce a new type called $Data_p$

$$[Data_p]$$

with an accompanying relation $\simeq_d$ defined on it, which is identical to $\simeq$ on *Message* in terms of meaning and intended use.

This allows us to be more explicit about the requirements on *Message* and how we intend to achieve them by means of $Data_p$. The ingredients required for this purpose include certain non-empty subsets of $Data_p$ as vocabularies to be used by individual nodes of the network defined as:

$$Vocabulary == Data_p / \simeq_d$$

and a certain fixed vocabulary called *External Data Representation* (EDR) to be used by all nodes of the network:

$$| \quad EDR : Vocabulary$$

It follows from the definition of *Vocabulary* that its elements, including *EDR*, are non-empty sets.

Since the presentation layer is not concerned with the meanings of messages and, hence, the semantics of the languages used for expressing them, it is only necessary to compare messages syntactically. For this purpose, we introduce below certain functions on $Data_p$ for transliteration between messages. These functions ensure the special status of *EDR*:

$$Translit == \{f : Data_p \rightarrowtail Data_p; \ voc : Vocabulary \mid$$
$$\mathrm{dom}\, f \subseteq voc \wedge \mathrm{ran}\, f = EDR \bullet f\}$$

Thus, each element in *Translit* is a finite injective function on $Data_p$, drawing a one-to-one correspondence between each and every element of *EDR* and the elements in each vocabulary. Functions in *Translit* can be designed with different objectives; they may even incorporate features for data *encryption* and *decryption*, required for secure data communication.

NOTE: ENCRYPTION and DECRYPTION: Cryptography involves 'encoding' the information to be communicated from its original intelligible form of *plaintext* to *ciphertext* – a form of 'scrambled' or unintelligible text – and 'decoding' the *plaintext* from *ciphertext* by its intended recipient. The process of 'encoding' is known as *encryption* and the reverse process of 'decoding' as *decryption*. Unlike the conventional coding of information from one form to another according to a fixed rule (for example, when digitising information according the ASCII code in computing) encryption and decryption involve secret keys known only to the transmitter of the information and its intended receivers.

With this, we may provide a more detailed representation of *Message* so that all messages may be transliterated to *EDR*:

$Message_p[Data_p]$
$content : \mathrm{seq}\ Data_p$

$fun : Translit$

$\mathrm{ran}\ content \subseteq \mathrm{dom}\ fun$

$\exists\, voc : Vocabulary \bullet \mathrm{ran}\ content \subseteq voc$

Note that $Message_p$ is to be regarded as a refinement of $Message_a$. Thus, each message is seen as a pair: a sequence of data as the content of the message, and a function for transliterating the content to and from EDR. Our abstraction is such that the message content is represented as a sequence of data items belonging to one language. The function *fun* in the above is for the internal use of any given host only. For security reasons, a public version of messages may be made available in the form below by hiding the transliteration function:

$$PublicMessage_p \mathrel{\widehat{=}} Message_p \setminus fun$$

Representation of messages in the more refined form $Message_p$ allows a new definition for $\approx$, namely as:

$$\approx_p: Message_p \leftrightarrow Message_p$$

$$\approx_p = \{m_1, m_2 : Message_p \mid$$
$$s_2 = f_2^{\sim} \circ f_1 \circ s_1 \wedge s_1 = f_1^{\sim} \circ f_2 \circ s_2 \bullet (m_1, m_2)\}$$

$$\text{where} \quad s_i = m_i.content$$
$$f_i = m_i.fun, \quad i = 1, 2$$

requiring that any two messages hold in this relation if and only if they can be mutually transliterated via EDR to each other and with no loss of message content. It is also possible to give a new meaning to $\simeq$ so that it can be used both on $Data_p$ and on $Message_p$. However, it is simpler to keep a separate version $\simeq_m$ on $Message_p$ and, where there is no confusion, to use just $\simeq$ for both. $\simeq_m$ can be defined as:

$$\simeq_m: Message_p \leftrightarrow Message_p$$

$$\simeq_m = \{m_1, m_2 : Message_p \mid \mathrm{dom}(m_1.fun) = \mathrm{dom}(m_2.fun) \bullet (m_1, m_2)\}$$

According to the above, two messages are regarded as being in the same language if they use the same vocabulary. Obviously, this may not be a strong enough definition in certain situations.

With the above, it is possible to give a new definition for $Script$ and, thus, to restrict the script used by each host to a single vocabulary so that it can be fully transliterated by a single transliteration function. This is left as an exercise for the reader.

We may also relieve the network from the task of maintaining message addresses globally by incorporating such information as part of the message. This is given in EDR-$Message$ below:

$$\underline{\quad EDR\text{-}Message_p \quad}$$
$PublicMessage_p$

$origin, destn : HostId \times ProcId$

$\mathrm{ran}\ content \subseteq EDR$

$host(origin) \neq host(destn)$

The above form of messages is to be used by the medium of transmission. The primary task of the presentation layer is to provide the following encoding and decoding operations on messages before handing over the message, as appropriate, to the layer below or the layer above.

```
┌─ Encode ────────────────────────────────────────────────
│ from?, to? : HostId × ProcId
│
│ mes? : Message_p
│
│ mes! : EDR-Message_p
├──────────────────────────────────────────────────────────
│ mes! ≈_p mes?
│
│ mes!.origin = from?
│
│ mes!.destn = to?
└──────────────────────────────────────────────────────────
```

```
┌─ Decode ────────────────────────────────────────────────
│ from!, to! : HostId × ProcId
│
│ mes! : Message_p
│
│ mes? : EDR-Message_p
├──────────────────────────────────────────────────────────
│ mes? ≈_p mes!
│
│ mes?.origin = from!
│
│ mes?.destn = to!
└──────────────────────────────────────────────────────────
```

The above specifications require the preservation of the equivalence of message content during the encoding and decoding of messages. The functionality of sending, receiving and transmitting messages as seen at this level may be formalised as below, by incorporating the new facilities with the ones defined in Section 7.4:

$$Send_p \; \hat{=} \; Send_a[Message_p] \gg Encode$$
$$Receive_p \; \hat{=} \; Decode \gg Receive_a[Message_p]$$

where $\gg$ is the piping operator of the schema language. The generic type *Message* in $Send_a$ and $Receive_a$ are now instantiated with the refined data type $Message_p$.

NOTE: Given that S and T are two schemas, S having an output variable of the form $x!$ and T having a matching input variable of the form $x?$, the schema piping $S \gg T$ is a schema where both $x!$ and $x?$ denote the same variable, while all other variables in both S and T remain unaffected. This amounts to passing the value of $x!$ from S as the value of $x?$ to T.

In order to define *Transmit*, we rely on *Transmit-aux_a* given on page 121:

$$
\begin{array}{|l}
\hline
\textit{Transmit-aux}_a[\textit{Message}_p] \underline{\hspace{5cm}} \\
\textit{Net-Update} \\[4pt]
\textit{Send}_p[\textit{Host}_1/\textit{Host}, \textit{Host}_1'/\textit{Host}', p_1/p, \textit{from}/\textit{from}!, \textit{to}/\textit{to}!] \\
\textit{Receive}_p[\textit{Host}_2/\textit{Host}, \textit{Host}_2'/\textit{Host}', p_2/p, \textit{from}/\textit{from}?, \textit{to}/\textit{to}?] \\[4pt]
\hline
(\textit{from}, \textit{to}) \in \textit{v-sessions} \\[4pt]
\textit{mes}! \approx \textit{mes}? \\
\hline
\end{array}
$$

using $Message_p$, $Send_p$, $Receive_p$ for $Message$, $Send_a$, $Receive_a$, and retaining the structure of definitions of $Host$ and Net as before. The definition of $Transmit$ in the presentation layer follows then as:

$$
Transmit_p[Message_p] \; \widehat{=} \; Transmit\text{-}aux_a[Message_p] \setminus h_1, h_2, p_1, p_2
$$

7.5.2 Proofs on Verification

It was stated in the specification of the application layer in Section 7.4 that $\approx$ is an equivalence relation, that is, it is reflexive, symmetric and transitive. The refinement of $Message$ by employing the lower level $Data_p$ must not violate this property. It may be noted that:

$$
\text{ran } content \subseteq \text{dom } fun
$$

in $Message_p$ is essential for ensuring reflexivity, and that:

$$
\text{ran } f = EDR
$$

in $Translit$ for transitivity. Possible repercussions of relaxation of these properties are the potential loss of message contents and the allowance of messages not recognised universally over the network, thus affecting the requirements of the initial high level specification. See Section 7.8 for a formal proof of the preservation of the property of equivalence of $\approx$.

7.6 Session Layer

The aspect selected here for further development is what is referred to as virtual sessions, or *v-sessions* in Net_a, and how these are to be established and supported. The extensions envisaged in this layer require the inclusion of additional types:

$$
[SessionId, SocketId, Report]
$$

where the elements of *SessionId* are for identifying virtual sessions, *SocketId* for relating these to connections available on machines, and *Report* is a set of error notifications for some limited exception handling. These allow a refinement of *Host* as:

$Host_s$ _____
$Host_a$

$sockets : \mathbb{F}\, SocketId$

$outSessions : SocketId \nrightarrow ProcId$

_____

$\mathrm{dom}\; outSessions \subseteq sockets$

$\mathrm{ran}\; outSessions \subseteq \{p : Process \mid p \in processes \bullet p.pid\}$

---

where the component *outSessions* is intended for decoupling the direct relationship between hosts and their processes.

With the notion of sockets, it is also possible to identify sessions as a relationship between pairs of different hosts and their sockets, namely as:

$$Session == \{ses : SessionId \nrightarrow (Host_s \times SocketId)^2;$$
$$(h_1, c_1), (h_2, c_2) : Host_s \times SocketId \mid$$
$$((h_1, c_1), (h_2, c_2)) \in \mathrm{ran}\; ses \Rightarrow h_1 \neq h_2 \bullet ses\}$$

Thus, the above disallows any host to use the network for communicating with itself. It follows trivially from the above that:

$$\forall\, ses : Session;\; (h, skt) : Host_s \times SocketId \bullet ((h, skt), (h, skt)) \notin \mathrm{ran}\; ses$$

Part of the service offered by the session layer are operations for a host to request a new session, accept a session request, withdraw an active session and decline a request. None of these are expected to affect the host as seen from the layer above.

Below is a partial specification shared by three of the above mentioned operations. It captures the scenario in which a process running on the initiating host proposes a new session to a process running on another host, by offering an unused socket along with the necessary identifiers.

$SessionProposal$ _____
$\Delta Host_s;\; \Xi Host_a$

$from!, to! : HostId \times ProcId$

$socket! : SessionId$

$p : Process$

_____

$from! = (hid, p.pid)$

$p \in processes$

$socket! \in sockets - \mathrm{dom}\; outSessions$

$sockets' = sockets$

Turning to the specific session operations, a session request is basically a proposal to another partner, but with the initiator updating its *outSessions* in order to be able to honour the proposal if accepted at the other end.

$$SessionRequest \mathrel{\widehat{=}} (SessionProposal \mid$$
$$outSessions' = outSessions \oplus \{socket! \mapsto p.pid\}) \setminus p$$

A session acceptance is analogous to the above, except that the operation should affect the recipient, that is:

$$SessionAccept \mathrel{\widehat{=}} SessionRequest[from?\setminus to!, to?\setminus from!]$$

The other two operations are:

SessionWithdraw

$\Delta Host_s;\ \Xi Host_a$

$socket! : SocketId$

$socket! \in \mathrm{dom}\ outSessions$

$outSessions' = \{socket!\} \lhd outSessions$

$sockets' = sockets$

SessionDecline

$\Xi Hist_s$

$rep! : Report$

$\neg\ ((SessionProposal[from?/to!, to?/from!])\setminus p)$

$rep! = \,'\text{Inappropriate Session!}'$

With the new definition of *Host*, we are obliged to provide a new definition for the network. Here we must show how the newly introduced components are to be integrated by relating them to the existing ones. In particular, this is the right moment to provide a more concrete specification for the virtual sessions *v-sessions* introduced at the application level. This is done as a pairing of hosts and processes relying on inter-host connections between sockets on the network boundary and intra host connections between sockets and processes within each host. The specification also prevents intra host communications taking place over the network.

$$\begin{array}{|l}
\hline
\_\_Net_s _____ \\
Net_a \\
\\
sessions : Session \\
\hline
\{h : Host_s; \ s : SocketId \mid (h, s) \in \text{fld (ran } sessions) \bullet h\} \subseteq hosts \\
\{h : Host_s; \ s : SocketId \mid (h, s) \in \text{fld (ran } sessions) \bullet s\} \subseteq \\
\qquad\qquad\qquad\qquad\qquad\qquad\qquad\qquad \bigcup_{h \in hosts} h.sockets \\
v\text{-}sessions = \{h_1, h_2 : Host_s; \ p_1, p_2 : Process; \ c_1, c_2 : SocketId \mid \\
\qquad ((h_1, c_1), (h_2, c_2)) \in \text{ran } sessions \wedge (c_1, p_1) \in h_1.outSessions \wedge \\
\qquad (c_2, p_2) \in h_2.outSessions \bullet ((h_1, p_1), (h_2, p_2))\} \\
\hline
\end{array}$$

The session operations at the network level are: *SessionGrant* for connecting two hosts, *SessionClose* for disconnecting and *SessionReject* for rejecting a session request. They are defined below.

$$Net\text{-}Update_s \;\widehat{=}\; Net\text{-}Update_a[Message_p]; \; s_1, s_2 : SocketId$$

$$\begin{array}{|l}
\hline
\_\_SessionGrant _____ \\
Net\text{-}Update_s \\
\hline
SessionRequest \\
\quad [Host_1/Host_s, Host_1'/Host_s', p_1/p, from/from!, to/to!, s_1/socket!] \\
SessionAccept \\
\quad [Host_2/Host_s, Host_2'/Host_s', p_2/p, from/from?, to/to?, s_2/socket!] \\
\hline
((h_1.hid, s_1), (h_2.hid, s_2)) \notin \text{ran } sessions \\
\exists \, sid : SessionId \bullet sid \notin \text{dom } sessions \wedge \\
\quad sessions' = sessions \oplus \{sid \mapsto ((h_1.hid, s_1), (h_2.hid, s_2))\} \\
\hline
\end{array}$$

$$\begin{array}{|l}
\hline
\_\_SessionClose _____ \\
Net\text{-}Update_s \\
\hline
SessionWithdraw \\
\quad [Host_1/Host_s, Host_1'/Host_s', p_1/p, from/from!, to/to!, s_1/socket!] \\
SessionWithdraw \\
\quad [Host_2/Host_s, Host_2'/Host_s', p_2/p, from/from?, to/to?, s_2/socket!] \\
\hline
((h_1.hid, s_1), (h_2.hid, s_2)) \in \text{ran } sessions \\
sessions' = sessions \rhd \{((h_1.hid, s_1), (h_2.hid, s_2))\} \\
\hline
\end{array}$$

__SessionReject__
$Net\text{-}Update_s$

$SessionRequest$
$\quad [Host_1/Host_s, Host_1'/Host_s', p_1/p, from/from!, to/to!, s_1/socket!]_s^s$

$\qquad Session\,Withdraw[Host_1/Host_s, Host_1'/Host_s', p_1/p,$
$\qquad\qquad from/from!, to/to!, s_1/socket!]$

$\Xi\, Host_s[Host_2/Host_s, Host_2'/Host_s']$

$p_2 : Process; \ s_2 : SocketId$

$SessionDecline[Host_2/Host_s, Host_2'/Host_s', p_2/p, from/from?,$

$\qquad\qquad\qquad\qquad\qquad\qquad to/to?, s_2/socket!] \ \vee$

$((((h_1.hid, s_1), (h_2.hid, s_2)) \in ran\ sessions\ \vee$

$dom\ sessions = SessionId) \wedge$

$rep! = \ 'Session\ already\ active\ or\ no\ free\ sessions!')$

The specification on transmission of messages in the session layer may be defined analogously to $Transmit_s$, but taking into account the new context and the dependency of the virtual session on sockets.

It can be given as:

__$Transmit\text{-}aux_s[Message_p]$__
$Net\text{-}Update_s$

$Send_p[Host_1/Host, Host_1'/Host', p_1/p, from/from!, to/to!]$

$Receive_p[Host_2/Host, Host_2'/Host', p_2/p, from/from?, to/to?]$

$((h_1.hid, s_1), (h_2.hid, s_2)) \in ran\ sessions$

$(s_1, p_1.pid) \in h_1.outSessions$

$(s_2, p_2.pid) \in h_2.outSessions$

$mes! \approx mes?$

---

and:

$$Transmit_s[Message_p] \ \hat{=} \ Transmit\text{-}aux_s[Message_p] \setminus h_1, h_2, p_1, p_2$$

7.7 Transport Layer

Let us now focus our attention on possible limitations on the message length, and the desirable features of the network discipline at both the transmitter's

and receiver's end. In order to retain the freedom for intermittent transmission as required by physical network components, and for other reasons
mentioned earlier, the messages handed over by the session layer have to be
decomposed into smaller units. Let us assume that the maximum permitted
unit size is specified in terms of the length of the message content, a message
being basically a sequence of data. The upper limit on the length of messages
in the transport layer is considered through the free variable *packing-length*:

$$| \quad packing\text{-}length : \mathbb{N}_1$$

Furthermore, in addition to those in $Data_p$, let us introduce some extra
values notSent, sent, acknowledged and endMessage to $Data$ for exclusive use
by the network. This can be done by creating a new free type $Data_t$ to be
used by the transport layer in the following manner:

$$Data_t ::= \text{notSent} \mid \text{sent} \mid \text{acknowledged} \mid \text{endMessage} \mid \text{pres}\langle\!\langle Data_p \rangle\!\rangle$$

where pres is a total injective function from $Data_p$ to $Data_t$.

Let us incorporate these additions to *EDR-Message* as:

$$EDR\text{-}Message_t \mathrel{\widehat{=}} EDR\text{-}Message_p[Data_t]$$

Messages are transported over the network in the form of packets. It is the
size of the packets which is limited by the predefined value of *packing-length*
introduced above. The concept of 'packet' may then be formalised as:

$$Packet \mathrel{\widehat{=}} [EDR\text{-}Message_t; \ pkid : \mathbb{N}_1 \mid \#content \leqslant packing\text{-}length]$$

where *pkid* is a packet identifier.

Let us turn our attention to packing and unpacking procedures. Packing
requires the last element in a packed sequence to carry a special message
with just endMessage. Other elements in a packed sequence are supposed to
only carry messages of type $Message_p$ and not any network specific message.
Note also that *pkid* reflects the relative position of each packet in the input
sequence.

$$
\begin{array}{|l}
\hline
\textit{Pack} \underline{} \\
\ mes? : EDR\text{-}Message_p[Data_p] \\
\ mes! : \text{seq } Packet \\
\hline
\ mes?.content =^\frown \backslash\{i : \mathbb{N}_1; \ p : Packet \mid \\
\qquad\qquad\qquad (i,p) \in (\{\#mes!\} \vartriangleleft mes!) \bullet (i, p.content)\} \\
\ \exists\, p : Packet \bullet p = mes!(\#mes!) \wedge p.content = \langle\text{endMessage}\rangle \\
\ \forall\, i : \mathbb{N}_1; \ p : Packet \bullet (i,p) \in mes! \Leftrightarrow p.pkid = i \\
\ \forall\, p \in \text{ran } mes! \bullet p.origin = mes?.origin \wedge p.destn = mes?.destn \\
\hline
\end{array}
$$

```
┌─ UnPack ─────────────────────────────────────────────────────
│ mes? : bag Packet
│
│ mes! : EDR-Message_p[Data_p]
├──────────────────────────────────────────────────────────────
│ ∀ p ∈ dom mes? • p.origin = mes?.origin ∧ p.destn = mes?.destn
│
│ {p : Packet | p ∈ dom mes? • p.pkid} = 1 .. #(dom mes?)
│
│ mes!.content = ⁀\{p : Packet; i : ℕ₁ |
│
│                     (p, i) ∈ {#mes?} ◁ mes? • p.content}
└──────────────────────────────────────────────────────────────
```

where $\frown\backslash s$ denotes the distributed concatenation of several sequences together.

The above two definitions specify the packing and unpacking disciplines, according to which the contents of messages received from, or to be delivered to, the session layer must already be in the presentation layer format.

The definition of *Host* at this level becomes:

```
┌─ Host_t ─────────────────────────────────────────────────────
│ Host_s
│
│ inPacks : bag Packet
│
│ outPacks : 𝔽 Packet
│
│ record : Packet ↠ Data_t
├──────────────────────────────────────────────────────────────
│ dom record = outPacks
│
│ ran record ∩ (Data_p ∪ {endMessage})) = ∅
│
│ ∀ p₁, p₂ : Packet • {p₁, p₂} ⊆ dom inPacks ⇒
│
│     p₁.destn = p₂.destn ∧ p₁.origin = p₂.origin
│
│ ∀ p₁, p₂ : Packet • {p₁, p₂} ⊆ outPacks ⇒
│
│     p₁.destn = p₂.destn ∧ p₁.origin = p₂.origin
└──────────────────────────────────────────────────────────────
```

where *inPacks* and *outPacks* contain the incoming and outgoing packets. The component *record* maintains the status of outgoing packets in the form of one of the values notSent, sent or acknowledged. Note that *inPacks* is defined as a bag in order to allow the deliveries of multiple copies. The packets contained in both *inPacks* and *outPacks* must be consistent with respect to the addresses in them. An implication of this requirement is that a host can serve at most one process at a time. In practice, this condition is likely to be too restrictive, but can be relaxed without too much difficulty. As a further simplification, the specification does not consider facilities for buffering messages.

The additional activities carried out by the transport layer with respect to sending and receiving may be composed from the following:

```
┌─ BeginDispatch ──────────────────────────────────
│ ΔHost_t; ΞHost_s
│
│ mes? : seq Packet
├──────────────────────────────────────────────────
│ outPacks = ∅
│
│ outPacks' = ran mes?
│
│ ran record' = {notSent}
└──────────────────────────────────────────────────
```

A dispatch may begin only if no dispatch is under progress and the beginning of a new dispatch initialises the record with the packets to be dispatched, but marked notSent.

```
┌─ KeepDispatching ────────────────────────────────
│ ΔHost_t; ΞHost_s
│
│ packet! : Packet
├──────────────────────────────────────────────────
│ record ≠ ∅
│
│ ran record ≠ {acknowledged}
│
│ packet! ∈ dom(record ▷ {acknowledged})
│
│ packet!.content = ⟨endMessage⟩ ⇒
│       ran({packet!} ◁ record) = {acknowledged}
│
│ record' = record ⊕ {packet! ↦ sent}
│
│ outPacks' = outPacks
└──────────────────────────────────────────────────
```

The choice of the packet to be dispatched at any time is nondeterministic, except that it must be an unacknowledged one. Obviously, the dispatch has to continue as long as there is any unacknowledged packet by the recipient. The packet with endMessage is only sent upon the acknowledgement of all other packets, that is, packets conveying the user's message. Despite these restrictions, the designer is left with important design decisions to make, for example, how to order and prioritise message dispatches, especially in relation to messages already sent but yet to be acknowledged and messages yet to be sent, etc.

___ *RecordAcknowledgement* _____
$\Delta Host_t$; $\Xi Host_s$

$acknow?$: $Packet$
_____
$record \neq \varnothing$

$\mathrm{ran}\ record \neq \{\mathsf{acknowledged}\}$

$\exists\, p : Packet \bullet (p, \mathsf{sent}) \in record \,\wedge$

$\qquad p.destn = acknow?.origin \,\wedge$

$\qquad p.origin = acknow?.destn \,\wedge$

$\qquad p.pkid = acknow?.pkid \,\wedge$

$\qquad acknow?.content = \langle \mathsf{acknowledged} \rangle \,\wedge$

$\qquad record' = record \oplus \{p \mapsto \mathsf{acknowledged}\}$

$outPacks' = outPacks$

The above operation is meant for accepting acknowledgements, but it can take place while dispatching packets.

___ *FinishDispatch* _____
$\Delta Host_t$; $\Xi Host_s$
_____
$\mathrm{ran}\ record = \{\mathsf{acknowledged}\}$

$outPacks' = \varnothing$

$record' = \varnothing$

The dispatch terminates upon the acknowledgement of all packets, emptying the record and the store of outgoing packets.

The next set of operations concerns what happens at the recipient's end. Since, according to our simplification, there is no buffering of messages, a delivery can begin only if there are none in progress.

___ *BeginReceiving* _____
$\Xi Host_t$
_____
$inPacks = \varnothing$

The recipient's other operations share the following schema:

CheckAndAcknowledge _____
$\Delta Host_t; \ \Xi Host_s$

$packet?, acknow! : Packet$

$\exists p : Process \bullet p \in processes \bullet packet?.destn = (hid, p.pid)$

$\forall p : Packet \bullet p \in \mathrm{dom}\ inPacks \Rightarrow p.destn = packet?.destn \wedge$
$$p.origin = packet?.origin$$

$acknow!.destn = packet?.origin$

$acknow!.origin = packet?.destn$

$acknow!.pkid = packet?.pkid$

$acknow!.content = \langle \mathsf{acknowledged} \rangle$

It ensures that all incoming packets are consistent with respect to the addresses, and specifies how the acknowledgement has to be drafted.

KeepReceiving _____
CheckAndAcknowledge

$packet?.content \neq \langle \mathsf{endMessage} \rangle$

$inPacks' = inPacks \uplus [\![packet?]\!]$

The recipient continues to receive packets and respond with acknowledgements for every packet delivered, even in the case of multiple copies.

FinishReceiving _____
CheckAndAcknowledge

$mes! : \mathrm{bag}\ Packet$

$packet?.content = \langle \mathsf{endMessage} \rangle$

$\#(1 .. (packet?.pkid - 1)) = \#(\mathrm{dom}\ inPacks)$

$mes! = inPacks$

$inPacks' = \varnothing$

Upon the receipt of the packet with endMessage, provided that it has received all the packets of the given sequence, the recipient outputs all packets except the last one to the layer above and empties the 'store' *inPacks* intended for incoming packets.

The following two operations incorporate the local activities of the transport layer at each host. First, the operation of sending a message:

$$Send_t \mathrel{\widehat{=}} Send_p \gg Pack \; _9^\circ \; BeginDispatch \; _9^\circ$$
$$((KeepDispatching \lor RecordAcknowledgement)^* \lor$$
$$FinishDispatching)$$

where the superscript $*$ denotes the iterative composition of the operation concerned on itself an unspecified number of times; see Section 2.10 for composition. Processing a message by the transport layer at the initiator involves converting it to a sequence of packets of an appropriate size, and dispatching packets and receiving acknowledgements as many times as necessary and in any order until all packets have been acknowledged.

On the other hand, the operation of receiving a message can be defined as:

$$Receive_t \mathrel{\widehat{=}} BeginReceiving \; _9^\circ$$
$$(KeepReceiving^* \lor FinishReceiving) \; _9^\circ$$
$$UnPack \gg Receive_p$$

Thus, the deliveries at the recipient's end begin if the recipient is not receiving deliveries from another host. Once started, the recipient continues to receive deliveries as many times as necessary until the receipt of the packet signifying the end of message.

Following the familiar style now, the whole operation of transmission at the network level may be defined by as:

$Transmit\text{-}aux_t[Message_p]$
$Net\text{-}Update_s$

$Send_t[Host_1/Host, Host_1'/Host', p_1/p, from/from!, to/to!]$

$Receive_t[Host_2/Host, Host_2'/Host', p_2/p, from/from?, to/to?]$

$Transmit_s$

---

and

$$Transmit_t[Message_p] \mathrel{\widehat{=}} Transmit\text{-}aux_t[Message_p] \setminus h_1, h_2, p_1, p_2$$

7.8 Selected Proofs

This section presents a proof on the preservation of the property of equivalence of the relation $\approx_a$ after its refinement by $\approx_p$ introduced in the presentation layer; see page 124. The proof consists of three sub-proofs dealing with:

- Reflexivity of $\approx_p$ (the proof is given in Section 7.8.1)
- Symmetry of $\approx_p$ (the proof is given in Section 7.8.2)
- Transitivity of $\approx_p$ (the proof is given in Section 7.8.3)

7.8.1 Proof of Reflexivity

Reflexivity of $\approx_p$ amounts to:

$$\vdash \forall m : Message_p \bullet m \approx_p m$$

which is equivalent to:

$$\vdash \forall m : Message_p \bullet s = f^\sim \circ f \circ s$$
$$\text{where } s = m.content$$
$$f = m.fun$$

<u>Proof of the above:</u> Given that

$$m : Message_p, s : \text{seq } Data, f : Translit$$

and

$$s = m.content \qquad\qquad f = m.fun$$

1.	$\text{ran } s \subseteq \text{dom } f$	– def. $Message_p$
2.	$f^\sim \circ f = \text{id}(\text{dom } f)$	– a theorem on composition
3.	$(x, y) \in s$	– assumption
4.	$y \in \text{ran } s$	– from 3; def. of ran
5.	$\forall y \bullet y \in \text{ran } s \Rightarrow y \in \text{dom } f$	– from 1; def. of set inclusion
6.	$y \in \text{ran } s \Rightarrow y \in \text{dom } f$	– from 5; elim. $\forall$
7.	$y \in \text{dom } f$	– from 4, 6; elim. $\Rightarrow$
8.	$(y, y) \in \text{id}(\text{dom } f)$	– from 7; def. of id
9.	$(x, y) \in s \wedge (y, y) \in \text{id}(\text{dom } f)$	– from 3, 8; intro. $\wedge$
10.	$\exists z \bullet (x, z) \in s \wedge (z, y) \in \text{id}(\text{dom } f)$	– from 9; intro. $\exists$
11.	$(x, y) \in (\text{id}(\text{dom } f) \circ s)$	– from 10; def. composition
12.	$(x, y) \in s \Rightarrow (x, y) \in (\text{id}(\text{dom } f) \circ s)$	– from 3, 11; intro. $\Rightarrow$
13.	$(x, y) \in (\text{id}(\text{dom } f) \circ s)$	– assumption
14.	$\exists z \bullet (x, z) \in s \wedge (z, y) \in \text{id}(\text{dom } f)$	– from 13; def. composition
15.	$(x, z) \in s \wedge (z, y) \in \text{id}(\text{dom } f)$	– from 14; elim. $\exists$
16.	$(z, y) \in \text{id}(\text{dom } f)$	– from 15; elim. $\wedge$
17.	$z = y$	– from 16; def. of id
18.	$(x, z) \in s$	– from 15; elim. $\wedge$
19.	$(x, y) \in s$	– from 17, 18; substitution of an equal
20.	$(x, y) \in (\text{id}(\text{dom } f) \circ s) \Rightarrow (x, y) \in s$	– from 13, 19; intro. $\Rightarrow$
21.	$(x, y) \in (\text{id}(\text{dom } f) \circ s) \Leftrightarrow (x, y) \in s$	– from 12, 20; intro. $\Leftrightarrow$

22. $s = (\text{id}(\text{dom} f) \circ s)$ – from 21; axiom of extension

23. $s = f^{\sim} \circ f \circ s$ – from 2; substitution of an

                                             equal

□

7.8.2 Proof of Symmetry

Symmetry of $\approx_p$ amounts to:

$$\vdash \forall m_1, m_2 : Message_p \bullet m_1 \approx_p m_2 \Rightarrow m_2 \approx_p m_1$$

<u>Proof of the above:</u> Given that:

$$m_1, m_2 : Message_p; \ s_1, s_2 : \text{seq } Data; \ f_1, f_2 : Translit$$

and

$$s_1 = m_1.content \qquad\qquad f_1 = m_1.fun$$
$$s_2 = m_2.content \qquad\qquad f_2 = m_2.fun$$

1. $s_1 \approx_p s_2$ – assumption

2. $s_2 = f_2^{\sim} \circ f_1 \circ s_1 \wedge s_1 = f_1^{\sim} \circ f_2 \circ s_2$ – from 1; def. of $\approx_p$

3. $s_1 = f_1^{\sim} \circ f_2 \circ s_2 \wedge s_2 = f_2^{\sim} \circ f_1 \circ s_1$ – from 2; commutativity of $\wedge$

4. $s_2 \approx_p s_1$ – from 3; def. of $\approx_p$

5. $s_1 \approx_p s_2 \Rightarrow s_2 \approx_p s_1$ – from 1, 4; intro. $\Rightarrow$

□

7.8.3 Proof of Transitivity

Transitivity of $\approx_p$ amounts to:

$$\vdash \forall s_1, s_2, s_3 : Message_p \bullet s_1 \approx_p s_2 \wedge s_2 \approx_p s_3 \Rightarrow s_1 \approx_p s_3$$

<u>Proof of the above:</u> Given that:

$$m_1, m_2, m_3 : Message_p; \ s_1, s_2, s_3 : \text{seq } Data; \ f_1, f_2, f_3 : Translit$$

and

$$s_1 = m_1.content \qquad\qquad f_1 = m_1.fun$$
$$s_2 = m_2.content \qquad\qquad f_2 = m_2.fun$$
$$s_3 = m_3.content \qquad\qquad f_3 = m_3.fun$$

1. $s_1 \approx_p s_2 \wedge s_2 \approx_p s_3$ — assumption
2. $\forall f : Translit \bullet (\text{id}(\text{ran} f)) \circ f = f$ — a theorem on composition
3. $s_1 \approx_p s_2$ — from 1; elim. $\wedge$
4. $s_2 \approx_p s_3$ — from 1; elim. $\wedge$
5. $s_2 = f_2^{\sim} \circ f_1 \circ s_1 \wedge s_1 = f_1^{\sim} \circ f_2 \circ s_2$ — from 3; def. of $\approx_p$
6. $s_2 = f_2^{\sim} \circ f_3 \circ s_3 \wedge s_3 = f_3^{\sim} \circ f_2 \circ s_2$ — from 4; def. of $\approx_p$
7. $s_2 = f_2^{\sim} \circ f_1 \circ s_1$ — from 5; elim. $\wedge$
8. $s_1 = f_1^{\sim} \circ f_2 \circ s_2$ — from 5; elim. $\wedge$
9. $s_2 = f_2^{\sim} \circ f_3 \circ s_3$ — from 6; elim. $\wedge$
10. $s_3 = f_3^{\sim} \circ f_2 \circ s_2$ — from 6; elim. $\wedge$
11. $s_1 = f_1^{\sim} \circ f_2 \circ f_2^{\sim} \circ f_3 \circ s_3$ — from 8, 9; substitution
12. $s_3 = f_3^{\sim} \circ f_2 \circ f_2^{\sim} \circ f_1 \circ s_1$ — from 10, 7; substitution
13. $s_1 = f_1^{\sim} \circ (\text{id}(\text{ran} f_2)) \circ f_3 \circ s_3$ — from 11; thm. on composition
14. $s_3 = f_3^{\sim} \circ (\text{id}(\text{ran} f_2)) \circ f_1 \circ s_1$ — from 12; thm. on composition
15. $s_1 = f_1^{\sim} \circ (\text{id}(\text{ran} f_3)) \circ f_3 \circ s_3$ — from 13; def. of $Translit$: $\text{ran} f_2 = \text{ran} f_3$
16. $s_3 = f_3^{\sim} \circ (\text{id}(\text{ran} f_1)) \circ f_1 \circ s_1$ — from 14; def. of $Translit$: $\text{ran} f_2 = \text{ran} f_1$
17. $s_1 = f_1^{\sim} \circ f_3 \circ s_3$ — from 2 (after eliminating $\forall$), 15
18. $s_3 = f_3^{\sim} \circ f_1 \circ s_1$ — from 2 (after eliminating $\forall$), 16
19. $s_1 = f_1^{\sim} \circ f_3 \circ s_3 \wedge s_3 = f_3^{\sim} \circ f_1 \circ s_1$ — from 17, 18; intro. $\wedge$
20. $s_1 \approx_p s_3$ — from 19; def. of $\approx_p$
21. $s_1 \approx_p s_2 \wedge s_2 \approx_p s_3 \Rightarrow s_1 \approx_p s_3$ — from 1, 20; intro. $\Rightarrow$

$\square$

7.9 Bibliographical Notes

There are a variety of formal approaches to protocol specification and design; see Bochmann and Sunshine [11], Tarnay [60] and King [29]. These approaches are based on formalisms such as finite state transition models [9, 10, 14], Petri nets [5, 14], process algebra approaches [48, 54], specification languages for communication (SDL), languages for architectural specification (Estelle) [62]), languages for temporal ordering (LOTOS) [55], state based formal specification languages (Z and its variants) [29] and temporal logic [53].

Among them, the languages based on process algebras, in particular, Communicating Sequential Processes (CSP) due to Hoare [24] and CCS due to Milner [38], have been found extremely effective in such applications. Given that a protocol is understood in sufficient detail, it is fairly straightforward to express it in an appropriate formalism, despite the extent of effort required in such tasks. However, the situation is different with regard to the design of network architectures and associated protocols from high level specifications. In this respect, the prevailing approach is that of successive refinement of high level specifications as expressed in, for example, Sharp [54], He-Jifeng [26] and Griffiths [19]. This suits the hierarchical (layered) view of networks and protocols well as manifested in solutions such as those due to the International Standards Organisation (ISO).

The maturity of state based approaches to formal specification and refinement, as well as their widespread use, popularity and accessibility makes this an attractive practical proposition. Furthermore, as evident from such works as Griffiths [19] and Woodcock [67], the process algebra and the state based views of systems may be linked by relating the trace of external events of the process concerned with the state transformations of its equivalent state based system. This combined approach allows one to express finer structural details in the state based style and to reason about them in traditional logic, and then to switch to process algebra style for dealing with issues such as concurrency.

Exercises

7.1 The definition of $Host_t$ on page 132 allows a host to serve only one process at a time. As mentioned there, this condition can be unnecessarily restrictive. Remove this restriction by redefining the operations of the transport layer. Note that, when catering for the needs of several processes at the same time, it may be necessary to have a facility to store, or buffer, messages intended for different processes.

7.2 For reasons of space, this chapter omitted the majority of the exception handling operations, some of which potentially have a crucial bearing on the behaviour of the network. Identify the five most important, in your view, exception handling operations missing in the specification, specify them and integrate them into the rest of the specification.

7.3 Extend the design formally to deal with some functions offered by the network layer. In particular, the design may cover bi-directional communication between two hosts using a connection that can serve only one direction at a time.

8. Object Oriented Specification

The object oriented approach is seen as a radically different approach to both programming and software design. As a paradigm of programming, object oriented programming shares certain features with other paradigms, namely imperative, declarative and functional programming; see, for example, Goldberg and Robson [17]. However, a feature which distinguishes it from the rest is the underlying model of computation, whereby a computation is viewed through the effects brought about by the interaction of computational objects on their internal states. The relevance of the object oriented approach in practical programming is evident from the increasing interest in programming languages such as C^{++}.

The benefits of object orientation are not limited to programming. Compared to other software design techniques, it offers a totally different view of a system, that is, a different form of abstraction, which supports a more natural link between the software and the world of physical or abstract objects that it purports to model. This chapter is about the application of the object oriented approach to specification, which, as highlighted in Chapter 1, is a critically important phase in the software development process. However, bearing in mind our greater familiarity with programming, the chapter motivates the discussion with a review of the benefits of object orientation in programming.

8.1 Object Orientation in the Narrow Sense

Historically, one of the early aims of object orientation was to achieve standard protocols for data handling, that is, the ability to handle different types of object through an agreed suite of general procedures and not any type specialised procedures. In today's terms, object orientation has a much broader range of objectives than this narrow view. Even in the above literal sense, however, object orientation offers a number of important benefits. In particular, object orientation facilitates data abstraction and, thereby, relieves the programmer from the burden of having to remember information specific to different types of object.

In order to demonstrate this, let us consider an example, where we outline two programming solutions for handling, say, four different kinds of object by a robot: trolley, cart, sledge and ball. Being physical objects, various kinds of operation are applicable on them, e.g., for moving them, loading them with other objects, turning them around, throwing them if it is an appropriate action, and so on. Here, we consider just one such operation, namely moving each of these items on a surface. We are not concerned with how this movement is performed, but with the general structure of a program intended for that purpose. The first solution is an attempt in the imperative style of programming. In order to define a general procedure *move* which is capable of moving an object belonging to any of the four types of object under consideration, the pseudo-code given below first proposes four different procedures, each specialised to handle objects of a particular type, and then invoking them as appropriate through a 'case' statement.

```
type Kind = (trolley, cart, sledge, ball);
     Place = · · · · · ·;

type Item = record
                typeOf : Kind
                location : Place
            end;

procedure move(object : Item, destination : Place);
     begin
          procedure push(object : Item, destination : Place);
                              ⋮

          procedure pull(object : Item, destination : Place);
                              ⋮

          procedure slide(object : Item, destination : Place);
                              ⋮

          procedure roll(object : Item, destination : Place);
                              ⋮

     end
begin
     case object.typeOf of
          trolley : push(object, destination);
          cart    : pull(object, destination);
          sledge  : slide(object, destination);
          ball    : roll(object, destination);
end
```

Although a program of the above structure may be adequate for the purpose, a critic may argue against its structure and elegance, suggesting that the routines *push, pull* and so on are specific to different object types and, therefore, should be defined as part of the type *Item*. Bearing in mind the possibility of this kind of criticism, let us try to revise the pseudo-code as indicated below:

```
type Kind      = ······
     Place     = ······;
     Proc_name = (push | pull | slide | roll);
type Item      = record
                      typeOf : Kind
                      location : Place
                      move : Proc_name
                 end;
procedure move(object : Item, destination : Place);
     begin
          procedure push(object : Item, destination : Place);

                    ⋮

          procedure pull ······
     end
begin
```

$$\underline{\text{apply}} \quad \underbrace{object.move}_{\text{an object orientation}} \quad (object, destination); \quad \left.\begin{array}{l} \text{a function taking} \\ \text{as its argument} \\ \text{another function} \end{array}\right\}$$

```
end
```

By encapsulating the method applicable for performing a given task as part of the definition of a relevant type, the above code attempts to invoke the procedure relevant to a particular object by means of a function called 'apply'. The code also illustrates a kind of object orientation too. When invoking the routine that moves an object, the programmer does not need to think about object–specific information at all; the code '*object.move* ···' sounds almost like the phrase 'move such and such an object to such and such a destination'. At least, that is the intention and it would be nice if it could be achieved. However, most programming languages do not support a function like 'apply'. The languages which support it belong to the category of declarative languages, for example, Lisp [65] and functional languages such as Miranda [61] and Haskell [7]. The following is an attempt to solve the above problem in the functional style.

Let us first introduce a few basic types by enumeration:

> *Name* ::= $s1 \mid s2 \mid s3 \mid s4 \mid \cdots$
> *Kind* ::= *trolley* | *cart* | *sledge* | *ball*
> *Place* ::= $p1 \mid p2 \mid \cdots$

a type for the Cartesian product of *Name* and *Place*:

> $Item == (Name, Place)$

and, finally, a function to identify specific objects according to their types:

> $typeOf :: Name \rightarrow Kind$
> $typeOf\ s1 = trolley$
> $typeOf\ s2 = cart$

$\vdots$

Consider now specialised functions for moving objects about:

> $push :: Place \rightarrow Item \rightarrow Item$
> $pull :: Place \rightarrow Item \rightarrow Item$

$\vdots$

> $push\ q\ (x, p) = (\cdots \text{function body} \cdots)$ ⎫
> $pull\ q\ (x, p)\ = \cdots\cdots$ ⎬ functions defining object
$\vdots$ ⎭ movements

In order to introduce a more general function for invoking the above specialised functions, let us consider an auxiliary function:

> $moveAux :: Kind \rightarrow Place \rightarrow Item \rightarrow Item$
> $moveAux\ trolley = push$
> $moveAux\ cart = pull$
> $moveAux\ sledge = slide$
> $moveAux\ ball = roll$

and then the 'type–insensitive' general version:

> $move :: Place \rightarrow Item \rightarrow Item$
> $move\ q\ (x, p) = moveAux\ (typeOf\ x)\ q\ (x, p)$

We have thus achieved an object orientation in the sense described earlier. The code appears to be clearer and, as expected in functional languages, it should be easier to reason about the correctness of the code. If required, the code can be further improved by localising some of the subsidiary functions used in defining others. However, even the above version has drawbacks. In the event of changes in the requirements, any revision could affect the above code quite extensively and not just in one or two places. Furthermore, such constructs as 'case' statements appear in the code in disguise. This kind of drawback calls for a more general approach to object orientation.

8.2 Object Orientation in the Wider Sense

Although uniformity in protocols for handling different kinds of object is desirable from the point of view of programming, as evident from the above, programs produced in imperative and declarative paradigms can suffer from a number of drawbacks. In general, these include the following:

- Modularity of programs is restricted to functional (operational) modularity.
- Procedures or functions specific to different types of object may be freely invoked anywhere in the code, although this can be overcome in functional languages by the use of definitions local to specific functions.
- With respect to functional languages, the notions of 'sameness' and 'change' cannot coexist. In other words, it is not possible to capture the notion that objects can undergo change, although as individuals they remain the same.
- Lack of correspondence between the program structure and the spatial structure of the actual or, possibly, the physical system being modelled.

The above drawbacks have serious implications in the software life cycle. New features, change of requirements, change of originally intended use, development in programming techniques and new algorithms are some of the things which often call for extensive revisions of software. However, cost implications and vulnerability of software to fresh faults during revision raise the question of the most effective way of conducting them. An object oriented approach in the wider sense addresses this need, not only at the implementation level but also at every other stage of the software life cycle.

Despite its frequent use, 'modularisation' is a heavily loaded term with different meanings. The notions of 'modules' and 'packages' are common in programming languages such as Modula2 and Ada. A module is taken to mean a largely independent but coherent collection of software with well-defined interfaces between different software components. Meyer [37] introduces several notions of modularisation. Modularisation may be motivated purely from the point of view of software construction where the emphasis is on the decomposition software such that the decomposed modules can be independently developed and, subsequently, put together to form the overall system. This can be further guided by conceptual modularity to promote better understanding, although in principle the latter can be an alternative in its own right. On the other hand, modularisation may be driven by software maintenance considerations, thus leading to a notion of modular extendibility of software. There can also be an operational perspective of modularisation aimed at modular protection – a notion encountered in fault tolerance with respect to the containment of run–time consequences of software faults.

Whatever the perspective, modularisation is closely related to abstraction, whether with respect to modelling or the treatment of detail. With respect to the former, that is, how a system is viewed abstractly, abstraction may exploit the modularity inherent in the problem. The treatment of the detail, on the other hand, concerns not only the establishment of the extent of detail to be considered, but also the separation of the information relevant to a problem from the rest. Both notions of abstraction are a product of analysis. In this respect, information hiding, that is, encapsulation of the chosen information relevant to an entity within it, is regarded as an effective software engineering principle. This involves division of information pertinent to an entity into 'private' and 'non-private' parts, and provision of a clear interface so that the world outside has access to services implied by the non-private information of the entity.

Object orientation fits in well with the aforementioned perspectives and considerations. As a design strategy it shifts emphasis from system function to system architecture built around the notion of an 'object'.

8.3 What are Objects?

The object oriented approach is based on modularisation of software along the lines of so–called 'objects'. Objects can be of different kinds. There are abstract mathematical objects such as the number '5', the set of integers, etc., which undergo no change. A more appropriate term to distinguish them from the kind of object we have in mind is to use the word *value*.

Exemplars of the kind of object we have in mind are objects such as bank accounts, games, organisations, individual persons, nations and countries which undergo change but still retain their identity. What characterises this kind of object is that each individual object has a certain *state* and any change takes place with respect to that state. Given a particular class of object with some shared characteristics, certain aspects may remain the same despite any change. For example, a bank savings account may be required to remain in credit, even though withdrawals and deposits of funds from the account will affect its state.

The notion of 'sameness' in this context means the aspects which remain true of all objects of the given class during change. Formally, this can be captured by the notion of a *state invariant*. On the other hand, the changes themselves can be seen as *transformations*, or *transitions*, of the state of the particular individual affected by the change. State transformations involve two kinds of information: *procedural information*, that is, information on how to perform a given transformation, which obviously is common to all objects of a class, and *state information*, which concerns the current state of specific objects. The notion of a *class* embodies the notion of a state invariant and the procedural component of state transformation. On the other hand, objects, i.e., specific instances of a class, are characterised by the state information unique to a given object.

8.4 Some Object Oriented Concepts

8.4.1 Software Reuse

Software reuse is not a concept unique to object orientation but is increasingly used in the object oriented context. The idea of software reuse has been around for some time, for instance, under the guise of software libraries – a concept which has been particularly successful in science and engineering in relation to numerical computing. Modular languages such as Modula2 and Ada also aim at greater software reuse. The object oriented approach even claims superior software reusability on the grounds of *inheritance, overloading, genericity* and *polymorphism*.

8.4.2 Inheritance

Inheritance is a way of avoiding the replication of information which is common to a number of different classes of object. Instead of replicating information under each class separately, the object oriented approach encourages the process of modelling to start with a single general class embodying the 'common denominator' of all the classes under consideration, and then to define more specific classes by the gradual introduction of information relevant to them. In some sense, class is a generalisation of the features underlying the notion of *module*. Meyer [37] characterises modules in the following manner:

- A module is a set of services on offer.
- A module is open in the sense that not all the services may be provided from the outset.
- A module is closed in the sense that any subsequent extension to it should not affect the services currently on offer.

Inheritance as a mechanism supports the same objectives as those of modules. It allows functionality to be extended without inadvertently affecting the services offered by the super–class. In practical terms of *software reuse*, inheritance therefore results in the following:

- Automatic inheritance of all services from super–classes.
- Opportunity to add any new operations.
- Opportunity to redefine any inherited operations.

Inheritance can also be seen as a *specialisation* of types through incorporation of new features. A rich source of examples illustrating inheritance is the natural world. The concept of an *animal* in the animal world corresponds to a highly general class, enabling the definition of more specific concepts such as *amphibians, invertebrates, birds, mammals, reptiles*, etc., by specialisation. These are subclasses of *animal* and introduce its possible variations. They in turn can be further specialised by, for example, defining the concepts of *toad, crocodile* and so on from *amphibians*. This process can be continued until every species of the animal kingdom has been identified. If our interest is restricted to the classification of animals purely on biological grounds, and not to environmental and regional considerations, species of animals may be seen as classes at the lowest level.

8.4.3 Overloading, Genericity and Polymorphism

One implication of introducing standard protocols for data handling is *operator overloading*, that is, the use of the same operation name with operations of different semantics. A typical example is the operator ' + ' used for adding numbers irrespective of their type, whether we are dealing with natural numbers, integers, rational numbers, real numbers or complex numbers.

Genericity is an attribute frequently used in relation to either parameterised modules, that is, modules with unspecified arbitrary parameters, or modules that can be used across different applications with suitable adjustments to, or instantiations of, their interfaces. It is also a term applied in relation to unspecified types of values. Meyer [37] makes an interesting comparison between overloading and genericity. According to him, overloading is intended for the convenience of the client programmer so that he can write the same *client code* in different implementations, whereas genericity is intended as a goal for the module implementor so that he can write the same *module code* with a view to using it in different implementations.

Polymorphism is a mechanism which allows the definition of functions or operations with no regard to the kind of values to be handled by them as arguments. In practice this is achieved by means of generic types when defining functions and instantiating with an appropriate specific type of values at the point of their use. In object oriented implementations, polymorphism has also implications at run–time, especially in resolving the specific types applicable to instances of objects at run–time and in working out any inherited features from more general super classes.

8.5 Abstract Data Types and Classes

A concept which, in some ways, resembles the concept of *class* is the notion of *abstract data type* (ADT). An ADT is a problem–oriented mathematical concept. Essentially, it describes what the data type is about in terms of the functionality of operations associated with it. As such, a definition of an ADT is not concerned itself with implementation details and does not address performance considerations such as time and space efficiency. In some cases such as numbers, an ADT may lack a full implementation of its values. The primary concern of an ADT is two–fold. On one hand, it conveys to the user how to use the data type correctly, and on the other hand, it provides the implementor of the data type with a specification against which the correctness of the implementation of the data type can be verified. ADTs deal with mathematical objects or values which, as mentioned in Section 8.3, do not undergo change.

By contrast, classes are a computational notion in the sense that each class has a role in the computational process. Because of their link with computation, implementation issues such as efficiency matter in classes. Classes are concerned with properties shared by a collection of objects, which, unlike values belonging to a data type, may undergo change.

However, ADTs and classes of objects exhibit some similarities; these should also become evident in Chapter 11, where a more detailed discussion of ADTs will follow. Both concepts have a similar structure and are developed on the basis of similar principles, in particular, encapsulation of operations within their definitions. These similarities may be exploited in using ADTs as an initial specification of classes. In this context, ADTs can facilitate an understanding of the behaviour of objects, although this is limited to an understanding of objects taken in isolation and not to their interactions.

8.6 Representation of Classes

From the point of view of our discussion, there are a number of important structural features of classes. The following syntax definition of classes is intended to outline these.

> class ⟨class name⟩
> inherit ⟨class name$_1$⟩ redefine ⟨feature$_a$⟩
>
>   ⋮
>
>   ⟨class name$_m$⟩ redefine ⟨feature$_z$⟩
> export ⟨externally visible feature and method names⟩
> features
>   ⟨feature$_1$⟩ : ⟨type$_1$⟩;
>
>   ⋮
>
>   ⟨feature$_n$⟩ : ⟨type$_n$⟩;
>   ⟨method$_1$⟩(⟨its arguments and their types⟩) is
>   ⟨definition of method$_1$⟩;
>
>   ⋮
>
>   ⟨method$_n$⟩(⟨its arguments and their types⟩) is
>   ⟨definition of method$_n$⟩
> end

Note that the inherit clause specifies other classes inherited by the class under consideration. However, inherited features or methods can be, if necessary, overridden by new definitions and this is achieved through a redefine clause. Clause export specifies the interface of the class with the outside world. Clause features introduces two categories of entities: *features* and *methods*. In conventional Z, the terms closest to the former are *component* or *state variable*, while the term closest to the latter is *operation*.

8.7 Object Oriented Specification Languages

Most formal specification languages are not intended for use in conjunction with a particular design methodology. Although the same is true of the algebraic specification languages discussed in Chapters 11 and 12, they can be a useful tool in object oriented design because of the features they have in common. Such an application is not surprising, especially in the light of how frequently algebraic specifications are used for specifying ADTs and the close links between ADTs and classes in the object oriented paradigm.

The motivation for extending formal specification languages to cope with object orientation is primarily due to their inadequacies for structuring specifications. This might be contentious, especially since extensions such as the schema language of Z are meant to address this need. Perhaps, such deficiencies are a matter of degree. A schema language, for example, enables the structuring of mathematical text and provides a convenient way to refer to mathematical text as specification entities, such as a specification of the general state of a system, a specification of an operation transforming its state, and so on. However, it lacks a mechanism for identifying specifications dealing with a particular part of a system, operations associated with a particular system or even specifications which are to be regarded as specifications of the system state. This is where object orientation offers a number of advantages through its notion of *class*. This is because, a class definition clearly identifies the general state of objects of that class, encapsulates all operations associated with its objects within its definition and makes a distinction between features and operations to be used only for internal purposes and those meant for both internal use and the outside world.

Limiting our discussion just to Z, we note that there are a number of object oriented 'dialects' of Z such as that of Schumann and Pitt [52, 51, 1], OOZE [2], Z^{++} [32] and Object–Z [46, 47]. A comparative study of these and other dialects may be found in [30], with a further discussion of the role of object oriented specification languages in software development in [31].

8.7.1 An Object Oriented Syntax in Z Style

Our case study is conducted in the object oriented extension of Z proposed by Schumann and Pitt [52, 51, 1]. Each object oriented variant of Z regards implicitly the standard non-object oriented Z as its core. Therefore, the boundary between the object oriented part and the non-object oriented part of such extensions to Z is quite clear. Thus, for example, the basic mathematical objects, namely sets, relations, functions, sequences and bags are to be used as in conventional Z.

Schumann and Pitt have adopted the following style for using schemas in an object oriented context. Typically, any object oriented schema, that is, a schema defining a class in this style, contains three sections (enclosed in boxes in visual presentations) and consists of:

- A class name followed by any generic types used by the relevant class and/or any parameters.
- Declaration of applicable features or state variables. This is made in the top section of the schema and follows the style of signature declarations in conventional Z.
- A class invariant, which is analogous to the state invariant in conventional Z. This is given in the second section of the schema.
- Initialisation specification of new objects. This is given in the third section of the schema.

Schumann and Pitt refer to methods as *events*, and define *event schemas* in the following manner. They use the dot notation to encapsulate or 'bundle' all the methods associated with the relevant class. The syntax of event schema consists of:

- An event name, which is prefixed by the class name using the dot notation and is followed by a parameter list. The parameter list consists of two kinds of parameters: arguments or inputs to the method and, if appropriate, its outputs. The inputs and outputs are separated by the symbol $\rightarrow$. The parameters are formal parameters used only for defining the method concerned and have no significance elsewhere.
- A precondition stating under what circumstances the method can be invoked.
- A postcondition stating the effect of invoking the method. The postcondition is stated in a new third section of the event schema. As in conventional Z, when specifying operations the postcondition uses the dashed and undashed feature names (component names) for specifying the effect of the method.
- An important convention in Schumann and Pitt approach is that, unless it follows from explicitly stated predicates, features remain unchanged during the application of any method. Note that this convention is the opposite of that in non–object oriented Z, where there is no guarantee that features remain unchanged during an operation unless it is stated explicitly. In other words, state changes in the Schumann and Pitt approach are minimal with respect to the specification. This has been introduced purely for

convenience but it is important to note the difference in interpretation of schemas in object oriented and non–object oriented contexts.

8.8 Object Oriented Version of Sequences

This section and Section 8.9 are devoted to a case study in object oriented specification.

Contrary to what was said earlier in respect of the boundary between object oriented and non–object oriented Z, let us begin our case study with an object oriented formalisation of sequences, a concept well within the latter. This is done purely as a convenient illustration of object oriented concepts. In order to illustrate the style of specification, we describe some of the initial schemas in some detail, and less so in subsequent schemas.

When treating sequences as objects, or abstract data structures, we note that each sequence has a certain state, namely its current content. Furthermore, there are various operations to manipulate sequences, for example, an operation to add an element at the front, an operation to concatenate another sequence at the tail end, and so on. Each of these operations affects the current state of any given sequence. Of course, there are other operations which allow various observations about any given sequence, for example, finding out the element at its tail end. Such operations return other mathematical objects such as numbers, sets or, for that matter, sequences as well. Therefore, in the object oriented formalisation of sequences, we introduce a 'class' definition for sequences by, on the one hand, specifying what is true of all sequences as objects of this class and, on the other hand, by encapsulating as part of sequences all operations relevant to them.

The state of every sequence as an object can be specified as:

$$
\begin{array}{l}
\rule{6cm}{0.4pt}\ Seq[X] \\
\quad f : \mathbb{N}_1 \nrightarrow X \dots\dots\dots\dots \text{declaration of a feature (a state variable)} \\
\rule{6cm}{0.4pt} \\
\quad \mathrm{dom}\ f = 1 \mathrel{..} \# f \dots\dots\dots\dots\dots \text{state invariant of sequences} \\
\rule{6cm}{0.4pt} \\
\quad f' = \varnothing \dots\dots\dots\dots\dots\dots \text{predicate defining the initialisation}
\end{array}
$$

The class Seq, which is defined with respect to a generic type X, consists of just one feature (a state variable), which is a finite function f from $\mathbb{N}_1$ to X. The state invariant specifies what is true of all objects belonging to this class, namely that in effect f 'indexes' the chosen elements of X with numbers drawn from a contiguous stretch of natural numbers starting from 1 and ending at the number of elements appearing in the sequence. In some sense, this definition is exactly the same as that in non–object oriented Z, except that it brings in the notion of state to sequences in order to characterise them as objects. The treatment of sequences as objects requires the definition of the initial state of sequences as objects, which is done in the third section of the class schema.

Below is a method, an operation, belonging to the class *Seq*. The naming of the schema as *Seq*[*X*].*cons* makes the point that the schema concerns the specification of a method called *cons* on objects belonging to the class *Seq*. Furthermore, the method *cons* takes only one argument (the formal parameter *a* appearing in the schema label), which, according to the first section of the schema, is an element of any type used in place of the generic type *X* appearing in the definition.

$$\begin{array}{l} \underline{Seq[X].cons(a)} \\ \quad a : X \ldots\ldots\ldots\ldots \text{formal name used for the argument, and its type} \\ \hline \quad true \ldots\ldots\ldots\ldots\ldots\ldots\ldots\ldots\ldots\ldots\ldots\ldots\ldots\ldots\ldots \text{precondition} \\ \hline \quad f' = \{1 \mapsto a\} \cup (pred \, \mathbin{\substack{\circ \\ \circ}} f) \ldots\ldots\ldots\ldots \text{postcondition defining the} \\ \qquad\qquad\qquad\qquad\qquad\qquad\qquad\qquad\qquad \text{effect on the object} \end{array}$$

The precondition of the method *cons* is vacuously true and, hence, the method can be invoked irrespectively of the current state of f or the value of the argument. The postcondition specifies the new value of f'. This definition of *cons* is closely related to that in the standard Z and allows the insertion of an element at the head of a sequence. By contrast, the method *snoc* allows the insertion of an element at the tail end of a sequence

$$\begin{array}{l} \underline{Seq[X].snoc(a)} \\ \quad a : X \\ \hline \quad true \\ \hline \quad f' = f \cup \{\#f + 1 \mapsto a\} \end{array}$$

Another method is *head*, which, as indicated by the symbol $\rightarrow$ in the schema label, returns as output an object of whatever the type used in place of X.

$$\begin{array}{l} \underline{Seq[X].head(\rightarrow a)} \\ \quad a : X \ldots\ldots\ldots\ldots\ldots\ldots \text{name used for the output and its type} \\ \hline \quad f \neq \varnothing \\ \hline \quad a = f(1) \end{array}$$

The functionality of the method *head* is obvious. It is a 'query method' since it enables an observation about a given sequence. An analogous query method is *front*, which returns an object of the same class as the sequence operated on.

$$\boxed{\begin{array}{l} \underline{\; Seq[X].front(\rightarrow s) \;} \\ s : Seq[X] \\ \hline\hline \text{true} \\ \hline\hline s = \{\#f\} \lhd f \end{array}}$$

The methods *last* and *tail* defined below are very similar to the two operations *head* and *front* introduced above.

$$\boxed{\begin{array}{l} \underline{\; Seq[X].last(\rightarrow a) \;} \\ a : X \\ \hline\hline f \neq \varnothing \\ \hline\hline a = f(\#f) \end{array}}$$

$$\boxed{\begin{array}{l} \underline{\; Seq[X].tail(\rightarrow s) \;} \\ s : Seq[X] \\ \hline\hline \text{true} \\ \hline\hline s = f \circ (\{0\} \lhd succ) \end{array}}$$

The method *concat* given below differs from methods introduced so far in that it not only operates on a sequence but also takes a sequence as its input. Given a sequence s as its argument, *concat* appends s at the end of the sequence it is operating on.

$$\boxed{\begin{array}{l} \underline{\; Seq[X].concat(s) \;} \\ s : Seq[X] \dots\dots\dots\dots\dots\dots\dots \text{an input which is a sequence} \\ \hline\hline \text{true} \\ \hline\hline f' = f \cup (pred^{\#f} \, \mathring{\,}_9\, s) \end{array}}$$

The generic nature of the class *Seq*, arising from the genericity of X in its definition, can lead to objects of some complicated internal structure. Below is a method *dconcat* on a class of sequences, the elements of which themselves are sequences with respect to X. *dconcat* stands for 'distributed concatenation' of a sequence of sequences.

$$\boxed{\begin{array}{l} \underline{\; Seq[Seq[X]].dconcat \;} \\ \text{true} \\ \hline\hline f \neq \varnothing \Rightarrow f' = f.tail.dconcat.concat(f.last) \end{array}}$$

Note the application of methods to objects using the period '.' and that the application of methods associates to the left. The above is a recursive definition and, therefore, requires the following:

$$f = \varnothing \Rightarrow f' = f$$

as an additional axiom as the terminating clause for recursion. Such an axiom would ensure that the value of f remains unchanged in the final recursive call of *dconcat*. However, according to the convention mentioned in Section 8.7.1, this is unnecessary, since anything not stated explicitly should have no effect.

Below is a method with no input/output parameters at all. It simply reverses the order of elements of the affected sequence.

```
┌─ Seq[X].rev ────────────────────────────────
│ true
├─────────────────────────────────────────────
│   f' = {i ↦ (#f − i + 1) | i ∈ 1 .. #f} ⨾ f
└─────────────────────────────────────────────
```

Each of the methods we came across above either modifies the sequence at which the method is directed or makes an observation about the sequence concerned by returning an object of another or the same class. Obviously, such observations are made in terms of classes themselves, that is, in the language of classes in our discourse.

By contrast, we also need to make observations in our meta–language about objects, especially when reasoning. Since our language of reasoning is predicate logic, we therefore introduce additional predicates for this purpose. Two such predicates are *in* and *not-in* introduced below:

$$in, not\text{-}in : X \leftrightarrow Seq[X]$$
$$\forall\, a : X;\ s : Seq[X] \bullet$$
$$a\ in\ s \Leftrightarrow a \in \operatorname{ran} s$$
$$a\ not\text{-}in\ s \Leftrightarrow a \notin \operatorname{ran} s$$

Other useful predicates on sequences are:

$$subseq, starts, ends : Seq[X] \leftrightarrow Seq[X]$$
$$\forall\, s, t : Seq[X] \bullet$$
$$s\ subseq\ t \Leftrightarrow \exists\, k : \mathbb{N} \bullet pred^{k} \mathbin{\substack{\circ \\ \circ}} s \subseteq t$$
$$s\ starts\ t \Leftrightarrow s\ subseq\ t \wedge s.head = t.head$$
$$s\ ends\ t \Leftrightarrow s\ subseq\ t \wedge s.last = t.last$$

as well as:

$$\forall\, s : Seq[X] \bullet is\text{-}empty(s) \Leftrightarrow s = \varnothing$$

where *pred* denotes the predecessor function on $\mathbb{N}$. The predicate *subseq* establishes whether one sequence is a subsequence of another sequence, *starts* whether one sequence is a subsequence at the beginning of another sequence, and *ends* whether one sequence is a subsequence at the end of another sequence.

Being predicates in the conventional sense, the above return truth values belonging to the domain of semantics. Obviously, introducing a new class for Boolean values, truth values themselves and, hence, the above predicates can also be 'implemented' using classes.

8.9 Text Processing

8.9.1 A Character Set

Relying on our discussion in the previous section, let us attempt to formalise text manipulation in different applications. One obvious such application is a text editor, but there could be others. First, let us introduce a type *Char*:

$$[\mathit{Char}]$$

representing a character set. It is generic only in the sense that its composition is yet to be defined fully but, otherwise, it is specific enough from the point of view of possible applications. It suffices to state at this stage that *Char* consists of an appropriate textual character set, punctuation symbols, and any other symbols required for text processing purposes. Some of the latter special elements in *Char* are:

$$' \sqcup ', \ ' \hookleftarrow ', \ ' \rhd ', \ ' \boxed{\mathrm{cr}} \ ' \in \mathit{Char}$$

As a simplification, we omit below the quotes on specific characters such as $' \sqcup '$ and $' \hookleftarrow '$. Informally, $\sqcup$ represents the space character, $\hookleftarrow$ a new line character, $\rhd$ a character showing a system prompt for user input, and $\boxed{\mathrm{cr}}$ a character to be typed by the user to signify an end of user entry of text.

8.9.2 Textual Objects

The new class *Text* introduced below is associated with all possible textual objects and can be based on the abstraction of class *Seq* of sequences introduced in the previous section. Thus, the following class schema is defined by 'inheriting' the class *Seq*:

```
┌─ Text ─────────────────────────────────────────────
│  Seq[Char][f \ text]
│
```

with some minor modifications, that is, instantiating the generic type X with the specific type *Char* and renaming the feature identifier f to *text*.

    Text is a general class and it inherits all methods applicable in *Seq*. It is possible to identify more specialised subclasses of *Text*, for example, a subclass *Line*:

```
┌─ Line ─────────────────────────────────────────────
│  Text
│  ──────────────────────────────────────────────────
│  ↩ in text ⇒ ↩ not-in text.front
```

for modelling individual lines of text. According to the above definition, a line is a piece of text which could possibly contain the new line character $\hookleftarrow$

but only at the very end. Note the use of *text.front* in the class definition of *Line* to apply the method *front*, inherited from *Seq*, to the only feature *text* in objects belonging to the class *Text*. Similarly, a subclass *Word*:

$$
\begin{array}{|l|}
\hline
\quad Word \underline{\hspace{9cm}} \\
\quad Line \\
\hline
\quad \sqcup \ in \ text \Rightarrow \sqcup \ not\text{-}in \ text.front \\
\hline
\end{array}
$$

may be introduced to introduce words, a textual object which could possibly contain either a space character $\sqcup$ or a new line character $\hookleftarrow$ but, again, only at the very end. Note that *Line*, and *Word* in its turn, rely on inheritance to identify the features in each class, standard properties as well as its methods.

8.9.3 Text as Scripts

Below, we introduce a more complex class *Script*. Informally, *Script* represents all kinds of textual objects and, in addition, identifies words and lines of each object explicitly. While inheriting *Text*, objects belonging to *Script* consist of just two additional features, namely *lines* and *words*.

$$
\begin{array}{|l|}
\hline
\quad Script \underline{\hspace{8cm}} \\
\quad Text \\
\quad lines \ \ : Seq[Line] \\
\quad words : Seq[Word] \\
\hline
\quad text = lines.dconcat \dotfill (SC1) \\
\quad text = words.dconcat \dotfill (SC2) \\
\quad lines = \{s : Seq[Word]; \ w : Word \mid s \ subseq \ words \ \wedge \\
\qquad\qquad (w \ in \ s.front \Rightarrow \ \hookleftarrow \ not\text{-}in \ w) \ \wedge \\
\qquad\qquad (w \ in \ s \ \wedge \ \hookleftarrow \ in \ w \Rightarrow \ w = s.last) \bullet s.dconcat\} \dots (SC3) \\
\hline
\end{array}
$$

Informally, *text* represents the whole body of text we are dealing with, while *lines* and *words* represent the same body of text but in terms of its lines and words respectively. As an object, the feature *lines* is a sequence of objects each belonging to *Line*. Since each line itself is a sequence of characters, it is obvious that *lines* represents a sequence of sequences of characters, to which the method *dconcat* is applicable. Thus, the axiom (SC1) states that, when all its constituent sequences are concatenated together, the sequence of characters resulting from *lines* becomes identical with the sequence *text*. The interpretation of the axiom (SC2) is analogous. On the other hand, the axiom (SC3) establishes the relationship between lines and words in the body of the text.

It is possible to identify other forms of textual script. An example is the kind of script displayed within a text window on a computer screen, where any lines longer than the window width are 'wrapped' around so that they display within the window boundary in full. The class *PrettyScript* is intended for dealing with scripts displayed in this manner and its definition contains a formal parameter *width*. In this respect, *PrettyScript* is a parameterised class definition.

```
┌─ PrettyScript(width) ────────────────────────────────────────
│  Script
│  width : ℕ₁ ............................. a parameter and its type
│ ────────────────
│  ∀ l : Line  • l in lines ⇒ #l ⩽ width
│  ∀ l : Line  • l in lines ∧ #l < width ⇒ l(#l) = ↵
└──────────────────────────────────────────────────────────────
```

Note that the axiom (SC3) in *Script* does not necessarily require each line to end with the newline character. This freedom is intended especially for defining classes such as *PrettyScript* so that it is unnecessary to insert the newline character as lines longer than *width* are wrapped around.

Another form of textual script is the kind entered by a computer user using a keyboard. Although such scripts are instantly displayed nicely on the user's computer screen as an object of *PrettyScript*, the script in 'raw' form lacks such features and consists internally of just lines. The class *ClientScript* represents this kind of textual script.

```
┌─ ClientScript ───────────────────────────────────────────────
│  Script
│ ────────────────
│  ∀ l : Line  • l in lines ⇒ ↵  not-in l.front
│  ∀ l : Line  • l in lines.front ⇒ l(#l) = ↵
└──────────────────────────────────────────────────────────────
```

So far, we have not introduced any methods on pieces of simple text such as a line or a word, or a more complex block of text with lines etc. Below is a method on objects belonging to class *ClientScript*. The aptly named method *wrap* has both an input and output: *width* and *wrapped*.

```
┌─ ClientScript.wrap(width, → wrapped) ────────────────────────
│  width : ℕ₁ ............................................... (USC1)
│  wrapped : PrettyScript(width) ........................... (USC2)
│ ────────────────
│  text = wrapped.text.dconcat ............................. (USC3)
└──────────────────────────────────────────────────────────────
```

Whatever the number supplied for the input *width*, *wrap* instantiates with it the formal parameter *width* of the parameterised class *PrettyScript*. Thus the declaration (USC2) specifies on its own the nature of the object to be output. However, the axiom (USC3) makes sure that the object to be output is not an arbitrary textual object but one which is identical to *text* in 'client script' once any line–wrapping done purely for display purposes has been removed.

Here is the complementary operation, but this method converts a 'pretty script' into a 'client script'.

$$\begin{array}{|l} \hline \text{\textit{PrettyScript.unwrap}}(\rightarrow \textit{unwrapped}) \\ \hline \textit{unwrapped} : \textit{ClientScript} \\ \hline \textit{unwrapped.wrap}(\textit{width}) = \textit{text} \\ \hline \end{array}$$

8.9.4 Text as Documents

Textual objects can also be viewed as *documents*, which mean here text as manipulated by a text editor. The class *Document* is an abstraction of a body of text in this sense and relies on the class *Script* introduced above. Inspired by the work due to Sufrin [58], we model the class in the following manner:

$$\begin{array}{|l} \hline \textit{Document} \\ \hline \textit{Script} \\ \textit{left} \quad : \textit{Script} \\ \textit{right} \quad : \textit{Script} \\ \hline \textit{text} = \textit{left.text.concat}(\textit{right.text}) \\ \hline \textit{left}'.\textit{text} = \varnothing \\ \textit{right}'.\textit{text} = \textit{text} \\ \hline \end{array}$$

where *left* and *right*, two objects of class *Script*, together model the cursor position within the document being edited. The cursor position can be moved further to its right, or to its left, by two methods on objects of class *Document*.

$$\begin{array}{|l} \hline \textit{Document.moveL} \\ \hline \textit{left.text} \neq \varnothing \\ \hline \textit{left}'.\textit{text} = \textit{left.text.front} \\ \textit{right}'.\textit{text} = \textit{right.text.cons}(\textit{left.text.head}) \\ \hline \end{array}$$

$$\begin{array}{|l} \hline \textit{Document.moveR} \\ \hline \textit{right.text} \neq \varnothing \\ \hline \textit{left}'.\textit{text} = \textit{left.text.snoc}(\textit{right.text.head}) \\ \textit{right}'.\textit{text} = \textit{right.text.tail} \\ \hline \end{array}$$

The above two methods move the cursor position by one character at a time.

Other operations required for editing files may be defined in an analogous manner. We leave these as an exercise for the reader. In connection with this, the reader may find Exercise A.1 in Appendix A helpful.

8.9.5 Text as Dialogue

Another view of textual objects is in the form of a dialogue between a computer and its user as in a 'command window'. In this context, the computer first prompts the user to enter a command and, after some processing, responds to the user's command by printing some text in the window in some intelligent manner and, at the end, prompts the user for the next command. We are not concerned here with the form of 'intelligence' in the computer's response, and thus limit ourselves to the exchange of texts between the two parties.

Any text produced by the computer on the screen belongs to a class called *Response*, which is defined as:

$$
\begin{array}{|l}
\hline
\;Response \underline{\hspace{8cm}}\\
\;\;Text\\
\hline
\;\;text.last = \rhd\\
\;\;\rhd\;\; not\text{-}in\;\; text.front\\
\;\;text.front \neq \varnothing \Rightarrow text.front.last = \hookleftarrow\\
\hline
\end{array}
$$

According to the above, a computer response consists of zero or more lines followed by the character $\rhd$ to prompt the user for his next command.

The user, on the other hand, may type some text in response to the prompt and, at some stage, may type the character $\boxed{\text{cr}}$ to signify the end of his command. The class *Command* captures this understanding.

$$
\begin{array}{|l}
\hline
\;Command \underline{\hspace{8cm}}\\
\;\;Text\\
\hline
\;\;\boxed{\text{cr}}\;\; in\;\; text \Rightarrow \boxed{\text{cr}}\;\; not\text{-}in\;\; text.front\\
\;\;text.last = \boxed{\text{cr}}\\
\hline
\end{array}
$$

In the context of a computer user interface, a dialogue is essentially an alternating sequence of computer responses and user commands, but each dialogue beginning with a computer response to start with. The class *Dialogue* consists of such textual objects and may be formalised as:

$$
\begin{array}{|l}
\hline
\;Dialogue \underline{\hspace{8cm}}\\
\;\;Script\\
\;\;dialogue : Seq[Text]\\
\hline
\;\;text = dialogue.dconcat\\
\;\;\forall s : Text \bullet s\;\; in\;\; dialogue \Rightarrow\\
\;\;\;\;(\exists k : \mathbb{N} \bullet even(k) \wedge s = dialogue.tail^k \Rightarrow s.head \in Command) \wedge\\
\;\;\;\;(\exists k : \mathbb{N} \bullet odd(k) \wedge s = dialogue.tail^k \Rightarrow s.head \in Response)\\
\hline
\;\;\#dialogue' = 1\\
\;\;head(dialogue') = \rhd\\
\hline
\end{array}
$$

8.9.6 Text Windows

Text displayed in the text window of a computer screen is another kind of textual object. Geometrically, a window is a rectangular area of the screen and, therefore, its features include a width and a height, measured respectively in terms of the maximum number of characters that can be displayed horizontally and the maximum number of lines that can be displayed vertically. A window displays as much text as possible of an associated textual object such as a document. Let us refer to the textual object associated with a given window and the piece of text as displayed at any time respectively as 'content' and 'display'. A window in this sense can be formalised as a class *Window*:

$$\begin{array}{|l}
\hline
\_\ Window\,(width, height)\ \underline{\hspace{5cm}} \\
\quad width, height : \mathbb{N}_1 \\
\quad content \qquad : ClientScript \\
\quad display \qquad\ : PrettyScript\,(width) \\
\hline
\quad \#\,display.text \leqslant height \\
\quad display.text.unwrap\ subseq\ content.text \\
\quad \#\,display.text < height \Rightarrow display.text.unwrap\ ends\ content.text \\
\hline
\quad content'.text = \varnothing \\
\hline
\end{array}$$

where, as a simplification, we use a 'client script' as *content*. Instead of letting the width and height be any two non-zero whole numbers, it would perhaps be more appropriate to specify a parameter for each as a minimum permitted lower bound.

Once created, there are different ways to associate a window with its content, for example, by letting the user enter the text manually into the window directly, or by letting him 'load' the content from a source such as a file. Just dealing with the latter, we introduce a method called *load* as:

$$\begin{array}{|l}
\hline
\_\ Window.load\,(in\text{-}text)\ \underline{\hspace{4cm}} \\
\quad in\text{-}text : ClientScript \\
\hline
\quad content.text = \varnothing \\
\quad in\text{-}text \neq \varnothing \\
\hline
\quad content' = in\text{-}text \\
\quad display'.text.unwrap\ starts\ content'.text \\
\hline
\end{array}$$

Two basic operations a user may wish to perform on a text window are to scroll up or down the associated textual object. The following two operations allow this to be done one line at a time as displayed.

```
┌─ Window.scroll-up ────────────────────────────────────┐
│  ¬ display.text.unwrap starts content.text             │
├────────────────────────────────────────────────────────┤
│   ¬ display.text.unwrap ends content.text ⇒            │
│         display′.lines.tail = display.lines.front       │
│  display.text.unwrap ends content.text ⇒               │
│         display′.lines.tail = display.lines             │
└────────────────────────────────────────────────────────┘
```

```
┌─ Window.scroll-down ──────────────────────────────────┐
│  display.text ≠ ∅                                       │
├────────────────────────────────────────────────────────┤
│   ¬ display.text.unwrap ends content.text ⇒            │
│         display.lines.tail = display′.lines.front       │
│  display.text.unwrap ends content.text ⇒               │
│         display.lines.tail = display′.lines             │
└────────────────────────────────────────────────────────┘
```

Exercises

8.1 Class *PrettyScript*, introduced in Section 8.9.3, is too 'loose' because it allows a line to be wrapped around at any of its characters even if the permitted line length would accommodate more words on the line. Tighten this specification so that the lines are only wrapped around at the end of a word and the inclusion of the next word in the text would result in the line exceeding the length specified by *size*.

8.2 Referring to the discussion in Section 8.9.4, extend the definition *Document* so that it forms an object oriented specification of a text editor with facilities for deleting text, inserting text, finding the location of a given string of characters in the document, etc.

8.3 Referring to the discussion in Section 8.9.6, specify a text window system with greater functionality, for example, with the capability to resize the window display area, drag the window to a different location on the screen, load additional text, etc.

8.4 Examine how to integrate the definition of *Document* resulting from Exercise 8.2 and that of *Dialogue* given in Section 8.9.5 with your answer to Exercise 8.3 so that the facilities concerned can be used in a window environment.

9. Specification of Safety

Prevailing approaches to ensuring safety in critical systems are based on two complementary strategies: prevention of failures and deployment of defensive techniques against failures. The former addresses safety concerns by eliminating design errors and by adhering to proven rules of operational practice. The latter, on the other hand, consists of various means to contain failures in hazardous processes and to mitigate the consequences of any failures. Formal methods are important in both respects, but are better established in the area of the former, namely in the elimination of design errors. However, there is no reason why formal methods cannot be employed the design of safety mechanisms that deal with failures. This chapter illustrates how this can be achieved in the specification area, giving at the same time some idea as to the nature of safety requirements.

This chapter relies on the material in Chapter 5 and, in particular, on Section 5.5.

9.1 Introduction

Safety critical systems are those which carry high penalties in the event of their failure, in terms of loss of human life, serious injury, environmental damage or destruction of property or other assets. Obviously, these penalties can occur in any combination. However, many systems often exhibit a dominant dimension of 'criticality', and this is usually underlined by more specialised terminology, typically by terms such as *life-critical, mission-critical, environmental-critical* and *cost-critical* systems.

From a design point of view, such systems have to operate in hazardous environments and under tight constraints regarding the use of resources. As is apparent from application areas such as avionics, nuclear power and radiation therapy, safety critical systems typically have a real–time dimension too, with the implication that the time available for taking any corrective action in the event of failure, especially in critical stages, is extremely limited. As a consequence of this, such systems have to operate within narrow margins for error, both in space and in time.

System attributes which complement safety include other notions, notably reliability and security – two notions also shared by other kinds of high integrity system. However, there are fundamental differences between these three attributes. For example, safety and reliability requirements may be distinct, or may even conflict with each other. A revealing example is the railway, the safest mode of operation of which is when all the trains are brought to a halt. However, the absence of any risk here is qualitatively different from the reliability requirement, which requires the railway to continue to provide the service required of it. This should not undermine the importance of reliability: on the contrary, as exemplified by scenarios such as air-borne aircraft and medical applications, reliability could often be a necessary condition for safety.

The distinction between reliability and safety is reflected at the requirements level. The concern of reliability is usually the function, whereas the concern of safety is the provision of means to exclude behavioural patterns that could lead to hazardous circumstances, prevent potential accidents and, should they ever occur despite all measures, manage such failures at run–time with minimal damage. The design of critical systems thus involves two independent sets of requirements: functional requirements and safety requirements.

The distinction between functional and safety requirements could serve as a basis for a systematic approach to the design of critical systems, by enabling the designer to focus attention on the two behavioural aspects separately, and then address possible logical inconsistencies between the two when considered together. It is worth noting that, in addition to the possibility of such inconsistencies at the specification stage, inconsistencies could also result from subsequent design decisions.

Formal methods are being successfully applied at present to the specification of functional requirements of sequential and concurrent systems. There are also important achievements with respect to their application in the remaining software development stages of such systems. The overriding concern of these endeavours has been the elimination of design errors – the greatest strength of formal methods. When dealing with safety critical systems, however, perhaps for pragmatic reasons, there are mixed feelings about the use of formal methods. Such concerns are understandable in the light of established views on safety critical systems design, in particular, a preference for simplicity and the use of tried-and-tested techniques. On the other hand, there is a growing realisation that formal methods are a necessary part of the design of important safety critical systems.

As was mentioned in the preamble to this chapter, the application of formal methods in the safety critical area may be seen from two different perspectives. The more established of these is their conventional use to eliminate design errors, and, thereby, to eliminate the system failures associated with them. The other perspective is their application, in addition to the latter use, to the study of safety issues, with a shift of strategy from failure prevention by design to coping with run-time failures. The former kind of application of formal methods, that is, how to deal with functional requirements, is better understood and, although limited to specification, is looked at elsewhere in this text. However, being one of the recent concerns of formal methods, the second kind is a less developed area of research. Most applications that are subjected to a formal design are often safety critical. Therefore, the bene- fits accrued from formality are limited if it does not encompass safety from both above points of view. This explains why this chapter is devoted to the specification of safety requirements and safety features of critical systems.

9.2 Specification Framework

9.2.1 Changes in States as Time Histories

The state of any system varies with time. In order to model the temporal behaviour of state-based systems, let us consider time histories of states. With this in mind, let us introduce a definition $\mathbb{H}[X]$ that captures the variation of some arbitrary state variable whose values are drawn from a set X over a a set of time values $\mathbb{T}$.

$$
\begin{array}{l}
\underline{\;\mathbb{H}[X]\;} \\
\quad history : \mathbb{T} \nrightarrow X \\
\quad init \quad\; : \mathbb{T} \\
\hline
\quad \mathrm{dom}\; history = \{t : \mathbb{T} \mid init \leqslant t < \Omega(\textsc{now})\}
\end{array}
$$

We refer to any object satisfying $\mathbb{H}[X]$ defined above as a 'time history function'. Given that h is a time history function, the notation h_t is an abbreviation for $h.history(t)$ and is defined subject to:

$$\forall\, h : \mathbb{H}[X] \bullet h_t = h.history(t) \Leftrightarrow t \in \mathrm{dom}\; h.history$$

The above notation can be extended to cover intervals of time as follows:

$$\forall\, \theta_c : \bar{\Gamma}_c \bullet h_{\theta_c} = h.history (\!\lvert\, \theta_c \,\rvert\!) \Leftrightarrow \theta_c \subseteq \mathrm{dom}\; h.history$$

Furthermore, given that $h_1, h_2, \cdots, h_n$ are several time history functions defining the evolution of the state of an object s, that is, $s : S$ and S is a state defined by a schema of the form:

$$
\begin{array}{l}
\underline{\;S[X_1, X_2, \cdots, X_n]\;} \\
\quad h_1 : \mathbb{H}[X_1];\; h_2 : \mathbb{H}[X_2];\; \cdots;\; h_n : \mathbb{H}[X_n] \\
\quad\quad \vdots \\
\quad (\text{other signature declarations}) \\
\hline
\quad (\text{a predicate involving } h_1, h_2, \cdots, h_n \text{ etc.})
\end{array}
$$

$p_t(s)$ expresses a predicate about the state of s at time t. Let us extend this to cover intervals of time as:

$$\forall \theta_c : \bar{\Gamma}_c \bullet p_{\theta_c}(s) \Leftrightarrow (\forall t : \mathbb{T} \bullet t \in \theta_c \Rightarrow p_t(s))$$

with $p_{\theta_c}(s)$ asserting that p holds for s over the whole interval of clock time θ_c. The following are some obvious consequences of the above convention:

$$(p \wedge q)_t \Leftrightarrow p_t \wedge q_t$$
$$(p \vee q)_t \Leftrightarrow p_t \vee q_t$$
$$(\neg p)_t \Leftrightarrow \neg (p_t) \Leftrightarrow \neg p_t$$
$$(p \Rightarrow q)_t \Leftrightarrow p_t \Rightarrow q_t$$

In other words, the time index has a higher precedence than logical connectives such as $\neg$, $\wedge$, $\vee$ and so on. Note, however, that this does not apply to indexing with time intervals. Thus, for the negation we have:

$$(\neg p(s))_{\theta_c} \not\Leftrightarrow \neg (p_{\theta_c}(s))$$

It is necessary sometimes to compare the time histories of state changes in different objects. Consider, for example, a representation maintained by a computer about an external object undergoing change. In its representation, the computer may not be able to account for the times of changes in the external object exactly, but only approximately to a certain degree of accuracy. Because of the unpredictability of the time taken by the communications between the external object and itself, the computer's time history may not be derived from a simple 'shift' of the actual time history of the object concerned by a constant amount. Despite this, there is a need to establish whether an internal representation is a reasonably accurate record of the actual time history. With this in mind, let us first define a function $\bar{h}$ taking an interval of time θ_c and returning h_{θ_c}, if h_{θ_c} is a singleton set with one element and θ_c is a 'maximal' (longest) interval with respect to the value of that element. The function $\bar{h}$ can be defined as:

$$\forall h : \mathbb{H}[X];\ \theta_c : \bar{\Gamma}_c, x : X \bullet$$
$$\bar{h}(\theta_c) = x \Leftrightarrow h_{\theta_c} = \{x\} \wedge \forall \theta'_c : \bar{\Gamma}_c \bullet \theta_c \subset \theta'_c \Rightarrow h_{\theta_c} \subset h_{\theta'_c}$$

Let us now define a predicate $shadows(h_1, h_2, \delta, \theta)$ to mean that the time history function h_1 shadows (or mirrors) the variation given by the time history function h_2, but with a 'delay' (an accuracy) of at most δ time units over the time interval θ; see Figure 9.1.

$$\forall h_1, h_2 : \mathbb{H}[X];\ \theta : \bar{\Gamma}_c \bullet shadows(h_1, h_2, \delta, \theta) \Leftrightarrow$$
$$(\exists f : \bar{\Gamma}_c \rightarrowtail \bar{\Gamma}_c \bullet \{\bigcup(\mathrm{dom}\ f), \bigcup(\mathrm{ran}\ f)\} \subseteq \bar{\Gamma}_c \wedge \bigcup(\mathrm{fld}\ f) = \theta \wedge$$
$$\forall \theta_1 : \bar{\Gamma}_c \bullet \theta_1 \in \mathrm{dom}\ f \Rightarrow$$
$$(\exists \theta_2 : \bar{\Gamma}_c;\ x : X \bullet f(\theta_1) = \theta_2 \wedge \bar{h}_1(\theta_1) = \bar{h}_2(\theta_2) = x \wedge$$
$$left(\theta_2) \leqslant left(\theta_1) \leqslant left(\theta_2) + \delta))$$

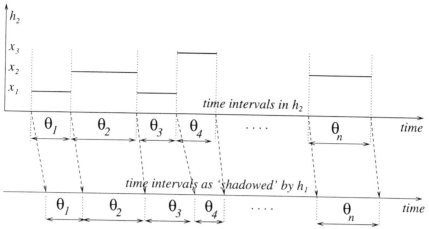

Fig. 9.1. 'Shadowing' of one time history function by another

According to the above definition, the domains of functions h_1 and h_2 each constitute a contiguous stretch of time, and taken together they cover the complete interval θ. There is a one-to-one correspondence between the intervals of time in the domains of h_1 and h_2, h_1 and h_2 return the same value for the corresponding intervals in their domains, and h_1 shadows every change in h_2 within a maximum tolerance of δ time units.

The above can be generalised into objects with several time varying attributes. For example, given that $s_1, s_2 : S$, S being the form of a schema as outlined above, we have:

$$shadows(s_1, s_2, \delta, \theta_c) \Leftrightarrow shadows(s_1.h_1, s_2.h_1, \delta, \theta_c) \wedge$$
$$shadows(s_1.h_2, s_2.h_2, \delta, \theta_c) \wedge$$
$$\vdots$$
$$shadows(s_1.h_n, s_2.h_n, \delta, \theta_c)$$

For convenience, let us also introduce an extended version of the notation h_t given earlier for dealing with functions defined in the form:

$$f : Y \nrightarrow \mathbb{H}[X]$$

where X and Y are some appropriate generic types. Given that $y : Y$ and $t : \mathbb{T}$, we write $f_t(y)$ for $(f\ y).history(t)$, provided that $t \in \mathrm{dom}(f\ y)$.

9.2.2 Representation of Equipments

We consider any system to consist of a *controlling system* (or the *controller*) and a *controlled system*. An implication of this is the need to ensure that the view held by the controller about the controlled system is consistent with the reality. As a result, the model of such a system requires two separate representations for each item of equipment; one modelling its actual behaviour and the other the behaviour as perceived by the controller. We refer to these two, respectively, as the representation of the equipment in the 'real environment' and the other as its 'internal' representation within the system. Decisions affecting the behaviour of the controller are based on this internal representation. For easy comparison, the two representations are assumed to have an identical structure.

Under normal operational conditions, that is, when there are no failures either within the equipment, the sensor monitoring it, the controller or the communication medium, these two representations must be 'nearly' the same. Any discrepancy between the two representations under normal operating conditions should therefore be confined to temporal aspects and not time invariant attributes such as location or any internal permanent fixture. However, the two representations could be at variance from each other in the presence of failures. For example, as discussed in Section 9.2.4, when a sensor fails the safest course of action at the disposal of the controller is to assume that the monitored equipment is in one of its highest risk states. Therefore, the actual state of the equipment and its internal representation within the controller could sometimes be totally different.

9.2.3 A Classification of Safety Requirements

As it was mentioned in Section 9.1, a systematic approach to the study of failures in the safety critical context is to consider the system behaviour from the functional and safety points of view separately and, in dealing with the latter, to consider the desired behaviour of each item of equipment, or the system as a whole, under the following headings:

(i) The behaviour of the rest of the system should any equipment fail.
(ii) The behaviour of the equipment if the controlling system fails.
(iii) Initialisation of the equipment when the system returns to service following a failure or a system shutdown.
(iv) The behaviour of each item of equipment as the system moves up to a state of higher risk in order to deliver a service.
(v) The behaviour of each item of equipment once the system has delivered the intended service, or in response to an unexpected hazardous set of circumstances.

The above are known in safety critical literature as fail–soft mechanisms, fail–safe mechanisms, safe initialisation of equipment, transitions from low to high risk states and transitions from high to low risk states respectively. They are different categories of safety requirements and, therefore, can be used as a basis for a systematic framework for specification of safety.

9.2.4 Specification of Safety Requirements

The following are some primitives used to specify the behaviours described above in order to ensure safety.

- Prohibitive low-to-high risk state changes
  The expression:

$$g \textbf{ prohibits } (p \rightsquigarrow q)$$

  is an abbreviation for:

$$\forall \theta_c : \bar{\Gamma}_c \bullet q_{\theta_c} \Rightarrow \exists \theta'_c : \bar{\Gamma}_c \bullet \theta'_c \textit{ meets } \theta_c \wedge p_{\theta'_c} \wedge \neg g_{\theta'_c}$$

  where $\bar{\Gamma} = \Gamma - \varnothing$. In other words, should the state specified by q ever prevail over any non-empty interval of time then it must have been the case just prior to it that p has prevailed but not g.
- Mandatory high-to-low risk state changes
  Given that l is a length of clock time interval, the expression:

$$p \textbf{ requires } q \textbf{ within } l$$

  is an abbreviation for:

$$\forall \theta_c : \bar{\Gamma}_c \bullet p_{\theta_c} \Rightarrow \exists t, t' : \mathbb{T}; \; \theta'_c, \theta''_c : \bar{\Gamma}_c \bullet t = \textit{left}(\theta_c) \wedge t' = \textit{left}(\theta'_c) \wedge$$
$$t' \leqslant t + l \wedge \theta_c \textit{ meets } \theta'_c \wedge q_{\theta'_c} \wedge$$
$$\theta''_c \textit{ finishes } \theta'_c \wedge \neg p_{\theta''_c}$$

  According to this kind of safety requirement, if p is to prevail at any time, and continues to do so, then within l time units of p's initiation q must prevail. Furthermore, q will continue to prevail until p ceases to prevail. Note that this allows for the possibility that both p and q prevail at certain times. It is clear that l is a deadline and its value can be chosen to match the desired response time.
- Unsafe equipment states (for managing sensor failures)
  In the event of a sensor failure, the safest course of action is to assume that the equipment monitored by the failed sensor happens to be in one of its highest risk states and act accordingly. Given an equipment E and a predicate p defining one or more of the highest possible risk states of E under normal operating conditions, we define the *fail–soft predicate* for E as:

$$\textbf{failure } E \textbf{ requires } p(E)$$

  with the meaning:

$$\forall \theta_c : \bar{\Gamma}_c \bullet \textit{faultySensor}_{\theta_c}(E) \textbf{ requires } p(E^i) \textbf{ within } T^E_{\textit{fail-soft}}$$

$T^E_{fail\text{-}soft}$ being the time limit set for the system to assume $p(E^i)$ when dealing with any requests involving E. Note that $faultySensor(E)$ is an appropriately defined predicate which captures the circumstances of failure of the sensor monitoring the state of the equipment E.

The category of safety requirements also applies to logical entities such as routes and subroutes in the case study that follows, should any sensor monitoring a piece of equipment on such an entity fail.

- Safe equipment states (for managing control signal failures)
  In the event of a failure of the controlling system, the most sensible course of action is to ensure that each item of equipment reverts to one of its safest states. Given equipment E, the behaviour required of E upon the failure of the controlling system can be defined as:

  failure *Controller* **requires** $p(E)$

  The above is the *fail–safe predicate* for E. It is to be interpreted as:

  $$\forall \theta_c : \bar{\Gamma}_c \bullet faultyController_{\theta_c} \textbf{ requires } p(E^r) \textbf{ within } T^E_{fail\text{-}safe}$$

  $T^E_{fail\text{-}safe}$ being the time limit set for E to return to any of the states defined by $p(E^r)$, which by implication is a safe state of E. A consequence of this requirement is that E is not permitted to respond to any requests so long as the controller is out of service. In this case, the predicate *faultyController* captures the circumstances of the controller's failure.

The above requirements of the form **prohibits** and **requires** appear to give the impression of 'enforcement' of requirements employing an appropriate 'agency'. However, according to the formalisation given above, this is not the case; they are simply declarative sentences describing the desired pattern of state changes.

9.3 Description of System State and Behaviour

This section defines the structure of equipment and other abstract entities applicable to railway signalling. The signalling system detects the presence of trains on the track and facilitates the correct movement of trains. It consists of two major components. The component *permanent way* comprises the tracks, the points and the signals on the ground; see Figure 9.2. The second component is the *interlocking*, which is a safety mechanism designed to prevent system operation resulting in hazardous circumstances or danger. It also monitors the permanent way in order to ensure a safe state.

9.3.1 Tracks

The position of trains on the tracks is identified with respect to *track circuits* – physically insulated individual sections of tracks each about 200 yards long.

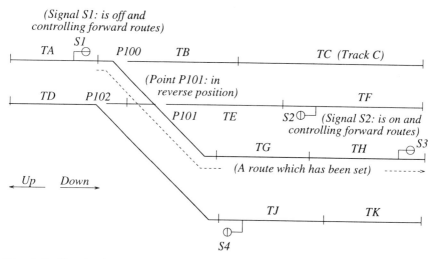

Fig. 9.2. Sketch of a permanent way

At any time, a track can be in one of the two states: *occupied* or *clear*, the former meaning that the given track is either occupied by a train, or assumed to be so, and the latter meaning the opposite. The state of the tracks is detected by means of *relays* located on each track circuit, which are activated by train movements.

In order to provide continuity for train movements, the adjacent track sections are linked. The linked tracks form two primary directions running opposite to each other which, according to British railway practice, are referred to as *up* and *down*; see Figure 9.2. These directions are intended as an indirect means of identifying the direction of train movements. Introducing a type Tid to identify track sections, this state of affairs is formalised in the schema $\Box\,Tracks$:

$$
\begin{array}{l}
\underline{\quad\Box\,Tracks\quad\rule{6cm}{0pt}} \\[4pt]
\quad\begin{array}{ll}
tracks & : \mathbb{F}\,Tid \\
up, down, bothDir & : Tid \leftrightarrow Tid \\
occupancy & : Tid \nrightarrow \mathbb{H}[\{\mathsf{clear}, \mathsf{occupied}\}]
\end{array} \\[4pt]
\underline{\rule{8cm}{0pt}} \\[4pt]
\quad\begin{array}{l}
tracks \neq \varnothing \\
up = down^{-1} \\
up \cap down = \varnothing \\
bothDir = down \cup up \\
\mathrm{id}\ tracks \cap bothDir = \varnothing \\
\mathrm{fld}\ bothDir = tracks \\
\mathrm{dom}\ occupancy = tracks
\end{array}
\end{array}
$$

Mathematically, the linked tracks form a connectivity graph, where the nodes are given by a set *tracks* essentially containing the tracks relevant to a given railway junction, and a relation *bothDir* on *tracks* formalising the interconnections between adjacent tracks. For obvious reasons, *bothDir* is symmetric and irreflexive. Partitioning of connections given by *bothDir* into two sets, *up* and *down*, thus allows us to capture the possible directions of train movements. The last axiom in *Tracks* ensures the state of each and every track at the junction is known.

9.3.2 Signals

Signals are the standard means for giving instructions to drivers about train movements. A signal typically displays three possible aspects with the following meanings:

- red - Do not proceed beyond this signal.
- amber - Expect the next signal to be at red.
- green - Expect the next signal to be at amber or at green.

Obviously, the display of these aspects depends on whether the lamp of a given signal is in working order or not. These can be captured by the inclusion of an additional value unlit to the set of possible aspects and by considering the two possible states of the signal lamp. Thus, the general state of signals may be specified as:

$$
\begin{array}{|l}
\hline
\;\Box Signal \rule{3cm}{0pt} \\
\quad \begin{array}{ll}
aspect & : \mathbb{H}[\{\text{red}, \text{green}, \text{amber}, \text{unlit}\}] \\
lamp & : \mathbb{H}[\{\text{in}, \text{out}\}] \\
location & : Tid \times Tid \\
berth, overlap & : Tid
\end{array} \\
\hline
\quad location = (berth, overlap) \\
\hline
\end{array}
$$

Using the above as a type for all possible signals, the following introduces certain predicates about the states of interest of any given signal $s : Signal$,

$$
\forall t, : \mathbb{T};\; s : \Box Signal \bullet
$$

$$
signalRed_t(s) \stackrel{def}{\Leftrightarrow} s.aspect_t = \text{red}
$$
$$
signalGreen_t(s) \stackrel{def}{\Leftrightarrow} s.aspect_t = \text{green}
$$
$$
signalAmber_t(s) \stackrel{def}{\Leftrightarrow} s.aspect_t = \text{amber}
$$
$$
failedSig_t(s) \stackrel{def}{\Leftrightarrow} s.lamp_t = \text{out}
$$

In a strict interpretation of the specification, the predicate $failedSig_t(s)$ above can be true if and only if the signal s has been turned off.

9.3.3 Points

Points provide the physical means for directing trains at junctions with multiple directions for forward movement. This is achieved by remote control of points into one of the two positions, *normal* and *reverse*. These two values are denoted by normalPos and reversePos respectively. A third possible state is *undetected* (or *out of correspondence*) – an intermediate state signifying that a given point is in the process of moving from the normal to the reverse position, or vice versa. However, a point can also be *broken*; a broken point is detected by its failure to reach a requested operational position, that is, either normal or reverse position, within a specified time limit T_{pt}^{max}. Once a point is moved to the desired position, it may be *locked* to prevent the issue of any command to change its position. The state of locking of the points is, therefore, entirely an internal concept and is not brought about by any real component on the ground. The points are also equipped with sensors for allowing the controlling system to know about the current positions of points. The state of a point, excluding any attached sensor, may be thus characterised as in the schema:

$$
\begin{array}{|l}
\hline
\Box Point \\
\hline
\quad trkSet \qquad\qquad : \mathbb{F}\,Tid \\
\quad normal, reverse : \mathbb{F}(Tid \times Tid) \\
\quad setting \qquad\qquad : \mathbb{H}[\{\mathsf{normalPos, reversePos, undetected, broken}\}] \\
\quad ptFixity \qquad\quad : \mathbb{H}[\{\mathsf{locked, free}\}] \\
\hline
\quad trkSet \neq \varnothing \\
\quad trkSet = \mathrm{dom}\,normal = \mathrm{dom}\,reverse \\
\quad \mathrm{ran}\,normal \cap \mathrm{ran}\,reverse = \varnothing \\
\hline
\end{array}
$$

The following predicates describe the possible states of any particular point $p : \Box Point$

$$isFreeNorPt_t(p) \stackrel{def}{\Leftrightarrow} p.ptFixity(t) = \mathsf{free} \wedge p.setting(t) = \mathsf{normalPos}$$
$$isFreeRevPt_t(p) \stackrel{def}{\Leftrightarrow} p.ptFixity(t) = \mathsf{free} \wedge p.setting(t) = \mathsf{reversePos}$$
$$isLockedNorPt_t(p) \stackrel{def}{\Leftrightarrow} p.ptFixity(t) = \mathsf{locked} \wedge p.setting(t) = \mathsf{normalPos}$$
$$isLockedRevPt_t(p) \stackrel{def}{\Leftrightarrow} p.ptFixity(t) = \mathsf{locked} \wedge p.setting(t) = \mathsf{reversePos}$$
$$brokenPt_t(p) \stackrel{def}{\Leftrightarrow} p.setting(t) = \mathsf{broken}$$

9.3.4 Subroutes

Legitimate train movements over individual track circuits are described by *subroutes*. Mathematically, subroutes are pairs of track sections reachable in a given direction via a third intermediate track section. Each subroute represents a possible train movement over a single track circuit.

Subroutes, as well as routes, are abstract (logical) entities founded on components of the permanent way allowing the operator or the system to manage the movement of trains on tracks safely. Safety is ensured by maintaining the subroutes and routes in one of the two distinct lock states: *locked* and *free*. With this in mind, let us introduce a type:

$LockState ::= \mathsf{locked} \mid \mathsf{free}$

Subroutes are locked in response to requests from the signal–person for a route. As a route is set, all the subroutes on it also become locked. As the train for which the route is intended passes through it the locked subroutes become free. Again, subroute locking is an internal concept. The intention is to prevent the allocation of a locked subroute to another route. The relationship between tracks and subroutes and the state of subroutes is formalised in the schema *Subroutes*.

```
┌─ Subroutes ─────────────────────────────────────
│  Tracks
│  subRoutes   : Tid ↔ Tid
│  subRtFixity : Tid × Tid ⇸ ℍ[LockState]
├─────────────────────────────────────────────────
│  subRoutes = up² ∪ down²
│  dom subRtFixity = subRoutes
└─────────────────────────────────────────────────
```

The component *subRtFixity* in the above schema contains the information on the lock state of each subroute.

9.3.5 Routes

A route is a section of a track in a given direction lying between two adjacent signals. It also includes all other ground equipment lying within its boundary, namely the signals and points, as well as the subroutes. Let us deal with these three aspects first in separate schemas: *RouteSignals*, *RoutePoints* and *RouteSubroutes*. The signals at the extremities of the route are referred to as *entry* and *exit*, while the track connections along the route as *routeCons*. Thus, the schema *RouteSignals* can be presented as:

```
┌─ RouteSignals ──────────────────────────────────
│  entry, exit : Signal
│  routeCons   : Tid ↔ Tid
├─────────────────────────────────────────────────
│  entry ≠ exit
│  {entry.location, exit.location} ⊆ routeCons
│  routeCons#routeCons = {(entry.berth, exit.overlap)}
└─────────────────────────────────────────────────
```

The components *normalPts* and *reversePts* in the schema *RoutePoints* denote the sets of points along the route in *normal* and *reverse* positions.

```
┌─ RoutePoints ──────────────────────────────────────────────
│ normalPts, reversePts :  𝔽 Point
│ routeCons                 : Tid ↔ Tid
├────────────────────────────────────────────────────────────
│ normalPts = {p : Point  |  p.normal ∩ routeCons ≠ ∅ • p}
│ reversePts = {p : Point  |  p.reverse ∩ routeCons ≠ ∅ • p}
└────────────────────────────────────────────────────────────
```

The information on the subroutes within a route includes the subroutes *routeSubs* forming the route, the first subroute *firstSub* on the route and an injective function *prevSub* on the set *routeSubs* giving the subroute immediately preceding a given subroute.

```
┌─ RouteSubroutes ───────────────────────────────────────────
│ routeSubs, routeCons : Tid ↔ Tid
│ firstSub                  : Tid × Tid
│ prevSub                   : Tid² ⤔ Tid²
│ routeTrks                 : 𝔽 Tid
├────────────────────────────────────────────────────────────
│ routeSubs = routeCons²
│ routeTrks = {t : Tid  |  trkSubs(t) ⊆ routeSubs}
│ firstSub ∈ trkSubs(entry.overlap)
│ firstSub ∈ dom prevSub
│ ran prevSub = routeSubs − {firstSub}
│     where
│     trkSubs    : Tid → 𝔽(Tid × Tid)
│     trkSubs(t) = {(t₁, t₂)  |  (t₁, t₂) ∈ routeSubs ∧
│                     {(t₁, t), (t, t₂)} ⊆ routeCons}
└────────────────────────────────────────────────────────────
```

We may define *prevSub* introduced in the above in the following manner:

$$prevSub : Tid^2 \rightarrowtail Tid^2$$
$$prevSub(t_1, t_2) = s$$
$$\text{such that}$$
$$t_1 = midTrk(s) \land s \in subRoutes \land$$
$$\exists\, t_3 \bullet s = (t_3, midTrk(t_1, t_2))$$

where,

$$midTrk(s) : Tid^2 \rightarrow Tid$$
$$midTrk(s) = y \, ,$$
$$\text{such that}$$
$$\exists\, x, z : Tid \bullet s = (x, z) \land \{(x, y), (y, z)\} \subseteq routeCons$$

The above three may be incorporated into a single specification giving the state of routes, but with an additional component recording the lock state of the route. Locking a route is similar to locking a subroute and is intended to prevent the allocation of a locked route to another route request.

```
┌─ Route ─────────────────────────────────────────────────────
│  Subroutes
│  RouteSignals
│  RoutePoints
│  RouteSubroutes
│  routeFixity       : LockState
└──────────────────────────────────────────────────────────────
```

```
┌─ Routes ────────────────────────────────────────────────────
│  routes       : 𝔽 Route
│  Subroutes
├──────────────────────────────────────────────────────────────
│  ⋃_{r∈routes}{r.entry, r.exit} = signals
│  ∀ s : Signal; r : Route • r ∈ routes ∧ s ∈ signals ⇒
│      (s.location ∈ r.routeCons ⇒ s = r.entry ∨ s = r.exit)
│  ∀ r : Route • r ∈ routes ⇒ (r.routeCons ⊆ up ∨ r.routeCons ⊆ down)
└──────────────────────────────────────────────────────────────
```

Within the context of a given route r, one may make the following observations as to whether a given subroute is locked or free:

$$\forall r : Route;\ s : Tid^2;\ Routes \bullet$$
$$isFreeSub_t(r, s) \stackrel{def}{\Leftrightarrow} subRtFixity_t(s) = \mathsf{free} \land s \in r.routeSubs \land$$
$$r.routeFixity_t = \mathsf{free}$$
$$isLockedSub_t(r, s) \stackrel{def}{\Leftrightarrow} subRtFixity_t(s) = \mathsf{locked} \land s \in r.routeSubs$$

Similar definitions may be introduced for route states:

$$\forall r : Route;\ s : Tid^2 \bullet$$
$$isFreeRoute_t(r) \stackrel{def}{\Leftrightarrow} r.routeFixity_t = \mathsf{free}$$
$$isLockedRoute_t(r) \stackrel{def}{\Leftrightarrow} r.routeFixity_t = \mathsf{locked}$$
$$isLockedRoute_t(r) \Rightarrow \forall s \bullet s \in r.routeSubs \Rightarrow isLockedSub_t(r, s) \land$$
$$\forall p \bullet p \in r.normalPts \Rightarrow isLockedNorPt_t(p) \land$$
$$\forall p \bullet p \in r.reversePts \Rightarrow isLockedRevPt_t(p)$$

Note that subroutes remain locked while routes remain locked.

9.4 System Behaviour in the Presence of Failures

This section deals with the specification of fail–soft and fail–safe behaviours in an individual item of equipment and other entities in the presence of failures. At the same time, it also outlines some general requirements on the pattern of equipment behaviour under normal operating conditions, that is, in the absence of failures. Obviously, the normal operational behaviour includes other aspects, in particular, the required response of the system to operator requests. Thus, our discussion deliberately excludes how the system responds to something like a route request by setting, as appropriate, the signal aspects, point positions and so forth.

Adopting the approach discussed in Section 9.2.3 and considering each item of equipment separately, Sections 9.4.3–9.4.5 first illustrate the specification of requirements belonging to categories (i)–(iii). Later, Sections 9.5.1–9.5.2 illustrate the specification of requirements belonging to categories (iv)–(v). Before moving on to this, however, it is necessary to have an abstract representation of sensors monitoring the equipment as well as an abstract representation of the controller. This is the subject of Sections 9.4.1 and 9.4.2.

Below is a summary of risk levels associated with equipment states and states of other entities. They are given with respect to their different attributes. These risk states are not unique and may be identified in relation to every equipment (and abstract entity).

Equipment (attribute)	Low Risk Value	High Risk Value
Signal (aspect)	red	amber, green
Point (setting)	normalPos, reversePos	normalPos, reversePos
Point (fixity)	locked	free
Subroute (fixity)	locked	free
Route (fixity)	free, locked	free, locked

These risk levels are used in Sections 9.4.3–9.4.5.

9.4.1 Behavioural Specification of Sensors

When looked at in sufficient detail, sensors themselves can be quite complex pieces of equipment. The process of establishing whether a sensor is working in the expected manner may also be quite complex. One of the reasons for this is the possible use of fault tolerance, that is, an extra layer of measures directed at increasing reliability of service. Note that for the purpose of fault tolerance, the system may employ several redundant sensors and take a 'vote' of their output in order to mask the output of any faulty sensors among them.

Although unlikely to occur in usual applications, it is conceivable, however, that all the sensors could fail simultaneously because, for example, of abnormal ambient conditions such as fire or electro-magnetic interference. The point being made here is that even the most reliable sensors can sometimes fail for different reasons. We assume that the system can detect such failures either by observing anomalies in sensor behaviour or by timeouts, that is, by observing the failure of the sensor to output its value at the right time, or the failure of the system to receive it on time because of persistent communication failures.

However, a detailed consideration of sensor behaviour is unnecessary here. What is relevant is some means of identifying whether a given sensor is in working order or is broken. Therefore, an abstract representation of sensors in the following form:

$$\boxed{\begin{array}{l} \textit{Sensor} \\ \hline \textit{sens-status} : \mathbb{H}[\{\mathsf{working}, \mathsf{broken}\}] \end{array}}$$

should suffice. For brevity, our representation of sensors does not deal with how the changes in sensor state are brought about either. Changes from working to broken are internal transitions, whereas those from broken to working take place following repairs. In other words, the former are nondeterministic in the nature of their occurrence and the latter occur as consequences of operations carried out by external agents. For convenience, let us define some useful predicates:

$$okSensor_t(s) \,\widehat{=}\, s : Sensor \mid s.sens\text{-}status_t = \mathsf{working}$$
$$faultySensor_t(s) \,\widehat{=}\, s : Sensor \mid s.sens\text{-}status_t = \mathsf{broken}$$

9.4.2 Behavioural Specification of the Controller

The safety of the system as a whole must anticipate the failure of the controller too. Unlike other equipment in the system, the number of failure modes of the controller, as well as their complexity, could be of a different scale altogether. Again, we adopt the simplest possible representation as given by:

$$\boxed{\begin{array}{l} \textit{Controller} \\ \hline \textit{cont-status} : \mathbb{H}[\{\mathsf{crash}, \mathsf{broken}\}] \end{array}}$$

and, as in the case of sensors, do not deal with how the possible state changes in this representation are brought about. Some useful predicates indicating whether the controller is working or is out of action are:

$$okController_t \,\widehat{=}\, Controller \mid cont\text{-}status_t = \mathsf{working}$$
$$failedController_t \,\widehat{=}\, Controller \mid cont\text{-}status_t = \mathsf{crash}$$

9.4.3 Behavioural Specification of Signals

Following the above discussion, a 'system view' of a signal consists of two separate views, one corresponding to the 'real' or the actual state of the signal and other being an 'internal image' of the former. Thus, a signal can be formally represented as:

$$Signal \,\widehat{=}\, \Box Signal^r; \Box Signal^i; Sensor \mid location^r = location^i$$

where the superscripts r and i identify, respectively, the state of the 'real' equipment and the state of its 'internal' representation. The additional predicate addresses the permanent aspects of the signal.

In specifying the safety requirements mentioned in Section 9.2.3 for any equipment, it is clear that they cannot be specified by considering the equipment concerned in isolation. However, let us consider initially the equipment of each different kind and the controller separately. We will return later to consider the interactions between all items of equipment as well as the services required.

When dealing with signals, we first consider the set of signals we are interested in and the controller. A suitable representation for this purpose is given by the schema:

$$
\begin{array}{|l}
\hline
\_SigSystem_____ \\
\quad Controller \\
\quad signals : \mathbb{F}\ Signal \\
\hline
\end{array}
$$

Under the normal operating conditions the expected behaviour must conform to the pattern given by:

$$
\begin{array}{|l}
\hline
\_SigSystem_{normal}_____ \\
\quad SigSystem \\
\hline
\quad \forall\, s \in signals;\ t : \mathbb{T} \bullet s.lamp_t^r = \mathsf{out} \Rightarrow s.aspect_t^r = \mathsf{unlit} \\
\quad \forall\, s \in signals;\ \theta_c : \bar{\varGamma}_c \bullet okController_{\theta_c} \wedge okSensor_{\theta_c}(s.Sensor) \Rightarrow \\
\qquad shadows(s.aspect^i, s.aspect^r, T_{com}^{sig}, \theta_c) \\
\hline
\end{array}
$$

The first predicate makes an obvious point; a signal on the ground does not show an aspect, i.e., it is unlit, if its lamp has failed. The second predicate makes a more technical point; it specifies the relationship between each signal and the controller. This is done with respect to the aspect as displayed on the real signal and the aspect as recorded in the system's internal representation. Since, by assumption, there are no failures, the aspect recorded in the internal representation must be, within limits, faithful to the external representation. The exact meaning of this has to be interpreted according to the definition of the predicate *shadows*, given in Section 9.2.1. T_{com}^{sig} is a timing parameter specific to signals.

We note the following conjecture as a possible consequence of the above specification:

$$
\forall\, s \in signals;\ \theta_c : \bar{\varGamma}_c \bullet okController_{\theta_c} \wedge okSensor_{\theta_c}(s.Sensor) \wedge
$$
$$
(s.aspect^r \neq s.aspect^i)_{\theta_c} \Rightarrow length(\theta_c) \leqslant T_{com}^{sig}
$$

According to the above, during all intervals of time longer than T_{com}^{sig}, the aspects in the two representations must be identical at some time within each interval, unless there is a failure either in the sensor or in the controller. The conjecture is left for the reader to validate.

The fail–soft behaviour of signals deals with situations involving failed sensors and is given by the specification

$$\begin{array}{|l}
\underline{\quad SigSystem_{failSoft}\ \underline{\hspace{6cm}}} \\
SigSystem \\
\hline
okController \wedge \forall\, s \in signals \bullet faultySensor(s.Sensor) \\
\qquad \textbf{requires}\ signalGreen(s.Signal^i)\ \textbf{within}\ T^{sig}_{sens\text{-}fail} \\
\end{array}$$

According to the above, the aspect recorded in the internal representation of every signal with a failed sensor must be green. The intention is to convey to the controller that such signals are to be treated as 'in use' and, thus, to prevent the controller allocating them to any route request made by the operator.

Fail–safe specification deals with scenarios in which the controller itself has failed. In this case, the specification requires that all signals revert to the safest possible state by displaying red and stay in that state as long as the controller remains failed.

$$\begin{array}{|l}
\underline{\quad SigSystem_{failSafe}\ \underline{\hspace{6cm}}} \\
SigSystem \\
\hline
faultyController \wedge \forall\, s \in signals \bullet okSensor(s.Sensor) \\
\qquad \textbf{requires}\ signalRed(s.Signal^a)\ \textbf{within}\ T^{sig}_{cont\text{-}fail} \\
\end{array}$$

$T^{sig}_{sens\text{-}fail}$ and $T^{sig}_{cont\text{-}fail}$ in the above specifications are timing parameters (unspecified here). Each specifies how quickly the relevant state should be brought about. In general, it is expected that this kind of response takes place 'immediately'. One way to achieve this to choose a sufficiently small value for the timing parameter, but this itself may not be sufficient. This is because the specification might allow, within the time interval concerned, events other than those required on safety grounds. This is not an aspect that can be addressed in our formalism, because it lacks the means to order events in such a way that, among the events possible at any instant, those concerned with safety have the highest priority and take place without failure.

9.4.4 Behavioural Specification of Points

Following the convention adopted when dealing with signals, a specification for points may be given as:

$$Point \,\hat{=}\, \Box Point^r;\ \Box Point^i;\ Sensor \mid trkSet^r = trkSet^i \wedge$$
$$normal^r = normal^i \wedge reverse^r = reverse^i$$

A representation for the set of points and the controller is given by the schema:

$$
\begin{array}{|l}
\hline
\_\,PtSystem\,\_\!\!\!\_ \\
\quad Controller \\
\quad points : \mathbb{F}\,Point \\
\hline
\end{array}
$$

Under the normal operating conditions the expected behaviour of *PtSystem* must conform with:

$$
\begin{array}{|l}
\hline
\_\,PtSystem_{normal}\,\_\!\!\_ \\
\quad PtSystem \\
\hline
\quad \forall\,p \in points;\ \theta_c : \bar{\Gamma}_c \bullet okController_{\theta_c} \wedge okSensor_{\theta_c}(p.Sensor) \Rightarrow \\
\qquad (p.setting^r_{\theta_c} \subseteq \{\mathsf{normalPos},\mathsf{reversePos}\} \Rightarrow \\
\qquad\qquad shadows(p.setting^i, p.setting^r, T^{pt}_{com}, \theta_c)) \\
\quad \forall\,p \in points;\ \theta_c : \bar{\Gamma}_c \bullet p.setting^i_{\theta_c} \cap \{\mathsf{normalPos},\mathsf{reversePos}\} = \varnothing \Rightarrow \\
\qquad p.setting^i_{\theta_c} \subseteq \{\mathsf{undetected},\mathsf{broken}\} \\
\quad \forall\,p \in points;\ \theta_c : \bar{\Gamma}_c \bullet p.setting^i_{\theta_c} \cap \{\mathsf{normalPos},\mathsf{reversePos}\} = \varnothing\ \wedge \\
\qquad length(\theta_c) > T^{max}_{pt} \Rightarrow \\
\qquad\qquad \exists\,\theta'_c, \theta''_c : \bar{\Gamma}_c \bullet length(\theta'_c) = T^{max}_{pt} \wedge \theta'_c\ starts\ \theta_c\ \wedge \\
\qquad\qquad \theta'_c\ meets\ \theta''_c \wedge \theta''_c\ finishes\ \theta_c \wedge p.setting^i_{\theta''_c} = \{\mathsf{broken}\} \\
\quad \forall\,p \in points;\ t : \mathbb{T} \bullet p.ptFixity^i_t = \mathsf{locked} \Rightarrow \\
\qquad p.setting^i_t \subseteq \{\mathsf{normalPos},\mathsf{reversePos}\} \\
\hline
\end{array}
$$

The axioms in the schema *Point* capture the temporal behaviour of points. The first axiom states that the internal representation of points follows the state of the actual points so long as the latter are in either normal or reverse position. The other two values in point settings are intended solely for use in the internal representation and are not relevant when dealing with the state of actual points. In this context, the second axiom states that whenever in the internal representation a point is not in either normal or reverse position then it must be recorded as being in the undetected position or as broken. The distinction between the two is made by the third axiom, according to which, as soon as the time limit T^{max}_{pt} on moving a point to an operational position expires without success, it is to be regarded in the internal representation as broken. The fourth axiom states that a point can be locked only in the normal or the reverse position.

The fail–soft state for points is the state in which they are broken since this would prevent the use of points with failed sensors. This is captured in the specification below.

PtSystem_failSoft
SigSystem

$okController \wedge \forall p \in points \bullet faultySensor(p.Sensor)$
requires $brokenPt(p.Point^i)$ **within** $T^{pt}_{sens\text{-}fail}$

Note that the settings of points have no significance from the safety point of view.

On the other hand, fail–safe requirements for points are such that all points are assumed to be locked so long as the controller remains in the failed state. Thus:

PtSystem_failSafe
PtSystem

$faultyController \wedge \forall p \in points \bullet okSensor(p.Sensor)$
requires $isLocked(p.Point^i)$ **within** $T^{pt}_{cont\text{-}fail}$

9.4.5 Behavioural Specification of Tracks

The specification for tracks may be based on:

$Tracks \mathrel{\widehat{=}} \Box\, Tracks^r;\ \Box\, Tracks^i;\ relays : Tid \nrightarrow Sensor\ |$
$\qquad tracks^r = tracks^i \wedge up^r = up^i \wedge down^r = down^i \wedge$
$\qquad bothDir^r = bothDir^i$

and

TrkSystem
Controller
Tracks

Under the normal operating conditions the expected behaviour of *TrkSystem* obeys the specification:

TrkSystem_normal
TrkSystem

$\forall tr \in tracks;\ \theta_c : \bar{\Gamma}_c \bullet okController_{\theta_c} \wedge okSensor_{\theta_c}(relays(tr))$

The highest risk state of a track is when it is occupied by a train. Therefore, should a track sensor fail, it is safer to assume the track in question is occupied. Thus, the fail–soft specification for tracks can be given as:

$$\boxed{\begin{array}{l} TrkSystem_{failSoft} \\[2pt] \hline TrkSystem \\[6pt] \hline okController \wedge \forall\, tr \in tracks \bullet faultySensor(relays(tr)) \\[4pt] \quad \textbf{requires } (occupancy^i(tr) = \text{occupied}) \textbf{ within } T^{trk}_{sens\text{-}fail} \end{array}}$$

On the other hand, there are no fail–safe requirements for tracks since they cannot be 'controlled' directly into any state.

9.5 Preventing and Averting Failures

Safety must address not only how to deal with on-going failures but also how to prevent failures and how to avert imminent failures.

The failure prevention measures considered here concern the circumstances that forbid a move from a low risk state to a high risk state. On the other hand, measures directed at averting imminent failures concern how to bring the system down swiftly from a high risk state to a low risk state. These safety requirements have been considered in general terms in Section 9.2.4. As stated there, the risk posed by different states of any equipment should not be assessed in isolation but in the context of the global system state. Thus, the risk should be examined in relation to: 1) overall system state, and 2) local states of equipment giving rise to extreme risks. The former either sanctions or forbids the transition while the latter determines local states posing different levels of risks.

These measures concern only the equipment which is in perfect working order, the behaviour of other equipment being addressed, as discussed in Sections 9.4.3–9.4.5, in a fail–safe or a fail–soft manner. As a consequence, it is unnecessary to make explicit below whether we are referring to the state of the real equipment and the state of its internal representation – the distinction made in Section 9.2.2. Therefore, as a simplification of the notation, we drop the decoration (superscript) i applied to state variables; they always refer to their values in the internal representation.

9.5.1 Low to High Risk State Transitions

Let us consider first the change of signals from red to either amber or green. Obviously, such a transition is sought in order to respond to a route request, which may be granted only after making sure of the overall safety. The requirements on overall safety may not be obvious from those written in natural language and the following is an interpretation of such a statement.

$$RouteSet_t(r) \overset{def}{\Leftrightarrow} isLockedRoute_t(r) \wedge r.exit.lamp_t = \text{in} \wedge$$
$$\forall\, tr : Tid \ \bullet \ tr \in r.routeTrks \Rightarrow tr.occupancy_t = \text{clear} \wedge$$
$$\forall\, p : Point \ \bullet \ p \in r.normalPts \Rightarrow p.setting_t = \text{normalPos} \wedge$$
$$\forall\, p : Point \ \bullet \ p \in r.reversePts \Rightarrow p.setting_t = \text{reversePos}$$

According to the above, a route is considered clear if and only if the route has been set by locking it, the signal at route exit is in working order, all tracks are clear and the points have been moved to their correct positions. Note that the predicate $\neg\, RouteSet_t(r)$ describes precisely the circumstances of a hazardous state. With this we may state the requirements on a safety action for setting the signal off to either **green** or **amber** from other possible values.

$$\neg\, RouteSet(r) \textbf{ prohibits } (signalGreen(r.entry) \vee signalAmber(r.entry))$$

The safety requirements on movements of points are more complex. The points are to be maintained locked in their correct positions during the passage of trains over any given route. Therefore, points are neither to be moved nor set free while a subroute passing over them remains locked or track sections where the points are located are occupied by a (stationary) train, resulting in what is called *dead–locking*. Let us formalise these circumstances separately.

The subroutes crossing over points and aligned with either the normal or the reverse point positions may be identified by means of the following predicates:

$$\forall\, Subroutes;\ s : Tid^2;\ p : Point\ \bullet$$
$$normalRunningSub_t(s,p) \stackrel{def}{\Leftrightarrow}$$
$$\quad s \in subRoutes \wedge p.setting_t = \mathsf{normalPos} \wedge midTrk(s) \in p.trkSet$$
$$reverseRunningSub_t(s,p) \stackrel{def}{\Leftrightarrow}$$
$$\quad s \in subRoutes \wedge p.setting_t = \mathsf{reversePos} \wedge midTrk(s) \in p.trkSet$$

where $midTrk$ is as defined in Section 9.3.5. The following predicate states whether a given point is, or is not, under the dead–locked condition because of the presence of a train above it.

$$DeadLocked_t(p) \stackrel{def}{\Leftrightarrow} \exists\, tr : Tid\ \bullet\ tr \in p.trkSet \wedge tr.occupancy_t = \mathsf{occupied}$$

The following two predicates establish whether any point is in a **locked** state by virtue of the fact that a subroute crossing the point is in a **locked** state:

$$\forall\, Routes;\ p : Point\ \bullet$$
$$NormalLockedSub_t(p) \stackrel{def}{\Leftrightarrow} \exists\, s : Tid^2\ \bullet\ \forall\, r : Route\ \bullet\ r \in routes\ \wedge$$
$$\quad normalRunningSub_t(s,p) \wedge isLockedSub_t(s)$$
$$ReverseLockedSub_t(p) \stackrel{def}{\Leftrightarrow} \exists\, s : Tid^2\ \bullet\ \forall\, r : Route\ \bullet\ r \in routes\ \wedge$$
$$\quad reverseRunningSub_t(s,p) \wedge isLockedSub_t(s)$$

Using the above predicates, it is possible to state formally the conditions under which the safety requirements on freeing points are violated either because of dead–locked points or locking imposed by route setting. Thus, it is forbidden to free points if the following condition prevails:

$Deadlocked(p) \lor NormalLockedSub(p)$ **prohibits** $isFreeNorPt(p)$
$Deadlocked(p) \lor ReverseLockedSub(p)$ **prohibits** $isFreeRevPt(p))$

Let us now turn our attention to subroutes. Changing subroute fixity from locked to free carries some risk because, as a consequence of any unwarranted freeing of subroutes, the points may be moved, potentially endangering any moving train, or damaging the points if the points are dead–locked by the presence of a train. Subroutes may be freed only if the route on which they lie and all preceding subroutes along the route are freed first.

$\forall Routes;\ r : Route;\ s : Tid^2 \bullet$

$clearRoute_t(r) \overset{def}{\Leftrightarrow} \forall tr \bullet tr \in routeTrks \Rightarrow tr.occupancy_t = \mathsf{clear}$
$safeToFreeFirstSub_t(r, s) \overset{def}{\Leftrightarrow}$
$\qquad\qquad isFreeRoute_t(r) \land clearRoute_r(r) \land s = r.firstSub$
$safeToFreeOtherSubs_t(r, s) \overset{def}{\Leftrightarrow} isFreeRoute_t(r) \land clearRoute_t(r) \land$
$\qquad\qquad s \in r.routeSubs \land isFreeSub_t(prevSub(s))$

The safety requirement on freeing subroutes is therefore:

$\forall r : Route;\ s : Tid^2 \bullet \neg\, (safeToFreeFirstSub(r, s) \lor$
$\qquad safeToFreeOtherSubs(r, s))$ **forbids** $isFreeSub(r, s)$

Let us now examine safety issues to be checked prior to locking a route. Firstly, none of the subroutes on the route must be locked for a route in the opposite direction. Secondly, the points along the route should not be locked.

$\forall Routes;\ r : Route \bullet$

$safeRoute(r) \overset{def}{\Leftrightarrow} (\neg \exists x : Route;\ s : Tid^2 \bullet s \in r.routeSubs^\sim \land$
$\qquad\qquad s \in x.routeSubs \land isLockedSub(x, s)) \land$
$\qquad\qquad (\forall p \bullet p \in r.normalPts \Rightarrow isFreeNorPt_t(p)) \land$
$\qquad\qquad (\forall p \bullet p \in r.reversePts \Rightarrow isFreeRevPt_t(p))$

If the above condition does not prevail, it is unsafe to lock a route. That is:

$\forall r : Route \bullet \neg\, safeRoute(r)$**prohibits** $isLockedRoute(r)$

9.5.2 High to Low Risk State Transitions

Transitions from high to low risk states may be motivated either by general strategic considerations to minimise risks, or by preparation for averting failures in the event of unforeseen hazards. More critical is the latter scenario, which invariably requires swift action on the part of safety monitoring agents. This means that such safety requirements necessarily involve timing constraints, usually in the form of deadlines. Let us again examine the change of signals, but from either amber or green to red.

$$\neg\, RouteSet(r) \text{ \textbf{requires} } signalOn(r.entry) \text{ \textbf{within} } T_{turn\text{-}red}$$

where $T_{turn\text{-}red}$ is the time limit for turning the signal at the entry to route r to the aspect red. An analogous safety assertion may be made with respect to points, obliging the controller to lock the points within a specified time limit if any of the points are found to be free while either a subroute over it remains locked or the point is effectively in a dead–locked condition. Thus,

$$(Deadlocked(p) \lor NormalLockedSub(p)) \land$$
$$isFreeNorPt_t(p) \text{ \textbf{requires} } LockNormal(p) \text{ \textbf{within} } t_{lock\text{-}pts}$$
$$(Deadlocked(p) \lor ReverseLockedSub(p)) \land$$
$$isFreeRevPt_t(p) \text{ \textbf{requires} } LockReverse(p) \text{ \textbf{within} } T_{lock\text{-}pts}$$

where $T_{lock\text{-}pts}$ is the time limit for locking the point p.

Concluding Remarks

This chapter has demonstrated an approach to the specification of safety features of realtime safety critical systems. Information on this approach may also be found in references [44, 42, 63]. Railway signalling, used here as an example, is a case study widely used in safety critical systems research, exhibiting a range of safety features found across many different applications. Obviously, such a specification requires a complementary functional specification. The behaviour of the system, therefore, has to be analysed under the requirements stated in both specifications.

Exercises

9.1 Below are descriptions of two safety critical scenarios. Review the safety requirements applicable to each, supplement them, if necessary, with any additional requirements, and formalise them using the approach presented in this chapter.

(a) *Radiation therapy machine*

Depending on the diagnosis of the patient under treatment, a radiation therapy machine can be used in one of two modes: electron mode or X–ray mode. Both use an electron beam, but differ in that the beam in X–ray mode is intercepted by a tungsten target in order to generate the X–rays. The machine can be used for treatment only in conjunction with a protection system intended to shield the operator and others from unwarranted radiation. The electron mode uses a low intensity beam and a low voltage, whereas the X–ray mode uses a high intensity beam and a high voltage. The intensity and voltage may be set independently of the mode selected, but because of potentially fatal consequences, turning the beam on with an incorrect setting for the selected mode is prevented by an interlocking system. Once the beam is turned on, the patient is exposed to the therapy for a preset duration: T_1 time units in the electron mode and T_2 time units in the X–ray mode. In order to minimise the risk, the settings are cancelled within T_3 time units after the therapy and the machine cannot be operated for T_4 time units after each cycle. As an added precautionary measure, a watchdog timer monitors the exposure times and, in the case of any violation, triggers the system to withdraw all the services and to shut itself down safely.

(b) *Industrial process control*

This safety critical application consists of a sensor monitoring a certain physical process and an actuator controlling its characteristics by regulating the flow of a coolant according to the sensor data. Although it is not the overriding objective, economical use of the coolant is an important concern in this application. The sensor samples the state of the process at regular intervals at a frequency of f Hz. When the system is functioning normally, the flow of coolant is increased or decreased by a certain amount, guided by the values read from the sensor. If necessary, the controlling system issues a control signal to the actuator within T_1 time units of receiving data from the sensor and the actuator obeys the instruction within T_2 time units. The sensor may, however, occasionally fail and the failure is detected by the controlling system through the irregularity of the sensor output. In this case, the control system abandons the objective of economising the coolant and starts providing the process with a predefined uniform flow of the coolant within T_3 time units of the detection to ensure safety. From then on the system makes no further use of the data provided by the sensor. Under its normal functioning mode the actuator regulates the flow as required. In the event of an actuator failure, that is when the actuator fails to obey an instruction issued by the controlling system within the permitted time, the controller simply shuts the system down within T_4 time units to ensure safety.

10. An Overview of VDM

This chapter presents an overview of the specification language known as the Vienna Development Method or VDM. The mathematical framework underlying it, and the domain of its application, are identical to that of Z and, as a result, there are remarkable similarities between the two languages. Our aim is to exploit these similarities to gain some familiarity, and a degree of competence, in VDM. Thus, our overview essentially compares and contrasts of some common syntactic features of VDM and Z with identical, or closely related, meanings.

Specifications in VDM exhibit a distinct style which makes the different aspects of the specification explicit. Although it is a subjective view, for various reasons, these stylistic differences may appeal to many practitioners. For example, thanks to the use of keywords based on English, it is easy to locate in a VDM specification the state invariant of a system, or the pre or postcondition of an operation. The language also makes explicit, very much like in a programming language, read and write access to different variables. These may not be of any material significance to many, but could help some to overcome the barrier posed by the more abstract mathematical symbolism of other specification languages.

10.1 Standard Mathematical Notation

This section considers the differences in notation as applicable to logic and set theory, and under the latter, a range of mathematical structures covering sets, relations and functions. For convenience, as well as for comparison, most of these differences are presented in tabular form.

10.1.1 A General Comment

First, here are some general notes on the notation. As mentioned in the prelude to this chapter, some of the notation in VDM is based on keywords borrowed from English. This book indicates these keywords with the textual font shown in pre. The symbol $\triangleq$ is identical to $\hat{=}$ in Z denoting syntactic equivalence and defines the term on its left with the expression on its right.

10.1.2 Logic

Major differences and similarities between the two languages with respect to logic are:

1. Propositional connectives
   VDM and Z do not distinguish between material and logical implications and thus use a single notation $\Rightarrow$ for both. The same applies to material and logical equivalences, the symbol used for them being $\Leftrightarrow$. Likewise, they share the same symbols for other propositional connectives.

2. Quantifiers
   Quantification in VDM has a simple and uniform syntax as in classical logic, but is typed as in Z. The examples below indicate the general syntax of quantified formulae in VDM and Z.

   $$\forall\, x, y : X \cdot p(x, y) \qquad\qquad\qquad - \text{VDM}$$
   $$\forall\, x, y : X;\; z : Y \mid q(x, y, z) \bullet p(x,\ y,\ z) \qquad - \text{Z}$$

   Note that $\exists!$ in VDM is the same as $\exists_1$ in Z and is used to quantify a unique object in a quantified formula.

3. Predicates
   See items 6 and 7 of Section 10.1.5.

10.1.3 Types

When dealing with different number systems, symbols such as $\mathbb{N}, \mathbb{N}_1, \mathbb{Z}, \mathbb{Q}$ and $\mathbb{R}$ are commonly encountered in both languages. Both languages also have an identical approach to introducing generic types, that is, types with potentially different interpretations of values or types without a formally defined representation for their values. Once formally introduced, types of other set theoretic origins such as the power set and Cartesian product may be defined in the usual manner. Table 10.1 presents some of the notational differences encountered when dealing with an arbitrary type T.

Table 10.1. Types and sets

Concept	VDM	Z
Generic types	T is not yet defined	$[T]$
Power set of T	$\mathcal{F}\ T$	$\mathbb{P}\ T$
Finite set of T	set of T	$\mathbb{F}\ T$
	T-set	
Functions and maps	(see below)	

10.1.4 Sets and Relations

The differences in the basic set theoretic notation are summarised in Table 10.2, S, S_1 and S_2 being some arbitrary sets of appropriate types.

Table 10.2. Sets (set theoretic operations) and relations

Concept	VDM	Z
Size (cardinality)	card S	$\#S$
Set theoretic operations	$\cup, \cap, -$ etc.	$\cup, \cap, -$ etc.
Symmetric set difference	$S_1 \diamond S_2$	$(S_1 \cup S_2) - (S_1 \cap S_2)$
Insertion of an element to a set; e.g. x to S	$x \oplus S$ (generator)	No equivalent notation
Relations	uses predicates only, (and that is using functions; see below)	uses predicates and sets.

10.1.5 Mathematical Functions

The treatment of mathematical functions in VDM is quite different from that in Z, as well as in traditional mathematics, although in this respect the differences between Z and traditional mathematics are insignificant. Because of the extent of the differences between VDM and Z, let us concentrate here on the distinctions that VDM makes in its treatment of functions.

VDM considers mathematical functions in terms of two different concepts: *function* and *map*. However, the underlying mathematical notion of associating a single value with each element in the domain is shared by both these new concepts. Note that the terms 'function' and 'mapping' are used as synonyms in mathematics, as well as in Z.

VDM Functions. In relation to its version of 'function', the following can be noted:

1. VDM functions imply a kind of a computation at the 'implementation level'.

   NOTE: The use of the word 'implementation' should not be misunderstood to mean that specification, design and implementation issues are mixed up in VDM.

2. VDM functions are defined only through an expression, or through an algorithm, and not by explicit enumeration of pairs of argument values and corresponding results (see 'maps' below).
3. VDM has no detailed classification of functions as in Z. For this reason, VDM has no extensive notation as in Z for identifying different types of function, such as bijective, surjective and so on. Therefore, it uses a uniform notation, namely → , in function type declarations.
4. VDM recognises the distinction between total and partial functions and, therefore, has a comprehensive theory of partial functions for dealing with situations when a function is not defined for certain values of its possible arguments.
5. The notation associated with VDM functions is given in Table 10.3.

Table 10.3. VDM functions

Concept	Notation
signature in function declaration	$f : X \rightarrow Y$
function application	$f(x)$
function abstraction using λ notation	$\lambda\, x \in X \bullet t$
conditional in function body	if ... then ... else
use of local variables in function definition	let $x = $ ... in ...

6. Function specification in VDM takes the form:

$$fun : X \times Y \rightarrow Z$$
$$fun\,(x, y)\ z : Z$$
$$\text{pre}\ \ p(x, y)$$
$$\text{post}\ \ q(x, y, z)$$

where x and y are the arguments of a function fun, z is the result returned by fun, p is a predicate specifying the permitted values of the arguments x and y, and q is a specification of the result z. The keywords pre and post make the role of p and q clear, in the usual terminology, as the pre and post conditions. As in Z, satisfaction of the precondition by the arguments ensures the correctness of the result with respect to the postcondition. Essentially, function specification in the above style is a way of specifying an algorithm as an input–output relation between the arguments and the result.
7. Predicates are also treated as (total) functions from appropriate domains to the domain $\mathbb{B}$ of Booleans. For example, a certain predicate named *pred* may be defined as:

$$pred : (X \times \ldots) \to \mathbb{B}$$
$$pred\ (x, \ldots)\ z : \mathbb{B}$$
$$\text{post } z \Leftrightarrow q(x, \ldots)$$

in the style of a function in terms of another predicate q involving variables x, ... etc.

VDM Maps. The following may be noted in relation to VDM 'maps':

1. At the implementation level 'map application' corresponds to retrieval of an already computed, or known, value from some (finite) data structure.
2. Maps are defined by explicit enumeration of pairs of values, or by map comprehension.
3. Operations associated with maps are similar to those of functions in Z. Except for a few exceptions, the notation is also similar. Table 10.4, which summarises this notation, uses M as a map, and A and B as sets, where necessary, with indices.

Table 10.4. VDM maps

Concept	Notation
signature in map declaration	$M = \mathsf{map}\ A \to B$, or
finite maps	$M\ :\ A \xrightarrow{m} B$
bi-directional (one-to-one) finite maps	$M : A \xleftrightarrow{m} B$
map application (M to x)	$M(x)$
empty map	$\{\mapsto\}$
generator	$\oplus$ (as in sets)
map enumeration	$\{a \mapsto b, c \mapsto e, f \mapsto d, \ldots\}$
map comprehension	$\{a \mapsto f(a) \mid predicate(a)\}$
domain	$\mathsf{dom}\ M$
range	$\mathsf{rng}\ M$
map merge (union)	$M_1 \overset{m}{\cup} M_2$
domain restriction (to the set A_1)	$A_1 \lhd M$
domain co-restriction (deletion)	$A_1 \ntriangleleft M$
range restriction (to the set B_1)	$M \rhd B_1$
range co-restriction (deletion)	$M \ntriangleright B_1$
map overwriting (M_1 by M_2)	$M_1 \dagger M_2$
composition (M_2 followed by M_1)	$M_1 \circ M_2$
iteration (n times)	$M_1 \uparrow n$

4. A map specification consists of a state specification and, depending on its use, may be accompanied by a specification of a set of appropriate operations. The state specification of a map in VDM has the general form:

$$M = A \xrightarrow{m} B$$

$$\text{inv } M(a) \triangleq predicate(a)$$

where inv introduces the predicate $predicate(a)$ as the invariant applicable to the map M, a being an arbitrary instance of the given map.

10.2 Specification of State Based Systems

10.2.1 Specification Structure

This section deals with the structure of VDM specifications for state based systems and the stylistic features which make it so distinct. As in Z, a specification consists of:

- The general state:
(1) The signature of each state variable
(2) The state invariant:
- For each operation:
(3) The signature of each input variable
(4) The signature of each output variable
(5) The state to be utilised, or affected, as an instance of the specification given above. The instance of the state specification is specified through a variable declared as an *external* variable having the same type as the general state. The declaration of an *external variable* is shown by the prefix ext. Alternatively, only a part of the state may be identified through a subset of the state variables. In this case, only the relevant state variables are declared in the external clause. Every external clause contains an extension for each variable: the extension Rd signifies that the variable concerned can be accessed in 'read only' mode, whereas the extension Wr that it can be accessed in 'both read and write' mode.
(6) A precondition on any input and external variables
(7) A postcondition potentially involving all variables, specifying the effect of the operation on the state
(8) Pre and post conditions of an operation may be referred to anywhere in the specification directly by prefixing, as appropriate, the operation name with either pre or post

- Initialisation:
  As in Z, initialisation is treated as a unique operation involving only one state, namely, the 'after state'. However, since no 'before state' is involved, the precondition of an initialisation specification may only refer to any inputs. The reader may also find in the literature two different styles of initialisation specification: as a predicate labelled by the keyword init under the state specification, or as a separate operation specification.

  NOTE: Analogously, termination of a system state can be defined as an operation with just a 'before state'.

- Exception handling:
  The required form of exception handling is specified through an errs clause in the operation specification.

10.2.2 A Comparison with Z

Tables 10.5 and 10.6 compare the general structure of specifications in VDM and Z. Note that in these tables st denotes an instance of a state S.

As Table 10.6 illustrates, in terms of presentation, operation specifications differ from state specifications to a greater extent. Note that the signature of operations in VDM ignores the fact that operations can have side effects on state variables.

10.3 Composite Objects

This section elaborates on some of the concepts mentioned in Table 10.5. A composite object is one with a number of fields taking values from specified domains. The names attached to these fields serve as selectors, or as accessor functions, each from the domain of the composite object to the domain of the relevant field. The selectors are generally used for reference to field values of concrete objects, using the selector name directly or as a function application to a concrete object.

The fields may also be referred to using a 'template' of variable names. A template is a way of decomposing an instance of a composite object into its components, but using named variables for referring to its different fields. As Table 10.5 shows, this is a device used in defining, for example, the state invariant. The same can be used in the specification of initialisation and other operations on the object concerned. A template can also be created using the so-called 'make function'.

The following notation applies to the specification, creation and modification of composite objects:

1. State model
   The state models of composite objects can be specified in several alternative ways, namely:

Table 10.5. Specification of general state

Concept	VDM	Z
Signature	Types of simple mathematical objects such as sets, maps, etc., are declared using the notations introduced earlier. In the case of composite objects, their constituents can be declared in several styles, one of them being: $$S :: x : A$$ $$y : B$$ $$z : C$$ In the above, S is the name of the composite object and expressions such as $y : B$ are field declarations.	Schema consisting of just the signature $\boxed{\begin{array}{l} S \\ \hline x : A \\ y : B \\ z : C \end{array}}$
Reference to constituents	1. In the case of an atomic object, any property described by a predicate is written as $pred(st)$, st being a variable denoting an arbitrary instance of the object concerned. 2. In the case of a composite object, a 'template' of variables written in the form (p, q, r) may be used. Alternatively, an instance of the object may be constructed using a 'make function'. Thus, mk-$S(p, q, r)$ constructs an object S with names of its components chosen as p, q and r. Both approaches are a way of decomposing an object into named components.	Directly using component names
Invariant	The signature is extended through a special clause, the following being the alternative forms: $$\text{inv-}S(p, q, r) \;\triangleq\; pred(p, q, r)$$ $$\text{inv}(\text{mk-}S(p, q, r)) \;\triangleq\; pred(p, q, r)$$ $$\text{inv } S(p, q, r) \;\triangleq\; pred(p, q, r)$$ which uses the keywords inv and mk.	Schema predicate $pred(x, y, z)$ as in $\boxed{\begin{array}{l} S \\ \hline x : A \\ y : B \\ z : C \\ \hline pred(x, y, z) \end{array}}$

Table 10.6. Specification of operations

Concept	VDM	Z
When modifying a state	ext Wr $st : S$	ΔS
When querying a state	ext Rd $st : S$	ΞS
	ext clause may identify only those state variables that need to be accessed by the operation.	
inputs and outputs	OP-NAME$(x:X)y:Y$	OP-NAME is the name of the operation schema
x – input		$x? : X$ in the schema signature
y – output		$y! : Y$ in the schema signature
operation signature in functional style	OP-NAME $: X \xrightarrow{o} Y$	
if no outputs	OP-NAME $: X \xrightarrow{o}$ OP-NAME $: X \xrightarrow{o} ()$	
if neither inputs nor outputs	OP-NAME $: () \xrightarrow{o}$ OP-NAME $: () \xrightarrow{o} ()$	
Predicates characterising the transformation	through two separate predicates labelled by keywords pre and post.	a single (composite) predicate linking state variables of 'before' and 'after' states, inputs and outputs.
Reference to 'before state' in the precondition	st	st
Reference to 'before state' in the postcondition	$\overleftarrow{st}$	st
Reference to 'after state' in the postcondition	st	st'
Reference to the precondition (or the postcondition) of an operation	By prefixing pre-(or post-) to the operation name	By applying the schema operators 'pre' (or 'post') to the operation schema
Exception handling	inclusion of clause errs $\langle$predicate$\rangle \rightarrow \langle$output$\rangle$ in the operation specification	A separate schema for each exception. A total operation is defined as the disjunction of primary operation and exception handling operations

(a) $\langle StateName \rangle :: \langle selector_1 \rangle : \langle FieldDomain_1 \rangle$
$\langle selector_2 \rangle : \langle FieldDomain_2 \rangle$
$\ldots\ldots$ $\vdots \ldots\ldots$

(b)   state $\langle StateName \rangle$ of
$\langle selector_1 \rangle : \langle FieldDomain_1 \rangle$
$\langle selector_2 \rangle : \langle FieldDomain_2 \rangle$
$\ldots\ldots$ $\vdots \ldots\ldots$
end

(c) $\langle StateName \rangle$ = compose $\langle StateName \rangle$ of
$\langle selector_1 \rangle : \langle FieldDomain_1 \rangle$
$\langle selector_2 \rangle : \langle FieldDomain_2 \rangle$
$\ldots\ldots$ $\vdots \ldots\ldots$
end

EXAMPLE 10.1 A composite object intended for recording the details of a person is:

$Name$ is not yet defined
$Date$ is not yet defined
$Person :: first\text{-}name : Name$
$surname \quad : Name$
$birthday \quad : Date$

$\heartsuit$

2. Make function
The so–called 'make function' of any composite object is represented by the symbol mk. It is used as a prefix to the name of the state model. The result is an arbitrary instance of the composite object concerned, with variables specified as arguments to the make function designating the components of the state model. The variables thus introduced may be used in predicates defining the state invariant, specification of operations, etc. On the other hand, if concrete (specific) values are used instead of variables, the make function results in a concrete instance of the composite object.

EXAMPLE 10.2 An invariant that may be applicable to the definition of $Person$ given in Example 10.1 is:

$\text{inv}(\text{mk-}Person(x, y, d)) \triangleq x \neq y$

x, y and d being variables denoting arbitrary but type compatible values. By contrast:

$lady\text{-}next\text{-}door = \text{mk-}Person(\text{Jane}, \text{Smith}, \text{12-Apr-70})$

with Jane, Smith and 12-Apr-70 denoting concrete values, may be used as a representation of a specific individual.   ♡

3. μ notation

This is a function which takes a specified instance of a composite object and a list of maplets (shown by $\mapsto$) from selectors to values, and modifies the values in the relevant fields to the newly specified values.

EXAMPLE 10.3 Changing the surname of the person represented by *lady-next-door* to Oakley may be achieved as follows:

$$a\text{-}married\text{-}lady = \mu(lady\text{-}next\text{-}door, surname \mapsto \mathsf{Oakley})$$
$$= \mathsf{mk}\text{-}Person(\mathsf{Jane}, \mathsf{Oakley}, \mathsf{12\text{-}Apr\text{-}70})$$

♡

10.4 Musical Chairs - An Example

This example illustrates the structure of a basic VDM specification. It is basic in the sense that the system is defined in terms of a single primitive state without identifying subsystems within it.

Refer to our earlier case study in Section 4.2 for an informal problem specification of this party game. Section 10.4.5 presents a formalisation of it in VDM in the form of a specification of a complete module, referred to as *Musical-Chairs*.

NOTE: For reasons of brevity, the narrative in this example is limited to an outline of linguistic features. The reader may treat this as an opportunity to provide his own interpretation.

10.4.1 State Model

A definition of the system state model of the game is given in lines 1.0–4.6 of the module *Musical-Chairs*; see Section 10.4.5. Lines 1.0-2.0 introduce two basic types *Player* and *Chairs* without formally giving any information about their representation; this point is emphasised by the keyword is not yet defined. *Report* in line 3.0 is another type used in the specification and denotes the set of output messages; its values will be enumerated later in the course of operation specification. The lines of 4. series introduce a formal representation of the game in terms of three state variables. The state variables *pl* and *ch* are, respectively, subsets of two sets *Player* and *Chair*. Their informal interpretation is clear from the names chosen. The third state variable, *occupiers*, is a bi-directional map, an injective function in the usual terminology (as in Z), from *Chair* to *Player*. It records the seating of players in chairs.

The state invariant in lines 4.4-4.5 expresses the interrelationships to be exhibited always by the state variables. It uses three distinct variable names, different from the selector names in the state model, to serve as a template. Obviously, this usage only makes sense if the order of variables listed in the template and in the state model are the same. The predicate on the right-hand side of $\triangleq$ constrains the values of the state variables as required by the informal specification.

10.4.2 Initialisation

Although initialisation specification can take, analogous to the invariant, the form of a predicate, we have chosen to specify it in this case as an operation. This is because of our decision to represent the parameters of the game, that is, values of state variables such as the number of players and chairs in a given setting, as inputs, so that these values can be altered with each game.

Lines of 5. series specifies the desired initialisation operation on the state of the game. According to the signature in line 5.0, the initialisation operation INIT takes a pair of inputs, a set from *pl*-set and another set from *ch*-set, and outputs a value through the variable *result* for reporting any error. Line 5.1 introduces the names of input variables to be used, alongside the state variables, in writing the precondition, the postcondition and the exception handling predicate. With the keyword wr for 'read and write access', lines 5.2-5.4 highlight the state variables, the values of which could be affected by this operation, in this case potentially those of the whole system. The input values must satisfy the precondition in line 5.5, whereas line 5.6 specifies the effect of initialisation on the state variables. The value of the output is defined by the predicate attached to a labelled error handling clause in lines 5.7-5.9.

10.4.3 Other Operations

Each round of the game consists of three sub operations: PLAY-MUSIC, STOP-MUSIC and ELIM-LOSER. PLAY-MUSIC defines the effect of playing music at the start of each round on the state of the game, STOP-MUSIC the immediate effect of stopping music on the state and, finally, ELIM-LOSER reconfiguration of the state following STOP-MUSIC in preparation for the next round. Obviously, there is a need for another operation in order to describe what happens when the game terminates; this has been left as an exercise for the reader.

The operations PLAY-MUSIC, STOP-MUSIC and ELIM-LOSER are specified respectively in lines of 6., 7. and 8. series. As discussed in Section 10.4.4, the lines in 9. series combine these suboperations, by a kind of composition, into a single operation PLAY-ROUND.

According to line 6.0, PLAY-MUSIC has neither inputs nor outputs and affects only the state variable *occupiers*. The postcondition in line 6.4 states the actual effect. In the representation this amounts to *occupiers* becoming the empty map, but in our abstraction to the state in which nobody is occupying a chair. The operation can fail if the precondition in line 6.3 is not satisfied, in which case the error clause in line 6.5 specifies the message to be output.

The operation STOP-MUSIC has access to all three state variables, but write access is restricted to *occupiers*. The operation has an output, which takes a value either from *Player* or *Report*, depending on whether the precondition is satisfied or violated. The latter case is handled by two possible error messages specified in lines 7.7-7.10. The postcondition states the value of the latter after the operation, as well as that of the output *result*, if the precondition is satisfied. As a result, if the operation succeeds, every chair in the given round will be occupied by exactly one player and the player left without a chair will be earmarked for elimination.

The operation ELIM-LOSER has an input, named as *loser* to mean that it stands for the player to be eliminated in the given round following STOP-MUSIC. It also has an output *result* and may modify all three state variables. The precondition in line 8.5 states that the input *loser* must be an element of the value of *pl* prior to the operation and that all chairs are occupied. The error clause in line 8.7 defines the value of the output in the event of the input not satisfying the precondition. The postcondition in line 8.6 specifies the values of *pl*, *ch* and, implicitly, *occupiers* after the operation is performed. The player identified as *loser* is eliminated from the game and the number of chairs is reduced by one. However, the specification does not forbid replacing chairs with other chairs, if necessary.

10.4.4 Execution Order of Operations

As was mentioned above, the operation PLAY-ROUND makes explicit how each round of the game should be played, in effect, the order of the three suboperations PLAY-MUSIC, STOP-MUSIC and ELIM-LOSER. This is expressed in the postcondition of PLAY-ROUND in lines 9.6-9.15.

Note the prefixing of operation names, as in pre-STOP-MUSIC and post-PLAY-MUSIC, to refer to the precondition or the postcondition of a given operation. Note also the use of variables as 'parameters' of these predicates in order to refer to inputs, the values of state variables in the before and, if appropriate, after states so extracted, and also to any output. In the case of any state variable with 'read only' access, only one instance of the variable appears as a parameter, whereas in the case of any state variable with both 'read and write' access, both the old instance (in the 'before' state) and the new instance (in the 'after' state) appear as parameters.

Being a formula in predicate logic, due to commutativity of some propositional connectives, the order of appearance of post-PLAY-MUSIC, pre-STOP-MUSIC, etc., in the postcondition cannot have any significance with respect to the actual permitted execution order of these operations. The desired execution order of these operations has to be expressed using 'templates of variables' as 'slots of connectors'.

In post-ELIM-LOSER(res-$stop$, $\overleftarrow{pl}$, pl, $\overleftarrow{ch}$, ch, occ-$stop$, $occupiers$, $result$), the predicate in lines 9.14-9.15, res-$stop$ denotes the input to ELIM-LOSER, $\overleftarrow{pl}$ and pl refer to the value of first state variable in the before and after states respectively, $\overleftarrow{ch}$ and ch to the value of the second state variable in the before and after states, and the last variable $result$ to the output of the operation. The values of the state variables, such as $\overleftarrow{pl}$ and pl, in the before and after states of ELIM-LOSER, as well as the existentially quantified variables such as occ-$music$ and occ-$stop$, have been used in the appropriate place to instantiate the pre and post conditions of the intermediate suboperations PLAY-MUSIC, STOP-MUSIC and ELIM-LOSER. As it is supposed to express the required order, the order of instantiation of the formal parameters of the different suboperations is important.

10.4.5 VDM Specification of Musical Chairs

module *Musical-Chairs*

definitions

types

1.0   *Player* is not yet defined;

2.0   *Chair* is not yet defined;

3.0   *Report* = ...   — see operation specifications below

4.0   state *Musical-Chairs* of
.1 $pl : Player$-set
.2 $ch : Chair$-set
.3 $occupiers : Chair \xleftrightarrow{m} Player$
.4   inv *Musical-Chairs*(p, c, o) $\triangleq$
.5   card p = card $c + 1 \wedge c \neq \{\,\} \wedge$ dom $o \subseteq c \wedge$ rng $o \subseteq p$
.6   end

operations

5.0   INIT : $Player$-set $\times$ $Chair$-set $\xrightarrow{o}$ $Report$
.1   INIT (p, c) $result : Report$
.2   ext wr pl : $Player$-set
.3   wr ch : $Chair$-set
.4   wr $occupiers$: $Chair \xleftrightarrow{m} Player$

.5	pre card p = card $c + 1 \wedge c \neq \{\}$
.6	post $pl = p \wedge ch = c \wedge occupiers = \{\mapsto\}$
.7	errs NUMBERS-WRONG :
.8	card $p \neq$ card $c + 1 \vee c = \{\} \rightarrow$
.9	$result =$ 'Wrong number of players or chairs, or no chairs!';

6.0	PLAY-MUSIC : () $\xrightarrow{o}$ ()
.1	PLAY-MUSIC ()
.2	ext wr $occupiers : Chair \xleftrightarrow{m} Player$
.3	pre card $pl > 1$
.4	post $occupiers = \{\mapsto\}$
.5	errs NO-PLAYERS : card $pl \leqslant 1 \rightarrow result =$ 'Not enough players!';

7.0	STOP-MUSIC : () $\xrightarrow{o} Player \mid Report$
.1	STOP-MUSIC () $result : Player \mid Report$
.2	ext rd pl : $Player$-set
.3	rd ch : $Chair$-set
.4	wr $occupiers : Chair \xleftrightarrow{m} Player$
.5	pre card $pl > 1 \wedge occupiers = \{\mapsto\}$
.6	post dom $occupiers = ch \wedge result \in pl -$ rng $occupiers$
.7	errs NO-PLAYERS :
.8	card $pl \leqslant 1 \rightarrow result =$ 'Players have disappeared!'
.9	SEAT-OCCUPIED :
.10	$occupiers \neq \{\mapsto\} \rightarrow result =$ 'Some players already sitting!';

8.0	ELIM-LOSER : $Player \xrightarrow{o} Report$
.1	ELIM-LOSER ($loser$) $result : Report$
.2	ext wr pl : $Player$-set
.3	wr ch : $Chair$-set
.4	wr $occupiers : Chair \xleftrightarrow{m} Player$
.5	pre $loser \in pl \wedge$ dom $occupiers = ch$
.6	post $pl = \overleftarrow{pl} - \{loser\} \wedge$ card $ch =$ card $\overleftarrow{ch} - 1$
.7	errs AN-OUTSIDER : $loser \notin pl \rightarrow result =$ 'An outsider!'
.8	EMPTY-CHAIR :
.9	dom $occupiers \neq ch \rightarrow result =$ 'Not all chairs occupied!';

9.0	PLAY-ROUND : $\xrightarrow{o} Report$
.1	PLAY-ROUND () $result : Report$
.2	ext wr pl : $Player$-set
.3	wr ch : $Chair$-set
.4	wr $occupiers : Chair \xleftrightarrow{m} Player$
.5	pre true

.6   post $\exists$ *occ-music* ·

.7   post-PLAY-MUSIC($\overleftarrow{occupiers}$, *occ-music*) $\wedge$

.8   pre-STOP-MUSIC($\overleftarrow{pl}$, $\overleftarrow{cl}$, *occ-music*) $\wedge$

.9 $\exists$ *occ-stop*, *res-stop* ·

.10   post-STOP-MUSIC($\overleftarrow{pl}$, $\overleftarrow{ch}$, *occ-music*,

.11   *occ-stop*, *res-stop*) $\wedge$

.12   pre-ELIM-LOSER(*res-stop*, $\overleftarrow{pl}$,

.13 $\overleftarrow{ch}$, *occ-stop*) $\wedge$

.14   post-ELIM-LOSER(*res-stop*, $\overleftarrow{pl}$, *pl*, *ch*,

.15   *ch*, *occ-stop*, *occupiers*, *result*)

.16   errs A-REAL-PROBLEM : (. . . not covered . . .)

end *Musical-Chairs*

10.5 An Indexed Filing System – A Case Study

One of the objectives of this case study is to illustrate features in VDM that enable the modular and hierarchical construction of specifications. Obviously, it relies on the experience gained in the previous example in Section 10.4 in defining simple states and operations on them. The case study is inspired by an analogous one given in Hayes [23] written in Z. The reader may therefore benefit from studying this section in conjunction with the latter work.

Section 10.5.1 outlines the requirements of the system informally. A complete specification of an indexed filing system in VDM is given in Sections 10.5.4, 10.5.5 and 10.5.7. Sections 10.5.2, 10.5.3, 10.5.5 and 10.5.6 provide a brief narrative explaining the different aspects of the specification.

10.5.1 An Informal Description of Requirements

In indexed files, information is kept as individual records against keys, the latter serving as a mechanism for retrieving records. This study considers four different operations for manipulating individual files: READ to read the record stored against a given key, WRITE to write a new record against an existing key, ADD to write a new record against a new key and, finally, DELETE to delete the record against an existing key.

At the system level, files are kept as named files. The above file operations can be performed only on files which are first opened using a system operation called OPEN. Other operations that can be invoked at the system level are: CLOSE to close an opened file, CREATE to create a new but empty file in the file store and REMOVE to remove a named file from the file store.

10.5.2 System Organisation

Obviously, it is unnecessary at the system level to know how individual file operations are performed. What is necessary at this level is the knowledge of services provided at the individual file level and, as a consequence, the kind of information required to invoke individual file operations on one hand and, on the other, the kind of information returned by the services offered at the individual file level. This suggests the appropriateness of considering two largely independent modules: *IndexedFile* and *FileSys*. The former, described in Section 10.5.3, deals with services offered at the individual file level, while the latter, described in Section 10.5.6, deals with the services provided at the system level.

10.5.3 Model of Individual Files

It follows from the outline given in Section 10.5.1 that, mathematically speaking, an indexed file can be viewed as a finite map from keys to records. Let us use the symbols *Key* and *Record* to refer to the sets of values (types) underlying this mathematical structure. As they can take many different forms in practice, the types *Key* and *Record* can be left undefined for the moment. Another type used in operation specifications, but not defined formally here, is *File-report*, which informally stands for all possible strings of characters used for error messages. Lines 1.0-3.0 in the module *IndexedFile* introduce these as types to be defined later.

The decomposition of the system into the modules *IndexedFile* and *FileSys* requires an understanding of the form of exchange of information between them. With this in mind, the specification introduces, in line 4.0, a composite type *File-op-type* and, in line 9.0, another composite type *File-result*. These take the form:

$$File\text{-}op\text{-}type = Read \mid Write \mid Add \mid Delete$$

$$File\text{-}result = Record \mid File\text{-}report$$

Each element of *File-op-type* is an abstract and, generally speaking, composite object consisting of actual parameters relevant to a given operation. Therefore, each of the types *Read, Write, Add* and *Delete* in *File-op-type* is defined in turn as a record structure; see lines 5.0-8.0. The intention is that the module *FileSys* uses an element of *File-op-type* each time it invokes an operation supported by the module *IndexedFile*. On the other hand, *File-result* consists of the basic types *Record* and *File-report*. Note that these types of value are used only for defining the communication interface between the two modules.

The complete functionality at the level of files is expressed in the specification of the module *IndexedFile* given in Section 10.5.4. Lines 10.0-10.3 define the representation of each individual file as a mapping from *Key* to *Record*. Line 10.3, which is an initialisation specification written in the form of a single predicate, makes the obvious point that all files are initially empty. The specifications of the file operations READ, WRITE, ADD and DELETE are given in lines of 11., 12., 13. and 14. series, and hardly require any explanation.

The operation FILE-OP defined in lines of 15. series integrates the above four operations into a single operation. It achieves this by using a case statement. Obviously, this is a construct borrowed from programming languages and has no direct counterpart in Z. However, it is possible to express the same as a conjunction of implications in Z. Note how the required postcondition is achieved by pointing to the postcondition of the relevant file operation with the prefix post. Each postcondition so prefixed has a list of parameters, consisting of the formal arguments appearing in the specification of the operation concerned, state variables listed in the specification as external parameters under ext clause, and any output. Note that this list of variables contains only one instance of any 'read only' variable, but both the old and new instances of any variable with both 'read and write' access.

10.5.4 VDM Specification of Indexed Files

module *IndexedFile*

definitions

types

1.0	*Key* is not yet defined;
2.0	*Record* is not yet defined;
3.0	*File-result* is not yet defined; — see op. specifications below
4.0	*File-op-type* = *Read*	*Write*	*Add*	*Delete*;
5.0	*Read* :: *key* : *Key* ;
6.0	*Write* :: *key* : *Key*
.1	*record* : *Record* ;
7.0	*Add* :: *key* : *Key*
.1	*record* : *Record* ;
8.0	*Delete* :: *key* : *Key* ;
9.0	*File-result* = *Record*	*File-report*

10.0	state *File* of
.1	*file* : *Key* $\xrightarrow{m}$ *Record*

.2   init $File(f) \triangleq f = \{\mapsto\}$

.3   end

operations

11.0   READ : $Key \xrightarrow{o} File\text{-}result$

.1   READ (key) $result : File\text{-}result$

.2   ext rd $file : Key \xrightarrow{m} Record$

.3   pre $key \in \text{dom } file$

.4   post $result = file(key)$

.5   errs UNKNOWN-RECORD :

.6 $key \notin \text{dom } file \rightarrow result = \ 'Key\ not\ in\ file!';$

12.0   WRITE : $Key \times Record \xrightarrow{o} File\text{-}report$

.1   WRITE (key, rec) $result : File\text{-}report$

.2   ext wr $file : Key \xrightarrow{m} Record$

.3   pre $key \in \text{dom } file$

.4   post $file = \overleftarrow{file} \dagger \{key \mapsto rec\} \wedge result = \ 'Done!'$

.5   errs UNKNOWN-RECORD :

.6 $key \notin \text{dom } file \rightarrow result = \ 'Key\ not\ in\ file!';$

13.0   ADD : $Key \times Record \xrightarrow{o} File\text{-}report$

.1   ADD (key, rec) $result : File\text{-}report$

.2   ext wr $file : Key \xrightarrow{m} Record$

.3   pre $key \notin \text{dom } file$

.4   post $file = \overleftarrow{file} \cup \{key \mapsto rec\} \wedge result = \ 'Done!'$

.5   errs EXISTING-RECORD :

.6 $key \in \text{dom } file \rightarrow result = \ 'Existing\ key!';$

14.0   DELETE : $Key \xrightarrow{o} File\text{-}report$

.1   DELETE (key) $result : File\text{-}report$

.2   ext wr $file : Key \xrightarrow{m} Record$

.3   pre $key \in \text{dom } file$

.4   post $file = \{key\} \vartriangleleft \overleftarrow{file} \wedge result = \ 'Done!'$

.5   errs UNKNOWN-RECORD :

.6 $key \notin \text{dom } file \rightarrow result = \ 'Key\ not\ in\ file!';$

15.0   FILE-OP : $File\text{-}op\text{-}type \xrightarrow{o} File\text{-}result$

.1   FILE-OP $(f\text{-}op)$ $result : File\text{-}result$

.2   ext wr $file : Key \xrightarrow{m} Record$

.3		post cases f-op :	
.4		$Read(key)$	$\rightarrow$ post-READ$(key, file, result)$,
.5		$Write(key, rec)$	$\rightarrow$ post-WRITE$(key, rec, \overleftarrow{file}, file, result)$,
.6		$Add(key, rec)$	$\rightarrow$ post-ADD$(key, rec, \overleftarrow{file}, file, result)$,
.7		$Delete(key)$	$\rightarrow$ post-DELETE$(key, \overleftarrow{file}, file, result)$
.8		end	

end $IndexedFile$

10.5.5 Model of the Module Interface

A specification of the module interface is given below. It includes all entities defining the module structure, entities the given module relies on but defined elsewhere in other modules and, finally, the services offered by the given module. These categories of entities appear in the interface specification under three headings: parameters (lines 16.0-18.3), imports (lines 19 and 20) and exports (lines 21 and 22).

From the point of any user module, which in this case is the module $FileSys$, the most important part of the interface is the items listed under export clause and contains file operations visible outside the module $IndexedFile$. Thus, according to line 22.0, user modules can use only the generalised operation FILE-OP, although the information specific to a required operation is provided to $IndexedFile$ in the form of a data item permitted by the type $File$-op-$type$ in line 21.0.

module $IndexedFile$

parameters

types

16.0	$Read :: key \quad : Key$
.1	$Write :: key \quad : Key$
.2	$record : Record$
.3	$Write :: key \quad : Key$
.4	$record : Record$
.5	$Delete :: key \quad : Key$

17.0	values $file : Key \xrightarrow{m} Record$

18.0	operations READ $: Key \xrightarrow{o} File$-$result$;
.1	WRITE, ADD $: Key \times Record \xrightarrow{o} File$-$report$;
.2	DELETE $: Key \xrightarrow{o} File$-$report$;
.3	FILE-OP $: File$-op-$type \xrightarrow{o} File$-$result$

imports

19.0	types $Key, Record$

20.0   values $file : Key \xrightarrow{m} Record$

        exports

21.0   types $File\text{-}op\text{-}type, Read, Write, Add, Delete, File, File\text{-}report$

22.0   operations FILE-OP : $File\text{-}op\text{-}type \xrightarrow{o} File\text{-}result$

        end $IndexedFile$

10.5.6 Model of the Filing System

Section 10.5.7 specifies the filing system as a separate module, but relying on the services provided by the module $IndexedFile$. In lines 3.0 and 4.0 it introduces two more basic types: $Name$ for file names and $Sys\text{-}report$ for system level messages. Lines 5.0-7.0 make explicit the services imported from the module $IndexedFile$, including the types $File\text{-}report$ and $File$. Lines 8.0-9.2, on the other hand, make explicit the services that the users of the module $FileSys$ can expect. Types such as Key and $Record$ are listed in line 8.0 as a reminder that the module must supply this information to the module $IndexedFile$.

Lines of 10. series formalise the general state of the filing system. It uses a mapping named $files$ from $Name$ to $File$ as a representation for the file store, but also maintains a subset $open$ of $Name$ as a record of files in the opened state at any given instance. Line 10.3 captures the system invariant that only the files in the file store can be opened. The initialisation specification given in line 10.4 forces both state variables of $FileSys$ to be empty initially.

Lines of series 11.-14. define the system level operations for manipulating files as complete entities, that is, the operations OPEN, CLOSE, CREATE and REMOVE. These are again fairly simple specifications and require little explanation. A point to note, however, is how the initialisation specification of $File$ is utilised in CREATE to define the state of files at the point of their creation; see lines 13.4-13.5.

The operation SYS-FILE-OP, defined in lines of 15. series, is a more complex operation. Using the generalised file operation FILE-OP on individual files, it integrates the services provided by the module $IndexedFile$ at the file system level. This is achieved by invoking FILE-OP but with an actual argument represented by an element of $File\text{-}op\text{-}type$.

The specification is still inadequate for dealing with multiple users etc. The reader is encouraged to extend the above definition in order to capture other desirable requirements and features.

10.5.7 VDM Specification of the Indexed Filing System

module *FileSys*

definitions

types

1.0   *Key* is not yet defined;

2.0   *Record* is not yet defined;

3.0   *Sys-report* is not yet defined;

4.0   *Name* is not yet defined

imports

5.0   from *IndexedFile*

6.0   types *File-op-type, Read, Write, Add, Delete, File, File-report*

7.0   operations FILE-OP

exports

8.0   types *Name, Key, Record, File-report*

9.0   operations OPEN, CLOSE, CREATE, REMOVE: $Name \xrightarrow{o} File\text{-}report$;

.1   SYS-FILE-OP : $File\text{-}op\text{-}type \times Name \xrightarrow{o}$

.2 $File\text{-}result \mid Sys\text{-}report$

10.0   state *FileSys* of

.1   *files* : $Name \xrightarrow{m} File$

.2   *open* : *Name*-set

.3   inv $FieSys(fs, op) \triangleq op \subseteq \text{dom } fs$

.4   init $Filesys(fs, op) \triangleq fs = \{\mapsto\} \wedge op = \{\}$

.5   end

operations

11.0   OPEN : $Name \xrightarrow{o} Sys\text{-}report$

.1   OPEN $(f\text{-}name)$ $result : Sys\text{-}report$

.2   ext wr *open* : *Name*-set

.3   rd *files* : $Name \xrightarrow{m} File$

.4   pre $f\text{-}name \notin open \wedge f\text{-}name \in \text{dom } files$

.5   post $open = \overleftarrow{open} \cup \{f\text{-}name\} \wedge result = {}'Ok'$

.6   errs ALREADY-OPENED :

.7 $f\text{-}name \in open \rightarrow result = {}'File\ already\ opened!'$

.8   UNKNOWN-FILE :

.9 f-name $\notin$ dom files $\rightarrow$ result $=$ $'Unknown\ file!'$;

12.0   CLOSE : $Name \overset{o}{\rightarrow} Sys\text{-}report$

.1   CLOSE $(f$-name$)$ result : $Sys\text{-}report$

.2   ext wr open : $Name$-set

.3   pre f-name $\in$ open

.4   post open $= \overleftarrow{open} - \{f\text{-}name\} \land$ result $=$ $'Ok'$

.5   errs NOT-OPEN :

.6 f-name $\notin$ open $\rightarrow$ result $=$ $'File\ is\ not\ opened!'$;

13.0   CREATE : $Name \overset{o}{\rightarrow} Sys\text{-}report$

.1   CREATE $(f$-name$)$ result : $Sys\text{-}report$

.2   ext wr files : $Name \overset{m}{\rightarrow} File$

.3   pre f-name $\notin$ dom files

.4   post $\exists file \cdot$ init-$File(file) \land$

.5   files $= \overleftarrow{files} \overset{m}{\cup} \{f\text{-}name \mapsto file\} \land$ result $=$ $'Ok'$

.6   errs FILE-EXISTS :

.7 f-name $\in$ dom files $\rightarrow$ result $=$ $'File\ already\ exists!'$;

14.0   REMOVE : $Name \overset{o}{\rightarrow} Sys\text{-}report$

.1   REMOVE $(f$-name$)$ result : $Sys\text{-}report$

.2   ext wr files : $Name \overset{m}{\rightarrow} File$

.3   rd open : $Name$-set

.4   pre f-name $\in$ dom files $\land$ f-name $\notin$ open

.5   post files $= \{f\text{-}name\} \vartriangleleft \overleftarrow{files} \land$ result $=$ $'Ok'$

.6   errs FILE-NON-EXISTENT :

.7 f-name $\notin$ dom files $\rightarrow$ result $=$ $'File\ does\ not\ exist!'$

.8   FILE-OPEN :

.9 f-name $\in$ open $\rightarrow$ result $=$ $'File\ in\ use!'$;

15.0   SYS-FILE-OP : $Name \times File\text{-}op\text{-}type \overset{o}{\rightarrow} File\text{-}result \mid Sys\text{-}report$

.1   SYS-FILE-OP $(f$-name$, f$-op$)$ result : $File\text{-}result \mid Sys\text{-}report$

.2   ext wr files : $Name \overset{m}{\rightarrow} File$

.3   rd open : $Name$-set

.4   pre f-name $\in$ open

.5   post $\exists \overleftarrow{file}, file : File \cdot \overleftarrow{file} = \overleftarrow{files}(f\text{-}name) \land$

.6   post-FILE-OP$(f\text{-}op, \overleftarrow{file}, file, result) \land$

.7   files $= \overleftarrow{files} \dagger \{f\text{-}name \mapsto file\}$

.8   errs NOT-OPENED :

.9 f-name $\notin$ open $\rightarrow$ result $=$ $'File\ not\ opened!'$

.10   UNKNOWN-NAME :
.11   *f-name* $\notin$ dom *files* $\rightarrow$ *result* = '*Unknown file name!*'

    end *FileSys*

Exercises

10.1 Section 10.4.3 on page 200 mentioned the need for another suboperation, in addition to the suboperations PLAY-MUSIC, STOP-MUSIC and ELIM-LOSER, to model the termination of the game with one of the players emerging as the winner. Define this operation and introduce it as an extra module operation, with the necessary modifications required elsewhere.

10.2 Sections 4.2 and 10.4 presented two specifications for the party game musical chairs, the former in Z and the latter in VDM. There are a number of differences between these specifications with regard to the requirements expressed in them.

(a) Identify these differences and critically evaluate their significance from the point of view of the normal rules of this game.
(b) Make the necessary improvements, if any, to the two specifications so that they both express the requirements according to the normal rules of the game.

10.3 Formalise in VDM the board game snakes and ladders covered in Section 4.3.

11. Algebraic Approach to Specification

This chapter presents an overview of the algebraic approach to specification. Like any specification, an algebraic specification is an abstract theory about some artifact. As a task, there are two aspects to algebraic specification: abstraction of data, or systems, in the form of such theories and their use in constructing more complex theories. This chapter is devoted to the former, while Chapter 12 is devoted to the latter. In terms of specification languages and the underlying mathematical concepts, the algebraic approach has several different variants. In this chapter, we consider a number of concepts commonly found in some of these languages.

The approach is not supposed to rely explicitly on the material covered so far, but we take limited advantage of our present knowledge of various notations and basic concepts covered elsewhere in this book.

11.1 Introduction

Algebraic approach is better known in data abstraction and, therefore, our study will be motivated by a brief discussion about its role in this particular area. Implementation of data types is a familiar activity in programming. However, its low level nature in programming tends to obscure the most essential features of data, namely how to use and manipulate data – the object of data abstraction. What is really required, especially at the specification level, is a concise and clear statement about the functionality of data without too much reference to the details of the representation. A question which arises immediately is the extent of detail which is desirable at this level, and it is this aspect which distinguishes algebraic techniques from the techniques we have studied so far. This is because algebraic techniques avoid abstract representations, even if such representations may have obvious mathematical roots.

In this respect, consider a specification written in Z. Such a specification makes use of mathematical structures such as sets, relations, functions, sequences, etc., in constructing an abstract model which exhibits the required functionality of the concrete artifact. It is for this reason that languages such as Z and VDM are dubbed model oriented languages. The model oriented approach goes quite a long way to providing a precise statement of what is required. As mentioned in Chapter 1, this is the most essential element for addressing the correctness of implementations and for providing a rigorous framework for reasoning about what is being specified or implemented.

However, as may be seen shortly, even such abstract mathematical representations are not essential for specifying what is required and, in certain cases, they may be seen as a hindrance to attaining an elegant and concise description. The techniques which do not rely on them come under the algebraic category. The basic tenet is that it is the operations that actually define data, and not the representation of data. The intended objects are specified by identifying the desired operations on them, and interrelating them in such a way that the requirements are stated implicitly through the properties of the operations. For this reason, specifications produced in this way are called 'implicit' specifications. The approach itself is known as 'algebraic' since an algebraic specification essentially axiomatises a class of algebra (a mathematical structure), which, when chosen appropriately, underpins the meaning of the specification precisely. It is important to realise that the associated algebra is separate from the specification itself. However, the requirements expressed in the specification need to be understood in terms of their meaning in the algebra. The model oriented and algebraic approaches to specification may be related to each other by treating a model oriented specification as an abstract implementation of an appropriate algebraic specification.

Algebraic approaches are widely used in the specification of *abstract data types* (ADT), non-dependence on particular mathematical representations being the characteristic of 'abstractness'; see, for example, Martin [35]. Furthermore, the kind of reasoning involved, namely equational and inductive reasoning, has a certain mathematical appeal, if not for being more intuitive than proofs in first–order predicate logic. From the practical point of view, the executability of such languages, or at least a major subset of each language (e.g. OBJ), is another attraction. As mentioned in Chapter 8, it may be worth noting that the algebraic approach has some features in common with the object oriented approach (most importantly, data encapsulation).

11.2 A Preliminary Comparison

The following is a superficial comparison of the model oriented and algebraic approaches in order to show their basic differences. It is based on a specification of a data type involving a finite set of integers. The specification consists of four operations: a primitive operation to create the initial value, operations to insert and remove an element to and from the set respectively, and an operation to query whether the set is empty.

11.2.1 Model Oriented Approach

The model based version, written using the standard notation of Z on predicate logic and set theory, relies explicitly and implicitly on set theoretic objects and notions. Explicit aspects concern the meaning given to all newly introduced operations and this is achieved by defining them in terms of such set theoretic operations as union, intersection, etc. The specification also relies implicitly on set theory in requiring the absence of multiple occurrences of elements in the integer set and in stipulating the irrelevance of the order of insertion of elements.

Initialisation

$$IntSet == \mathbb{F}\,\mathbb{Z} \qquad \qquad \text{The objects}$$
$$\forall\, S : IntSet \bullet S_{init} \;=\; \varnothing \qquad \text{Initial value as a nullary operation}$$

Other Constructor operations

$$Insert, Remove \; : \; \mathbb{Z} \times IntSet \rightarrow IntSet$$
$$\forall\, i : \mathbb{Z};\; S : IntSet \bullet$$
$$\quad Insert(i, S) = S \cup \{i\}$$
$$\quad Remove(i, S) = S - \{i\}$$

Observations made through other types

$$\_\, is\text{-}member \,\_ \; : \; \mathbb{Z} \leftrightarrow IntSet$$
$$\forall\, i : \mathbb{Z};\; S : IntSet \bullet$$
$$i \; is\text{-}member \; S \Leftrightarrow i \in S$$

11.2.2 Algebraic Approach

The algebraic version as written here refers to no objects other than Boolean values, consisting of two values *true* and *false*, and integers. Algebraic specifications must be self contained and, therefore, the specification should include the latter two kinds of objects. They are omitted here for brevity. The specification consists of three components: an introduction of sorts (type names) of data being used or specified, a syntactic specification of the domain and range of named operations, and a collection of equations characterising the operations.

Sorts $Intset, \mathbb{Z}, Bool$
Syntax of Operations
$\quad empty : \rightarrow IntSet$ (A nullary operation; note that there is no explicit reference to an object)
$\quad Insert, Remove : \mathbb{Z} \times IntSet \rightarrow IntSet$ (constructor operations)
$\quad is\text{-}member : \mathbb{Z} \times IntSet \rightarrow \mathsf{Bool}$ (observations)

Equations

$$Remove(i, empty) = empty$$
$$Remove(i, Insert(i, S)) = S$$
$$Remove(j, Insert(i, S)) = Insert(i, Remove(j, S))$$
$$is\text{-}member(i, empty) = false$$
$$is\text{-}member(i, Remove(i, S)) = false$$
$$is\text{-}member(i, Insert(j, S)) = (i == j) \lor is\text{-}member(i, S)$$

NOTE: The symbol '=' used in writing equations denotes equality of terms, whereas '==' denotes identity of objects denoted by terms.

The above specification does not deal with multiple occurrences of elements in the integer set and the order of insertion of elements into it. Since there is no underlying mathematical discipline and, therefore, no reliance can be placed implicitly on anything, the two requirements have to be stated by additional equations as given below:

$$Insert(i, (Insert(i, S))) = Insert(i, S)$$
$$Insert(j, (Insert(i, S))) = Insert(i, Insert(j, S)))$$

11.3 Algebraic Notions

An algebra is an abstract mathematical structure consisting of one or more non-empty sets of some objects, referred to often as carriers or phyla, and some finite set of finitary (taking a finite number of arguments) total operations (functions) on those sets. The following sub-sections consider the structure of algebras of varying complexity.

11.3.1 Some Basic Algebras

An algebra commonly encountered in mathematics is the notion of 'group'. Groups have a number of different variants forming a hierarchy of algebras. The lowest in this hierarchy is the semi-group, having just one non-empty set of elements A and a single associative binary operation $*$

$$* : A \times A \to A$$

on the set A. Given three arbitrary elements x, y, and z in A, the associativity of $*$ requires that:

$$(x * y) * z = x * (y * z)$$

The above mathematical structure is shown as a pair $(A, *)$.

Such structures arise naturally in computer science. For example, the concatenation operation $\frown$ on sequences or lists of items, such as character strings, satisfies associativity. Therefore, given that SEQ denotes the set of all sequences concerned, from the mathematical perspective, the pair:

$$(\text{SEQ}, \frown)$$

is a semi-group, that is, an algebraic structure of a specific kind.

As we confer more specific properties on either of its constituents, a semi-group acquires another status. For example, a monoid $(A, *, e)$ is defined as a semi-group with an identity element e such that $e \in A$ and for every element $x \in A$:

$$x * e = e * x = x$$

The identity element in the case of SEQ is the empty string $\langle \rangle$ and, as a result, $(\text{SEQ}, \frown, \langle \rangle)$ is a monoid.

The next in this hierarchy is the notion of group, which is defined as a monoid $(A, *, e)$, characterised by the additional property that every element of its carrier set A has an inverse. That is, for every element $x \in A$, there exists another element $x' \in A$ such that:

$$x * x' = x' * x = e$$

Thus, every basic algebraic structure identifies the association of a set with an operation, which together exhibit one or more particular desirable properties. These algebras are found in many applications as diverse as wave mechanics, stress analysis and computer science. As mathematical structures, their prime objective is to abstract away from the detail peculiar to such application domains and to study their mathematical characteristics independently of the application concerned.

Generally, most structures in computer science consist of not just one, but collections of sets and operations. Queues and stacks are some typical examples, with operations for creation, insertion and removal of elements at quite specific locations in the data structure, retrieval of elements from it, and making observations about them. The additional complexity of these structures requires a corresponding increase in the complexity of the algebras. Furthermore, these structures may be required to satisfy other desirable properties. The structurally more complex algebras may be classified in the following manner.

11.3.2 Homogeneous Algebras

A homogeneous algebra may be viewed as a pair:

$$A = \langle C, F \rangle$$

where:

(a) C – the carrier (the phylum)
(b) F – the set of operations, each indexed with elements from a set $\mathcal{I}$ and having a known arity n

$$F = \{f_{j.n} : C^n \to C \mid j \in \mathcal{I} \wedge n \in \mathbb{N} \bullet f_{j.n}\}$$

Thus, each element in F is a function $f_{j.n} : C^n \to C$, where n is the arity of the function, and C^n is therefore the n-fold Cartesian product of C with itself.

The best known homogeneous algebra is that of natural numbers. Its carrier consists of the natural numbers themselves and its operations the successor function, the arithmetical operations for addition and subtraction, etc. Another is the set of Boolean values with operations corresponding to propositional connectives.

The best known homogeneous algebra is that of natural numbers, whose carrier is the set of natural numbers and the operations are the successor function, the arithmetical operations for addition and subtraction, etc. Another is the set of Boolean values with operations corresponding to propositional connectives.

11.3.3 Heterogeneous Algebras

Heterogeneous algebras have multiple carriers and operations on and between them. Thus:

$$A = \langle V, F \rangle$$

where:

(a) V – a family of non-empty carrier sets (phyla) each indexed with elements from another index set $\mathcal{S}$.

$$V = \{i \in \mathcal{S} \bullet V_i\}$$

In this case, the set V is said to be $\mathcal{S}$-sorted, and the elements of $\mathcal{S}$ as 'sorts'; see Section 11.4.1. Another notation used later for referring to V in a given algebra A is:

$$\mid A \mid = V$$

(b) F – a set of operations, each indexed with elements from a set $\mathcal{I}$ and having a known arity n:

$$F = \{f_{j.n} : V_{i_1} \times V_{i_2} \times \ldots \times V_{i_n} \to V_k \mid$$
$$j \in \mathcal{I} \wedge i_1, i_2, \ldots, i_n, k \in \mathcal{S} \wedge n \in \mathbb{N} \bullet f_{j.n}\}$$

The stacks and queues mentioned earlier are some typical examples. For example, the carrier set in the algebra corresponding to queues contains the set of items we have in mind (e.g. integers, messages, or whatever), the set of queues made up of those items, and the set of Boolean values since, invariably, we wish to make various observations about them. The operations in the operation set may be those for creating a queue, enqueuing and dequeuing items, and checking whether a given queue is empty or full.

EXAMPLE 11.1 The operations required for a data type *Queue* of integers are:

$$empty : \rightarrow Queue$$
$$enqueue : Queue \times \mathbb{Z} \rightarrow Queue$$
$$next : Queue \rightarrow \mathbb{Z}$$
$$dequeue : Queue \rightarrow Queue$$
$$is\text{-}empty : Queue \rightarrow \mathsf{Bool}$$

and, therefore, the constituents of the corresponding algebra may be identified as:

$$\langle \{ Queue, \mathbb{Z}, \mathsf{Bool} \}, \{ empty, enqueue, next, dequeue, is\text{-}empty \} \rangle$$

♡

11.3.4 Type Algebras

Type algebras are a special kind of heterogeneous algebras, but with a distinguished carrier called 'type of interest' (TOI) such that for each function:

$$f_{j.n} : V_{i_1} \times V_{i_2} \times \ldots \times V_{i_n} \rightarrow V_k$$

in F:

$$\mathrm{TOI} \in \{ V_{i_1}, V_{i_2}, \ldots, V_{i_n}, V_k \}$$

In other words, TOI must be one of the operands of $f_{j.n}$, or its result.

In the case of the abstract data type for queues, the type *Queue* is regarded as TOI. According to the above requirement on type algebras, every operation in F must have some direct relevance to TOI and, thus, each specification concentrates on this single type. As a result, type algebras are clearer about the object of specification. This is acceptable in the specification of ordinary abstract data types, but is unnecessarily restrictive in the specification of systems in general.

However, the single type–oriented view enables an often useful classification of operations on the basis of the effect of each operation on TOI. For instance, in a type algebra there must be at least one operation of the form:

$$f_n : V_{i_1} \times V_{i_2} \times \ldots \times V_{i_n} \to \text{TOI}$$

such that the operands in the cross product in the argument of f_n satisfy the following:

$$\{ V_{i_1}, V_{i_2}, \ldots, V_{i_n} \} \subseteq V - \{\text{TOI}\}$$

Such operations are called *primitive constructors*, and if there is only one such operation then it plays the role of the 'mother' of all objects of TOI. Likewise, one may characterise other operations and this is best done by partitioning F as a whole into:

- A set containing exactly those operations whose range is TOI, that is:
  (i) *Primitive constructors* (as introduced above)
  (ii) *Combinational constructors* – for creating and modifying the values of TOI, and thereby delivering the new ones
- And another set containing operations whose ranges are other types:
  (iii) *Accessors* – for distinguishing the values in TOI

The type algebras constitute the basis of a major approach to algebraic specification. The absence of accessor operations is regarded in this approach as a deficiency which makes the type algebra on TOI totally 'uninteresting'. This view has significant theoretical implications and, therefore, has to be adopted as a premise of the underlying approach rather than a general statement; see Section 11.9.

All three categories of algebras presuppose the existence of the definition of other types and, in particular, the sort Bool for Boolean values (for making the types being specified meaningful) and the natural numbers $\mathbb{N}$.

11.4 Many–sorted Algebra

Sets such as Bool and $\mathbb{Z}$ may be represented or visualised as:

Bool $= \{true, false\}$
$\mathbb{Z} = \{\ldots, -1, 0, 1, 2, \ldots\}$

We are accustomed to thinking of them in terms of the symbols we customarily use to denote them. For example, when dealing with numbers we use, without any confusion, numerals such as '0', '1', '2', etc., to denote the corresponding abstract numbers. In this respect, the types such as *Queue* are rather unconventional. This is because there is no readily available form for representing their values, although they are well understood in the abstract sense. What we mean here is the absence of an 'atomic' symbol for representing each distinct value of data types such as *Queue*. Therefore, it is important to find a way to relate syntactic expressions of our representation with the values as we understand them. This requires a clear separation to be made between the abstract concepts we have in mind and the syntactic means used to represent them. The former may be conveniently and precisely captured in the form of an algebra. The latter is what we call a *specification*. Potential relationships between the two, however, are not unique. Establishing an appropriate relationship is a subjective task and, as a consequence, it results in different approaches to algebraic specification. Prominent among them are 'initial algebra' (covered in Section 11.8) and 'terminal algebra' (covered in Section 11.9) approaches.

11.4.1 Signatures

A specification is a syntactic object. Every specification consists of what is referred to as *signature*. A given signature can serve more than one specification and a specification may consist of just the signature. Such a specification is the simplest possible of its kind. A signature consists of:

(i) A set S of names called 'sorts' for data types
(ii) A set Ω of operation symbols (names), each with a specification of their domain names and the range names from those given under sorts. In order to distinguish the 'operations' given in specifications from the actual operations (or functions) in the algebra, we use the terminology *operation pattern* for the former and *operation* or *function* for the latter. Thus, 'operation patterns' are symbolic representations of actual operations used in the signature. Other terms such as 'domain' are used indiscriminately both in relation to actual operations and operation patterns.
The domain of each operation is specified as a finite string of sort names using, if desired, intervening punctuation symbols such as brackets or commas. All possible strings of domain sorts may be denoted by S^*, with λ denoting the empty string and $\lambda \in S^*$. Therefore, Ω may be thought of as a family of operation (function) patterns.

$$\Omega = \{\Omega_{w,s} : w \to s \mid w \in S^* \wedge s \in S \centerdot \Omega_{w,s}\}$$

Those operation patterns with $w = \lambda$ do not have any domain sort and, therefore, are nullary operation patterns. They are an alternative way of representing constants of the sort. The symbol *empty* in the example below is such an operation pattern.

A common notation used for signatures is Σ, with Σ_{sorts} and Σ_{opns} denoting, respectively, the sorts and operation patterns introduced in Σ. Thus, a signature is a pair as shown below:

$$\Sigma = \langle \Sigma_{sorts}, \Sigma_{opns} \rangle = \langle S, \Omega \rangle$$

EXAMPLE 11.2 The signature ΣQ for the data type *Queue* in Example 11.1 can be presented as:

> sorts *Queue*, Integer, Bool
>
> opns *empty* : $\to$ *Queue*
> $\quad\quad$ *enqueue* : Integer, *Queue* $\to$ *Queue*
> $\quad\quad$ *next* : *Queue* $\to$ Integer
> $\quad\quad$ *dequeue* : *Queue* $\to$ *Queue*
> $\quad\quad$ *is-empty* : *Queue* $\to$ Bool

Components of ΣQ include the sorts:

$$\Sigma Q_{sorts} = S = \{\, Queue, \text{Integer}, \text{Bool} \,\}$$
$$\Sigma Q_{opns} = \Omega = \{\, empty, enqueue, next, dequeue, is\text{-}empty \,\}$$

and the operation patterns

$$\Sigma Q_{\lambda, Queue} = \{\, empty \,\}$$
$$\Sigma Q_{Queue, Queue} = \{\, dequeue \,\}$$
$$\Sigma Q_{\text{Integer } Queue, Queue} = \{\, enqueue \,\}$$
$$\Sigma Q_{Queue, \text{Integer}} = \{\, next \,\}$$
$$\Sigma Q_{Queue, \text{Bool}} = \{\, is\text{-}empty \,\}$$

with subscripts of ΣQ indicating the domain and the range of the operation patterns concerned. $\quad\quad\quad\quad\quad\quad\quad\quad\quad\quad\quad\quad\quad\quad\quad\quad\quad\quad\heartsuit$

11.4.2 Signature Associated Algebra

The syntactic relationship between algebras and specifications is established in the following manner. Here, we treat the signature as a kind of a template, with names playing the role of labels for viewing the algebra. Any doubts, if they exist, may concern only the specification and the algebra is supposed to be a well understood abstract object. An algebra A is said to be a (many–sorted) Σ-algebra if it has the same syntactic structure as Σ. In terms of Σ, the constituents of algebra A may be identified in the following manner:

- The carrier set $\mid A \mid$ is $\mathcal{S}$-sorted. That is, its constituent sets may be referred to as $\mid A \mid_{s_i}$, where $s_i \in \mathcal{S}$, thus treating the sort name s_i as an index.
- For each operation pattern f of the form:

$$f : s_{i_1}, s_{i_2}, \ldots, s_{i_n} \to s_{i_k}$$

in the signature, the algebra A contains a function f_A of the type:

$$f_A : \mid A \mid_{s_{i_1}} \times \mid A \mid_{s_{i_2}} \times \ldots \times \mid A \mid_{s_{i_n}} \to \mid A \mid_{s_{i_k}}$$

where each s_{i_j} is in $\mathcal{S}$.

Note that operation symbols subscripted with the identifier of the algebra correspond to an *interpretation* of operation symbols in Σ as actual functions in A.

EXAMPLE 11.3 A signature Σ and an associated algebra:

Signature Σ	Σ-algebra A
sorts *face*	$\mid A \mid_{face} = \{ ☺, ☹ \}$
opns *smile* : $\to$ *face*	$smile_A = ☺$
frown : $\to$ *face*	$frown_A = ☹$
change : *face* $\to$ *face*	$change_A = \{ ☺ \mapsto ☹, ☹ \mapsto ☺ \}$
compromise :	$compromise_A =$
face, face $\to$ *face*	$\{ (☺, ☺) \mapsto ☺, (☺, ☹) \mapsto ☺,$
	$(☹, ☺) \mapsto ☺, (☹, ☹) \mapsto ☹ \}$

♡

11.4.3 Subalgebras

An algebra B is said to be a Σ-subalgebra of a Σ-algebra A if and only if the constituents of $\mid B \mid$ are closed under the operations designated by $\Sigma_{w,s}$. In other words, for each $f \in \Sigma_{s_1 s_2 \ldots s_n, s}$

$$a_1 \in \mid B \mid_{s_1} \wedge \; a_2 \in \mid B \mid_{s_2} \wedge \ldots \wedge \; a_n \in \mid B \mid_{s_n} \Rightarrow$$
$$f_A(a_1, a_2, \ldots, a_n) \in \mid B \mid_s$$

that is, the operations of B are exactly as those in A, but are restricted to operating on the carriers of B. A subalgebra B of A is said to be a 'proper subalgebra' of A if $B \neq A$.

11.5 Homomorphisms

The adoption of signatures as a template for viewing algebras obliges us to clarify how different algebras are supposed to relate to each other when viewed through the same signature. Our task amounts to providing a mapping as understood in set theory, but it is complicated by the fact that we are no longer dealing with such homogeneous atomic objects as elements in sets but with structured objects – algebras. Hence, the term 'homomorphism'.

A *homomorphism* is essentially a sorted collection of mappings. However, a homomorphism cannot be arbitrary but must satisfy an important condition, which amounts to 'preservation of operation application' as designated in the signature, that is, the interpretation provided by the algebras for the signature. This *homomorphism condition* may be stated formally as follows.

Given two Σ-algebras A and B, Σ-homomorphism is a function h:

$$h :\mid A \mid \rightarrow \mid B \mid$$

sorted by Σ_{sorts}. For $s \in \Sigma_{sorts}$ and $a \in \mid A \mid_s$, we write:

$$h(a) \overset{def}{=} h_s(a)$$

where $\overset{def}{=}$ denotes 'equality by definition'. The left hand side of the above amounts to a 'homomorphism application'. Each function $h_s :\mid A \mid_s \rightarrow \mid B \mid_s$ for $s \in \Sigma_{sorts}$ is such that:

$$f \in \Sigma_{s_1 s_2 \ldots s_n, s_k} \wedge$$
$$a_1 \in \mid A \mid_{s_1} \wedge a_2 \in \mid A \mid_{s_2} \wedge \ldots \wedge a_n \in \mid A \mid_{s_n} \Rightarrow$$
$$h_{s_k}(f_A(a_1, a_2, \ldots, a_n)) = f_B(h_{s_1}(a_1), h_{s_2}(a_2), \ldots, h_{s_n}(a_n))$$

The above basically says that it is immaterial whether to first apply the function designated by f in A to the appropriate arguments in A as designated by f's type and then to take the result to B using h, or first to take the relevant arguments in A as designated to B using h and then to apply the function designated by f in B; the result in both cases should be the same.

For constants, that is, for $f \in \Sigma_{\lambda, s_k}$, we have the special case:

$$h_{sk}(f_A) = f_B$$

NOTE: Example 11.4 below uses the notation $[\![a_1, a_2, \ldots, a_n]\!]$ for bags or multi-sets. Abstractly, a *bag* is a mathematical structure similar to a *set*, but allows multiple occurrences of its elements. The notation given above is from Z, according to which the bag $[\![a_1, a_2, \ldots, a_n]\!]$ is a function of the form $\{(a_1, k_1), (a_2, k_2), \ldots, (a_n, k_n)\}$, where each k_i denotes the number of occurrences of the element a_i. We use below $size(b)$ for the total number of elements in the bag b.

EXAMPLE 11.4 Consultation of the famous Chinese oracle *I Ching* (Book of Changes; see [64]) is based on the ancient concepts *Yang* and *Yin*, which also have two additional complementary concepts called *Moving Yang* and *Moving Yin*. There are two alternative ways of establishing these on a random basis: with the help of yarrow stalks or, alternatively, by tossing three coins. As the outcome of the former we have adopted a number for each concept. These concepts are then integrated to form what is called a *Trigram* by considering three concepts at a time and in the order of their generation. Here is a formalisation of an aspect of *I Ching* to illustrate the idea of homomorphism. It deals with how to relate random events to abstract concepts such as *Yang*, *Yin*, *ch'ien*, *tui*, *li*, *chên*, etc.

Signature *Iching*

sorts   *metric, concept, trigram*

opns   *yang* $: \to concept$
         yin $: \to concept$
         m-yang $: \to concept$
         m-yin $: \to concept$
         ch'ien, tui, li, chên, sun, k'an, kên, k'un $: \to trigram$
         situation : *concept, concept, concept* $\to$ *trigram*

The methods of establishing the trigrams are given below as two algebras with the above as a common signature.

Iching-Algebra *Stalk*	*Iching*-Algebra *Coin*
$metric_{Stalk} = \mathbb{Z}$	$metric_{Coin} = \{head, tail\}$
$concept_{Stalk} =$ $\{6,7,8,9\}$	$concept_{Coin} = a,$ where a : bag $metric_{Coin}$ $size(a) = 3$
$yang_{Stalk} = 7$	$yang_{Coin} = [\![tail, tail, head]\!]$
$yin_{Stalk} = 8$	$yin_{Coin} = [\![tail, head, head]\!]$
$m\text{-}yang_{Stalk} = 9$	$m\text{-}yang_{Coin} = [\![head, head, head]\!]$
$m\text{-}yin_{Stalk} = 6$	$m\text{-}yin_{Coin} = [\![tail, tail, tail]\!]$
$ch'ien_{Stalk} = ☰$	$ch'ien_{Coin} = ☰$
$tui_{Stalk} = ☱$	$tui_{Coin} = ☱$
$li_{Stalk} = ☲$	$li_{Coin} = ☲$
$chên_{Stalk} = ☳$	$chên_{Coin} = ☳$
$sun_{Stalk} = ☴$	$sun_{Coin} = ☴$
$k'an_{Stalk} = ☵$	$k'an_{Coin} = ☵$
$kên_{Stalk} = ☶$	$kên_{Coin} = ☶$
$k'un_{Stalk} = ☷$	$k'un_{Coin} = ☷$

$situation_{Stalk}$: $situation_{Coin}$:

(arguments)			(result)	(arguments)			(result)
7	7	7	☰	$[\![tail, tail, head]\!]$	$[\![tail, tail, head]\!]$	$[\![tail, tail, head]\!]$	☰
7	7	8	☱	$[\![tail, tail, head]\!]$	$[\![tail, tail, head]\!]$	$[\![tail, head, head]\!]$	☱
7	8	7	☲	$[\![tail, tail, head]\!]$	$[\![tail, head, head]\!]$	$[\![tail, tail, head]\!]$	☲
7	8	8	☳	$[\![tail, tail, head]\!]$	$[\![tail, head, head]\!]$	$[\![tail, head, head]\!]$	☳
8	7	7	☴	$[\![tail, head, head]\!]$	$[\![tail, tail, head]\!]$	$[\![tail, tail, head]\!]$	☴
8	7	8	☵	$[\![tail, head, head]\!]$	$[\![tail, tail, head]\!]$	$[\![tail, head, head]\!]$	☵
8	8	7	☶	$[\![tail, head, head]\!]$	$[\![tail, head, head]\!]$	$[\![tail, tail, head]\!]$	☶
8	8	8	☷	$[\![tail, head, head]\!]$	$[\![tail, head, head]\!]$	$[\![tail, head, head]\!]$	☷

Obviously, there is much more to the procedure which enables the reader of *I Ching* to begin a consultation process.

The homomorphism *h* shown below is from *Coin* to *Stalk*.

$$
\begin{aligned}
h \quad & : \; Coin \rightarrow Stalk \\
h_{concept} \quad & = \{\llbracket tail, tail, head \rrbracket \mapsto 7, \llbracket tail, head, head \rrbracket \mapsto 8, \\
& \qquad \llbracket head, head, head \rrbracket \mapsto 9, \llbracket tail, tail, tail \rrbracket \mapsto 6\} \\
h_{trigram} \quad & = \mathrm{id}\{\equiv, \eqcirc, \equiv, \equiv, \equiv, \equiv, \equiv\} \\
h(situation_{Coin}) \quad & = situation_{Stalk}
\end{aligned}
$$

Note that *metric* is peripheral to the discussion and, therefore, is ignored in the definition above.

It may be seen that the above satisfies the homomorphism condition. For example:

$$
h_{trigram}(situation_{Coin}(\llbracket tail, tail, head \rrbracket, \llbracket tail, tail, head \rrbracket,
$$
$$
\llbracket tail, tail, head \rrbracket)) = \equiv \tag{11.1}
$$

and

$$
situation_{Stalk}(h_{Coin}(\llbracket tail, tail, head \rrbracket), h_{Coin}(\llbracket tail, tail, head \rrbracket),
$$
$$
h_{Coin}(\llbracket tail, tail, head \rrbracket))
$$
$$
= situation_{Stalk}(7, 7, 7)
$$
$$
= \equiv \tag{11.2}
$$

Thus, the function application on the left hand side of (11.1) gives the same result as that in (11.1). The process can be continued for all arguments of $situation_{Stalk}$ and $situation_{Coin}$, thus verifying the homomorphism condition. ♡

11.5.1 Characterisation of Homomorphism

Being collections of mappings, set theoretic notions remain applicable to various components of homomorphisms and, as a result, the set theoretic concepts such as composition, identity, inverse, injection, surjection and bijection may also be extended to homomorphisms. These extensions being quite natural, no distinction has been made here in the notation, and the relevant operator symbols are overloaded with both set theoretic and algebraic notions. For example, the symbol ∘ on the left hand side in (i) below is a binary operator on algebras, whereas the same on the right is a binary operator on functions. Given S-sorted Σ-algebras A, B and C, these concepts may be defined as below.

(i) The *composition* of Σ-homomorphisms $g : A \rightarrow B$ and $h : B \rightarrow C$ (read as h over g) is defined such that for each $s \in S$:

$$
(h \circ g)_s \overset{def}{=} h_s \circ g_s
$$

(ii) The *identity at A* is a Σ-homomorphism $A \rightarrow A$ such that for each $s \in S$:

$$
(\mathrm{id}\,A)_s \overset{def}{=} \mathrm{id}\,A_s
$$

(iii) The *inverse* of the Σ-homomorphism $g : A \to B$, if it exists, is defined as the unique Σ-homomorphism $g^{-1} : B \to A$ such that:

$$(g \circ g^{-1}) \stackrel{def}{=} \text{id } A \qquad \text{and} \qquad (g^{-1} \circ g) \stackrel{def}{=} \text{id } B$$

(iv) Given the Σ-homomorphisms $g : A \to B$ and $h : B \to A$ such that:

$$(h \circ g) = \text{id } A$$

then g is said to be *surjective* and h *injective*. Homomorphisms which are both surjective and injective are called *bijective*. Other interesting properties follow from set theory; for example:

(a) If $(h \circ g)$ is surjective then h is surjective.
(b) If $(h \circ g)$ is injective then g is injective.

(v) Two Σ-homomorphisms $g : A \to B$ and $h : B \to A$ are said to be *isomorphisms* if they satisfy both:

$$(h \circ g) = \text{id } A \qquad \text{and} \qquad (g \circ h) = \text{id } B$$

Note the relationship of the above with the definition of *inverse*. Thus, a homomorphism is an isomorphism if and only if it is bijective.

(vi) The existence of a Σ-subalgebra B of a Σ-algebra A is equivalent to an injective Σ-homomorphism $h : B \to A$, since B is isomorphic to its image in A.

Isomorphism characterises algebras with a common signature which are abstractly the same – hence, its importance in *abstract data types* because their definition is not concerned with representational issues.

11.6 Term Algebras

The term algebra corresponding to a given signature Σ contains in its carrier set all the expressions that may be generated by the operation patterns in Σ, if Σ is treated as the grammar of a formal language. The significance of term algebras lies in the fact that they serve as an intermediate algebraic structure 'bridging' the gap between any given specification and the algebras targeted by it.

The term algebras are best illustrated with the use of signatures intended for describing abstract data types. For the time being, we restrict ourselves to specifications consisting of signatures only, that is, those without any axiom.

11.6.1 Well Formed Terms

First, let us give a more general definition of well formed terms (*wft*). *Wfts* are syntactically permissible sequences of operator symbols and argument symbols in the order given in the operation pattern. These expressions may contain variable names – a topic to be covered in Section 11.7.1. The expressions not containing variable symbols within them are called *grounded*. Those with at least one variable are known as *parameterised wfts*. A *parameterised wft* may be grounded by replacing, as appropriate, all its variables with *grounded wfts* or constant symbols. Grounded and parameterised *wfts* taken together are also called *words*. *Wfts* are also sorted by the sorts in the relevant signature. The sort name of a *wft* is, by definition, the same as the range sort of the outermost operation symbol of the *wft*.

It is possible to define an equivalence relation on the set of *wfts* such that a pair of *wfts* is in that relation if and only if they are equivalent to each other. The objects in the sort-indexed carrier set may then be identified with the elements of the quotient formed by the equivalence relation on *wfts*.

11.6.2 Natural Numbers as a Homogeneous Data Type

Let us first turn our attention to the most familiar and important algebra of all – the algebra of natural numbers $\mathbb{N}$. We may identify $\mathbb{N}$ through the signature given below.

> **sorts** *nat*
> **opns** *zero* : $\rightarrow$ *nat*
>   *succ* : *nat* $\rightarrow$ *nat*

Our intentions are obvious; *zero* is supposed to denote a constant and the operation pattern *succ* is intended to designate the successor function on $\mathbb{N}$. Restricting ourselves to the given signature, we may successively generate its grounded well formed terms *wfts* as:

$$zero, succ(zero), succ(succ(zero)), succ(succ(succ(zero))),$$
$$succ(succ(succ(succ(zero)))), \ldots$$

Our objective is to draw a correspondence between the terms generated above with our intuitive notion of numbers as represented by the numerals:

$$0, 1, 2, 3, 4, \ldots$$

However, in order to do this, we must be sure that the following two important conditions are met:

(i) Each term of the form $succ(succ(\ldots succ(succ(zero))\ldots))$ corresponds to a different number in $\mathbb{N}$.

(ii) There are no numbers in $\mathbb{N}$ which cannot be defined by such terms.

The above two properties amount to the notions introduced in Section 11.8, namely (i) to 'no confusion', and (ii) to 'no junk'.

If the above two conditions hold, then we can conceive a homogeneous algebra whose carrier set consists of just those terms. The algebra does not have an operation for generating *wfts*, but this is of less importance to our discussion here. Such an algebra is called a *term algebra*.

The carrier set of the term algebra T_Σ, corresponding to an arbitrary homogeneous signature Σ with just one sort s such that $\Sigma_{sorts} = \{s\}$, may be defined inductively as:

1. $\Sigma_{\lambda,s} \subseteq |\ T_{\Sigma,s}\ |$
2. For each $f \in \Sigma_{w,s} \wedge w \in s^n \wedge t_1, t_2, \ldots, t_n \in |\ T_{\Sigma,s}\ | \Rightarrow$
$$f(t_1, t_2, \ldots, t_n) \in |\ T_{\Sigma,s}\ |$$
3. These are the only members of $|\ T_{\Sigma,s}\ |$.

The importance of the term algebra T_Σ is that it allows us to visualise an abstract algebra. Note that $T_\Sigma = T_{\Sigma,s}$ since Σ is homogeneous. This algebra, however, is quite specific and is determined solely by the signature and the two properties mentioned. The elements in $|\ T_\Sigma\ |$ may therefore be treated as an indirect, yet convenient, way of identifying the elements in the algebra, such as the elements in $\mathbb{N}$. That is, given a homogeneous Σ-algebra A, and an appropriate mapping, namely a Σ-homomorphism $h : T_\Sigma \to A$, then $h(t)$ represents the element of A corresponding to the term $t \in |\ T_\Sigma\ |$.

11.6.3 Heterogeneous (Many-Sorted) Abstract Data Types

Heterogeneous data types, that is, those involving more than one data type may be subjected to an analogous treatment. The difference is in the multiplicity of term algebras, one for each sort.

EXAMPLE 11.5 As an illustration, the following are the well formed terms (*wfts*) of the signature given in Example 11.2. The first *wft* is of type Integer, whereas the second is of type *Queue*.

$next(enqueue(6, (enqueue(5, (enqueue(4, empty))))))$
$dequeue(enqueue(6, (enqueue(5, (enqueue(4, empty))))))$

♡

The carrier sets of the term algebra corresponding to an arbitrary heterogeneous signature may be defined inductively as follows. For each $s_k \in \Sigma_{sorts}$:

1. $\Sigma_{\lambda,s_k} \subseteq |\ T_{\Sigma,s_k}\ |$
2. $f \in \Sigma_{w,s_k} \wedge w \in s^n \wedge$
$\qquad t_1 \in |\ T_{\Sigma,s_1}\ | \wedge t_2 \in |\ T_{\Sigma,s_2}\ | \wedge \ldots \wedge t_n \in |\ T_{\Sigma,s_n}\ | \Rightarrow$
$\qquad\quad f(t_1, t_2, \ldots, t_n) \in |\ T_{\Sigma,s_k}\ |$

3. These are the only members of each $\mid T_{\Sigma, s_k} \mid$.

The term algebra T_Σ generated by the whole signature may then be defined such that T_Σ is S-sorted and:

$$\mid T_\Sigma \mid_s = T_{\Sigma, s}$$

As in the case of the abstract data type *nat*, the *wfts* so generated may be identified with the abstract values of what we have in mind and, in particular, with those objects (such as queues) we are unable to represent by conventional means. However, there is a difference! In relation to Example 11.2, both:

$$enqueue(5, (enqueue(4, empty)))$$
$$dequeue(enqueue(6, (enqueue(5, (enqueue(4, empty))))))$$

are expected to represent the same queue value. This contravenes condition (i) stated earlier with respect to $\mathbb{N}$, namely that the objects of $\mathbb{N}$ may be brought to a one-to-one correspondence with the elements of the term algebra of the signature for *nat*. Hence the need for *equations*.

11.7 Equations

Adherence to the rule that each term points to a different object in the desired algebra works only in a limited number of cases and, in general, may result in 'confusion'. This is because of the possible presence of multiple terms in the term algebra intuitively corresponding to the same object in the target algebra. In general, this situation arises in the case of heterogeneous data types, but also occurs in homogeneous data types with multiple operations, where properties such as commutativity, associativity, etc., are desired.

Returning to Example 11.2 on *Queue*, in order to fully define it as an abstract data type it is necessary to supplement the proposed signature with equations. The objective of introducing equations is to force different terms in the term algebra to denote the same object. Equations are written using the conventional equality '=' sign. For example, in order to avoid the situation pointed out earlier, we may write:

$$dequeue(enqueue(i, q)) = q$$

using variables i and q ranging, respectively, over Integer and *Queue*. Note that the variables i and q are universally quantified and, therefore, the above is to be read as:

$$\forall i, q \bullet dequeue(enqueue(i, q)) = q$$

With the introduction of the notion of equation, however, we now have to extend the enterprise developed so far in order that it can handle variables. This involves:

- Extending the definition of term algebras to include variables
- Providing a system of equational deduction

11.7.1 Variables

Our task here is to incorporate variables into the algebraic framework developed so far. This may be done by introducing a new S-sorted set X, where, for $s \in S$, each X_s is a set containing *variable symbols* of sort s. Analogous to the treatment of constants as nullary operation patterns, we may treat each variable name as a nullary operation pattern. This would allow the incorporation of X into Σ with the result of a new extended signature $\Sigma(X)$. Thus:

$$(\Sigma(X))_{sorts} = \Sigma_{sorts}$$

and

$$(\Sigma(X))_{\lambda,s} = \Sigma_{\lambda,s} \cup X_s$$
$$(\Sigma(X))_{w,s} = \Sigma_{w,s} \qquad \text{for } w \neq \lambda$$

With the above signature $\Sigma(X)$, we may go on to define its term algebra $T_{\Sigma(X)}$ in exactly the same way as T_{Σ}. Another way to look at $T_{\Sigma(X)}$ is $T_{\Sigma}(X)$, that is, as if T_{Σ} is parameterised with respect to X.

EXAMPLE 11.6 Given that:

$$X = \{\{i, \ldots\}, \{q, \ldots\}\}$$

let X be sorted as:

$$X_{\mathsf{Integer}} = \{i, \ldots\}$$
$$X_{\mathsf{Queue}} = \{q, \ldots\}$$

Then the term algebra $T_{\Sigma(X)}$, corresponding to the signature in Example 11.2 on *Queue*, contains terms such as:

$$dequeue(enqueue(i, q)),$$
$$next(enqueue(i, empty)),$$

Thus, $i, q, \ldots$ introduced via X are variables in the above parameterised *wfts*.

11.7.2 Algebras and Equations

Our objective here is to establish the role of equations in determining algebras or, in other words, what is meant by an algebra satisfying a set of equations. It is easily seen that an equation is a pair of *wfts*, usually parameterised with appropriate variables.

A data type with no equations may be dealt with satisfactorily by ensuring the two properties of 'no confusion' and 'no junk', that is, by ensuring a unique Σ-homomorphism $h : T_\Sigma \to A$, when the data type is viewed as an Σ-algebra A. Thus, when there are no equations, no two distinct *wfts* are mapped to a single object in the algebra.

A data type with just grounded equations (involving only grounded *wfts*) may be dealt with by requiring, additionally, that for each equation of the form:

$$t_1 = t_2$$

where $t_1, t_2 \in |\ T_\Sigma\ |_s$

$$h_s(t_1) == h_s(t_2)$$

That is, two distinct *wfts* may correspond to the same object in the algebra if the two *wfts* express an equation.

However, the presence of variable makes our task slightly more complex. What is required is an assignment of objects in A for variables in X. Let this assignment be an S-sorted mapping, or a valuation, $v : X \to A$. It may be easily seen that the homomorphism $h : T_\Sigma \to A$ and the mapping v together completely determine what is required for interpreting $T_\Sigma(X)$. Let this extended interpretation be $v^\sharp : T_\Sigma(X) \to A$. Obviously:

$$v_s^\sharp(x) = v_s(x)$$

for $s \in \mathcal{S}, x \in X_s$. Elsewhere, for any term $t \in |\ T_\Sigma(X)\ |_s$ and $s \in \mathcal{S}$, let $v_s^\sharp(t)$ denote the value of t in A as valued by v. The algebra A is then said to *satisfy* an equation of sort s:

$$\forall(X) \bullet t_1 = t_2$$

with $t_1, t_2 \in |\ T_\Sigma(X)\ |_s$, and any variables explicitly introduced by the quantifier, if and only if:

$$v_s^\sharp(t_1) == v_s^\sharp(t_2)$$

for every assignment v. Given a set of Σ-equations E, the Σ-algebra A is said to *satisfy* E if and only if A satisfies every equation in E.

11.7.3 Other Related Terminology

A Σ-algebra A satisfying a set of Σ-equations E is also referred to as a *model* of E. Also, such an algebra is said to be a (Σ, E)-algebra, and the class of (Σ, E)-algebras (i.e. the models of E) form what is called a *variety*. The pair (Σ, E) is referred to as an *equational presentation*. An *equational theory* is the set of all equations satisfied by each algebra in the class of (Σ, E)-algebras.

11.7.4 Equational Deduction

An important requirement in equational deduction is that the sorts of all variables used in equations are declared. For convenience, let t, u and v be terms of $T_\Sigma(X)$, $T_\Sigma(Y)$ and $T_\Sigma(Z)$ respectively, the latter being associated in turn with sorted sets of variables X, Y and Z respectively. Note that with t, u and v we also use subscripts and single quotes, as necessary.

Rules of equational deduction, most of which are quite intuitive, are as follows. For any term $t, t', t'' \in| T_\Sigma(X) |_s$ and $s \in \mathcal{S}$:

(i) Reflexivity: For any *wft t*

$$\forall X \centerdot t = t$$

is derivable.
(ii) Symmetry: If for *wfts t* and t'

$$\forall X \centerdot t = t'$$

then

$$\forall X \centerdot t' = t$$

is derivable.
(iii) Transitivity: If for *wfts t*, t' and t''

$$\forall X \centerdot t = t' \quad \text{and} \quad \forall X \centerdot t' = t''$$

then

$$\forall X \centerdot t = t''$$

is derivable.
(iv) Substitutivity: If

$$\forall X \centerdot t_1 = t_2$$

is derivable and is of sort s and

$$\forall Y \centerdot u_1 = u_2$$

is derivable and is of sort s' and, furthermore, $x \in X_{s'}$ (i.e. x of sort s') then

$$\forall Z . v_1 = v_2$$

is also derivable, with $Z = (X - \{x\}) \cup Y$, $v_i = t_i(x \leftarrow u_i)$ for $i = 1, 2$. The notation $t(x \leftarrow u)$ denotes the result of substituting u for x in t.

EXAMPLE 11.7 In relation to Example 11.2 on *Queue*, given the following equations:

$$\forall X . \ next(enqueue(j, r)) = next(r)$$
$$\forall Y . \ dequeue(enqueue(i, q)) = q$$

of sort Integer and *Queue* respectively, with $X_{\text{Integer}} = \{j\}$, $X_{Queue} = \{r\}$, $Y_{\text{Integer}} = \{i\}$ and $Y_{Queue} = \{q\}$, the following equation:

$$\forall Z . \ next(enqueue(j, dequeue(enqueue(i, q)))) = next(q)$$

is derivable. The above equation is of sort Integer, with $Z_{\text{Integer}} = \{j\}$, $Z_{Queue} = \{q\}$. ♡

(v) Abstraction: If

$$\forall X . t = t'$$

is derivable, and $y \notin X_s$ but y is of sort s then so is

$$\forall(X \cup \{y\}) . t = t'$$

EXAMPLE 11.8 In relation to Example 11.2 on *Queue*, given the equation

$$\forall \varnothing . \ next(enqueue(j, empty)) = j$$

then the following:

$$\forall X . \ next(enqueue(j, empty)) = j$$

where $X_{\text{Integer}} = \{j\}$ and $X_{Queue} = \varnothing$, is derivable. ♡

(vi) Concretion: If

$$\forall X . t = t'$$

is derivable, $x \in X_s$ but does not appear in either side of the equation, and $T_{\Sigma,s} \neq \varnothing$ then

$$\forall(X - \{x\}) . t = t'$$

is derivable.

EXAMPLE 11.9 In relation to Example 11.2 on *Queue*, given the equation

$$\forall X \bullet next(enqueue(j, q)) = j$$

where $X_{\mathsf{Integer}} = \{j\}$ and $X_{Queue} = \{q\}$, the following

$$\forall X' \bullet next(enqueue(j, q)) = j$$

where $X'_{\mathsf{Integer}} = \{j\}$ and $X'_{Queue} = \varnothing$, is derivable. This is because; $T_{\Sigma Q, Queue} \neq \varnothing$. ♡

11.8 Initial Algebras

Sections 11.6 and 11.7 have already laid the necessary foundations for our discussion here on initial algebras.

The notion of the *initial algebra* is an important concept linking the algebraic concepts given earlier and the approach to specification bearing the same name – the *initial algebra approach*. A corner stone of the approach lies in what is called a 'standard model' – a unique model defined up to renaming of data items.

11.8.1 The Motivation for Initial Algebras

Consider, for example, the signature *BoolSeq* given below:

Signature $\Sigma BoolSeq$

sorts	*bool, seq*	
opns	*true, false*	$: \rightarrow bool$
	empty	$: \rightarrow seq$
	unit	$: bool \rightarrow seq$
	join	$: seq, seq \rightarrow seq$
eqns	$join(empty, s)$	$= s$
	$join(s, empty)$	$= s$
	$join(join(s, t), u)$	$= join(s, join(t, u))$

and two algebras *Nums* and *BitSeq*, both satisfying the above specification.

$\Sigma BoolSeq$-Nums
$\mid Nums \mid_{bool} = \{0, 1\}$
$\mid Nums \mid_{seq} = \mathbb{Z}$
$true_{Nums} = 1$
$false_{Nums} = 0$
$empty_{Nums} = 0$
$unit_{Nums} = \mathrm{id}$
$join_{Nums} = +$

$\Sigma BoolSeq$-BitSeq
$\mid BitSeq \mid_{bool} = Bits$
where $Bits = \{zero, one\}$
$\mid BitSeq \mid_{seq} = seq\ Bits$
$true_{BitSeq} = one$
$false_{BitSeq} = zero$
$empty_{BitSeq} = \langle\rangle$
$unit_{BitSeq} = \{zero \mapsto \langle zero \rangle, one \mapsto \langle one \rangle\}$
$join_{BitSeq} = \frown$

In the above, 'id' denotes the identity relation, 'seq' the set of all sequences and $\frown$ the concatenation operator on sequences. It may be verified that:

$$(unit(false))_{Nums} = (empty)_{Nums} = 0$$
$$(join(unit(true), unit(false)))_{Nums} = (join(unit(false), unit(true)))_{Nums} = 1$$

in the algebra *Nums*, although these equalities do not follow from the equations in the specification $\Sigma BoolSeq$. In other words, in each case two distinct terms in the term algebra $T_{\Sigma BoolSeq}$ refer to the same object in the algebra *Nums*. As a result, the specification causes unwarranted confusion of objects in *Nums*. Also, there are objects in *Nums* which may not be referred to using terms in $T_{\Sigma BoolSeq}$; see Example 11.10.

On the other hand, no two terms in $T_{\Sigma BoolSeq}$ point to the same object in the algebra *BitSeq*, unless the equations in $\Sigma BoolSeq$ compel it. Also, every object in *BitSeq* can be denoted by an appropriate term in $T_{\Sigma BoolSeq}$. Thus, the algebra *BitSeq* is the initial algebra satisfying $\Sigma BoolSeq$, considered to be the most appropriate by the initial algebra approach for capturing the meaning of the specification $\Sigma BoolSeq$.

11.8.2 The Definition of Initiality

The so–called *standard model* is therefore an algebra defined through two important properties, expressed often through the catch phrases 'no confusion' and 'no junk'. These properties are as follows:

(i) There is 'no confusion' in the sense that no object in the algebra is denoted unintentionally by more than one expression. In other words, two data items are identical to each other if and only if this fact is deducible from the specification, namely the signature taken with equations.

(ii) There is 'no junk' in the algebra with respect to the signature or, more formally, every object in the target algebra is reachable through an appropriate *wft*. This amounts to ensuring structural induction so that one can reason about every item in the algebra through expressions resulting from the signature.

By definition, an algebra A is said to be an *initial algebra* in a class of algebras C with a common signature if and only if A is in C and there is a unique homomorphism from A to each algebra in C. In this connection, the algebra A must satisfy certain 'minimality' conditions, namely that the algebraL

(i) contains the minimal number of data items.

(ii) satisfies the minimal number of equations involving grounded *wfts*, that is, the given algebra is the least constrained.

An implication of the initiality in the above sense is that an initial algebra does not have any proper subalgebra in its class (i.e. the class of algebras with the same signature).

EXAMPLE 11.10 In relation to the example in Section 11.8.1, let us define the homomorphism from *BitSeq* to *Nums* and illustrate how to determine whether it satisfies the homomorphism condition stated in Section 11.5.

Homomorphism $h : | BitSeq | \rightarrow | Nums |$

$$h_{bool} : | BitSeq |_{bool} \rightarrow | Nums |_{bool}$$
$$h_{seq} : | BitSeq |_{seq} \rightarrow | Nums |_{seq}$$

$$h_{bool} = \{zero \mapsto 0, one \mapsto 1\}$$
$$h_{seq} = \{s : seqBits \bullet s \mapsto \#s\}$$
$$h_{bool}(true_{BitSeq}) = h_{bool}(one)$$
$$= 1$$
$$= true_{Nums}$$
$$h_{seq}(empty_{BitSeq}) = h_{seq}(\langle\rangle)$$
$$= 0$$
$$= empty_{Nums} = false_{Nums}$$
$$h_{seq}(join_{BitSeq}(s, t)) = h_{seq}(s \frown t)$$
$$= \#(s \frown t)$$
$$= \#s + \#t$$
$$= join_{Nums}(\#s, \#t)$$

$\heartsuit$

The last line in the above illustrates a deficiency in the algebra *Nums* in relation to the given signature $\Sigma BoolSeq$, namely that there are no terms in $T_{\Sigma BoolSeq}$ for referring to the numbers given by $\#s$ and $\#t$ when they are greater than 1.

11.9 Terminal Algebras

Since our account up to now has been geared towards an exposition of the initial algebra approach, the reader should exercise some care in relying on the material covered so far in the study of terminal algebras.

11.9.1 The Motivation for Terminal Algebras

The basic tenet in the initial algebra approach is that two distinct *wfts* in the term algebra of a given signature correspond to different objects, unless it may be deduced otherwise from the equations. As mentioned in Section 11.4, this is a stance taken on a subjective basis. An alternative would be to insist that, unless the specification points to the contrary, two distinct *wfts* in the term algebra correspond to the same object. A justification for this may be seen in the approach to specification based on *type algebras*, introduced in

Section 11.3.4. Suppose that the specification contains no accessor operation described there, that is, an operation with non-TOI range. In this case, there is no technical means to distinguish between the objects in TOI and, therefore, one may argue that the objects concerned are nothing but the same object. In some cases, the result could be a trivial algebra where everything collapses into a single object.

11.9.2 Reasoning About Inequalities

In contrast to the reasoning about equalities conducted in Section 11.7.4, this sub-section considers a rather unusual need – how to reason about inequalities.

Recall that 'type-algebraic' heterogeneous specifications Σ_{sorts} may contain one and only one TOI although, if required, there can be other more primitive sorts such as nat, Bool, etc. The *wfts* of each sort s are given in the carrier $| \ T_\Sigma(X) \ |_s$ of the term algebra. Let s be a non-TOI sort and, therefore, be independently defined through a suitable subsidiary algebra. The *wfts* of type s in carrier $| \ T_\Sigma(X) \ |_s$ may be of two kinds: those without any operation pattern involving TOI (*primitive wfts*), and those with such operation patterns (*non-primitive wfts*). The following are two examples:

$succ(succ(succ(succzero)))$
$succ(next(enqueue(j, empty)))$

respectively, for each.

Two *wfts* t_1 and t_2 of type TOI are said to be not equivalent to each other, that is, $t_1 \not\approx t_2$ by definition, if and only if there exists a non-primitive *wft* $u \in | \ T_\Sigma(X) \ |_s$ parameterised with respect to $x \in X_{\text{TOI}}$ and two distinct primitive *wfts* $p_1, p_2 \in | \ T_\Sigma(X) \ |_s$ such that:

$u(x \leftarrow t_1) = p_1$
$u(x \leftarrow t_2) = p_2$

but

$p_1 \neq p_2$

where, as before, $u(x \leftarrow t)$ denotes the value of u after substitution of t for x. That is, $t_1 \not\approx t_2$ if and only if an accessor with a non-TOI range is able to distinguish between t_1 and t_2. [Note that '$\not\approx$' does not stand for the negation of $\approx$. In fact, we have not introduced a symbol '$\approx$' in this chapter.]

EXAMPLE 11.11 The terms:

$next(enqueue(6, empty))$
$next(enqueue(7, empty))$

may be distinguished if and only if the following follows from the equations:

$$next(enqueue(6, empty)) = 6$$
$$next(enqueue(7, empty)) = 7$$

and on the grounds that $6 \neq 7$ in *nat*, which is a non-TOI type.   ♡

An algebra T is said to be a *final algebra* in a class of algebras $\mathcal{C}$ with a common signature if and only if T is in $\mathcal{C}$ and there is a unique homomorphism from each algebra in $\mathcal{C}$ to T.

11.10 Bibliographical Notes

Sources on algebraic specification include the books by Horebeek and Lewi [25] and Loeckx, Ehrich and Wolf [34]. In this respect, the reader may find Martin [35] a useful text with many practical examples on the specification and implementation of data types.

The material in this chapter is based on the works cited below. Zilles [68], Liskov and Zilles [33], and Guttag and Horning [21] represent some of the earliest works and address issues such as consistency and completeness of algebraic specifications. Major sources of the initial algebra approach may be found in Goguen and Burstall [12] Goguen [15], Goguen, Thatcher, and Wagner [16], Meseguer and Goguen [36] and Sannella [50]. Other major accounts of algebraic techniques include Birkhoff and Lipson [8], Bertizz and Thatte [6], and Guttag [20].

12. Algebraic Specification in CLEAR

Chapter 11 introduced some of the basic concepts in algebraic approach to specification but primarily from the point of view of abstract data types. This chapter extends this discussion to the specification of systems in general. In this respect, it relies on the specification language CLEAR developed at the University of Edinburgh in the 70s and the 80s. Despite the absence of much activity in its development now, CLEAR serves our purpose quite well, that is, to illustrate the issues encountered in the construction of large algebraic specifications, obviously, dealing with more complex problems than simple data types.

12.1 Data Types and Systems

Specification of systems is outside the traditional application area of the algebraic specification, namely, the specification of data types. Therefore, it is instructive to understand the relationship between the two.

Data types are concerned with abstract objects with no notion of change. The number represented by the numeral '5', for example, never undergoes any change. Systems, or machines, on the other hand, are inconceivable without change, which is manifested both internally with respect to its state and externally with respect to its environment, for example, through the exchange of data as input and output. In the specification of data types, the focus of attention is on the characterisation of data items, whereas in systems the objective is to characterise the behaviour of a system. In sequential systems, this concerns the characterisation of behaviour through inputs and outputs.

When dealing with data types, as other kinds of specification, an algebraic specification helps both to understand how to use a data type and as a basis for its implementation. Although a data type may have several different representations, what is important from the user's point of view is whether they are *isomorphic*, in other words, whether they are abstractly the same.

When dealing with machines, however, the algebraic notion of isomorphism could – unnecessarily – be too rigid a requirement. This is because, from the user's point of view, what matters in a system is its external behaviour in terms of its input and output, and not any effect of the latter on

the state of the machine. As an abstract machine, the algebraic specification
of a sequential system takes the form

$$\text{sorts } \alpha, \omega, state$$
$$\text{opns } input : \alpha, state \rightarrow state$$
$$output : state \rightarrow \omega$$
$$init : \rightarrow state$$
$$\text{eqns } \quad \ldots \ldots$$

The external behaviour of the system is to be characterised by input and
output communication of two types of data: input data of type α and output
data of type ω. Its internal behaviour is to be represented by relying on
another type of data, *state*, the values of which are abstract representations
of the possible states of the machine. The description of its overall behaviour
may be given by certain operations: *input* (an input operation which may
bring about a state transformation), *output* (an output operation) and *init*
(initialisation of the state). Obviously, its behaviour may be seen externally
as an invocation of *init*, followed by an interleaving of the operations *input*
and *output*, resulting in communication of data values of types α and ω with
the outside world.

If our primary concern is this interaction with the outside world, the
role of the state is immaterial. Moreover, it is possible that totally different
implementations, affecting the state differently, produce the same behaviour.
Thus, although an algebraic specification of a machine relies on the notion of
state in describing its behaviour, it is unnecessary to be concerned with its
state when examining the correctness of its implementations.

12.2 Views of Specifications

Any specification may be viewed differently at different levels. Each view
facilitates a certain function; certain views deal with how to write a specification correctly while others deal with how to interpret a specification.
Sannella and Tarlecki [49] present the classification given in Table 12.1. The
textual and presentation levels concern the syntax of the specification, the
theory level deals with formal reasoning and the model level deals with how
to relate a specification to its models. The higher level views in this hierarchy,
obviously, subsume the lower level ones.

12.3 An Introduction to CLEAR

This section presents a brief informal account of CLEAR; see Section 12.5 for
bibliographical sources with more detailed and precise accounts. Our account,

Table 12.1. Views of specifications

Level	Description
Textual Level	Being the lowest in the hierarchy, this is the least interesting view of a specification, namely, as a script of symbols and characters.
Presentation Level	This view may provide detailed syntactic structures employed in writing the specification. In the algebraic approach, it involves the signature, axioms and other linguistic constructs enabling the specification of complex syntactic structures from simpler ones. Being a document, the number of axioms should be finite or, in the case of axioms employing recursion, enumerable.
Theory Level	This view includes not only statements made explicitly in the presentation level but also all the consequences that may be inferred from the specification using the deductive apparatus provided by the language. In algebraic specifications that rely only on equations, the theory level includes all equations that may be deduced from explicitly stated equations using the equational deduction discussed in Section 11.7.4.
Model Level	Being the highest in the hierarchy, this view includes all the above and the algebraic models satisfying the specification.

where the emphasis is on how to build complex specifications from simpler specifications, relies significantly on the syntax of CLEAR as applicable to specification building operators. We refer to various syntactic categories in the definitions in the style '⟨category-indicator⟩', but in ordinary text without the hyphenation. Keywords of CLEAR are shown in sans serif type font as, for example, in 'theory'.

12.3.1 Sorts, Operators, Terms and Equations

The most basic syntactic categories of CLEAR are: sort names, operator names, variables and theory names. Knowing these, more general expressions of sorts and operators may be constructed as:

⟨sort-expr⟩   ::= ⟨sort-name⟩ | ⟨sort-name⟩ of ⟨theory-name⟩
⟨operator-expr⟩ ::= ⟨operator-name⟩ | ⟨operator-name⟩ of ⟨theory-name⟩

EXAMPLE 12.1 Given that *bool* is a sort name of a theory *Bool*, both '*bool*' and '*bool* of *Bool*' are sort expressions. Likewise, given that *not* is one of the operation names of *Bool*, '*not* of *Bool*' is an operator expression.   ♡

An operator is declared according to the following syntax:

⟨operator-declartion⟩ ::= ⟨sort-expr⟩, . . . , ⟨sort-expr⟩ → ⟨sort-expr⟩

and, using the above, a term expression may be defined as:

⟨term-expr⟩ ::= ⟨variable⟩ | ⟨operator-expr⟩(⟨variable⟩, . . . , ⟨variable⟩)

That is, a variable, or an operator applied to its arguments, is a term expression.

A declaration of a list of variables follows the usual style:

⟨variable-declaration⟩ ::= ⟨variable⟩ : ⟨sort-expr⟩, . . . , ⟨variable⟩ : ⟨sort-expr⟩

EXAMPLE 12.2

(a) Given that *dequeue* and *enqueue* are two appropriately defined operators on sorts *queue* and *item*, and q and i are variables of the sorts *queue* and *item* respectively, both '*dequeue*(*enqueue*(i, q))' and 'q' are term expressions.

(b) Given that *nat* and *bool* are two sorts, '$m, n : nat, b : bool$' is a specific variable declaration.

♡

An equation consists of a universally quantified variable declaration and a pair of term expressions. It has the general syntax:

⟨equation⟩ ::= all ⟨variable-declartion⟩ . ⟨term-expr⟩ = ⟨term-expr⟩

A variable declaration common to a set of equations does not need to be repeated for each equation, but instead can be placed at the beginning. Where it causes no confusion, a variable declaration may also be omitted.

EXAMPLE 12.3 An example of an equation is:

all $i : nat, q : queue$. *dequeue*(*enqueue*(i, q)) = q

where, as in Example 12.2, *queue* is a sort name, and *dequeue* and *enqueue* are two operators. ♡

In deriving new theories from existing ones, sort names and operator names can be renamed. This is achieved by a signature mapping (change) using expressions of the form:

⟨sort-change⟩   ::= ⟨sort-name⟩ is ⟨sort-name⟩, . . . ,
                               ⟨sort-name⟩ is ⟨sort-name⟩
⟨operator-change⟩ ::= ⟨operator-name⟩ is ⟨operator-name⟩, . . . ,
                               ⟨operator-name⟩ is ⟨sort-name⟩
⟨signature-change⟩ ::= ⟨sort-change⟩, ⟨operator-change⟩

EXAMPLE 12.4 A signature change, that maps character names $\{1,\ 2,\ \ldots,$ $9,\ A, B, \ldots Z\}$ to a numerical code drawn from $\mathbb{N}$, is given by

1 is $1, 2$ is $2, \ldots, 9$ is $9, A$ is $10, B$ is $11, \ldots, Z$ is 25

$\heartsuit$

12.3.2 Simple Theories

A specification at the presentation level consists of a signature and a set of equations on that signature. In addition, an equational theory consists of all other equations that follow from equational deduction. Despite this, CLEAR uses the flag **theory** to refer to specifications as 'theories'. Furthermore, theories can be *enriched*, or extended. For this reason, any theory can be regarded as an enrichment of an 'empty theory'. With this in mind, CLEAR has two syntactic categories: enrichment and enrichment body. These have the syntax:

⟨enrichment-body⟩ ::= **sorts** ⟨sort-name⟩, . . . , ⟨sort-name⟩
                        opns ⟨operator-declartion⟩
                              $\vdots$
                              ⟨operator-declartion⟩
                        eqns ⟨equation⟩
                              $\vdots$
                              ⟨equation⟩
⟨enrichment⟩   ::= ⟨enrichment-body⟩ | **data** ⟨enrichment-body⟩

Note that an enrichment body conforming to the above syntax corresponds to an algebraic specification of an ADT that we came across in Chapter 11.

CLEAR uses **data** to add new sorts and operators to a specification. It also has the effect of extending the specification with an extra *identity operator*

$== \ : s, s \to bool$

for every new sort s, *bool* being a sort consisting of Boolean truth values.

A feature of greater significance of **data** is, however, that it acts as a constraint on how to interpret a specification. Note that some specifications such as *Bool* (specifying Boolean truth values) and *Nat* (specifying natural numbers) specify particular structures such that possible different representations of each are isomorphic. However, there are other specifications, for example, those dealing with sequences and partially ordered sets, which apply to all kinds of structures possessing the characteristics required by the specification. When specifying sequences, for example, it is unnecessary to know whether the specification concerns a sequence of numbers or a sequence of databases.

The theories resulting from specifications dealing with particular structures are referred to as *canonical* theories, whereas theories that apply to any structure as long as it satisfies the axioms of the specification concerned are called *loose* theories. The *data constraint*, specified by the flag data, requires the theory concerned to be interpreted canonically with respect to another theory, including an empty theory. Since canonical theories are interpreted according to *initial algebra* semantics (see Section 11.8), data makes it explicit where a specification conforms with an initial algebra. Thus, when the keyword data is present, a pair of distinct operators in the theory concerned are not equal to each other unless this fact follows as a consequence from the equations of the theory.

By playing a role similar to equations, data constraint also extends the logical consequences of a specification. Consider a case such as the data type sequence, involving an empty sequence, a unit and concatenation operator. Since the data constraint assures the reachability of all possible values of this data type, it is possible to reason about such a specification inductively. In this case, the reasoning about a theory involves not only equational reasoning but also inductive reasoning.

EXAMPLE 12.5 Consider the specifications (note that the construct theory ... endth is to be introduced in Section 12.3.3)

theory $Bool =$
    sorts $bool$
    opns $true : \rightarrow bool$
        $false : \rightarrow bool$ endth

and

theory $Machine =$
    sorts $\alpha, \omega, state$
    opns $input : \alpha, state \rightarrow state$
        $output : state \rightarrow \omega$
        $init : \rightarrow state$
    eqns   ...... endth

outlined on page 242 in describing a machine abstractly.

There is an important difference between the two. The intention is that *Bool* is to be interpreted in no other way than a structure consisting of two specific binary values, corresponding to what we understand as truth values. By contrast, *Machine* is supposed to be used in different contexts using different interpretations. CLEAR makes this distinction by prefixing *Bool* with the keyword data, while leaving *Machine* as shown above with the effect that its sorts are interpreted loosely.   ♡

12.3.3 Complex Theories

This section deals with features of CLEAR that help the construction of more complex theories from simpler ones. An arbitrary theory expression can take any of the forms permitted by the following syntax:

⟨theory-expr⟩ ::=   ⟨theory-name⟩
                | theory ⟨enrichment⟩ endth
                | ⟨theory-expr⟩ + ⟨theory-expr⟩
                | enrich ⟨theory-expr⟩ by ⟨enrichment⟩ enden
                | derive ⟨enrichment⟩
                        using ⟨theory-expr⟩, . . . , ⟨theory-expr⟩
                        from ⟨theory-expr⟩
                        by ⟨signature-change⟩ endde
                | let ⟨theory-name⟩ = ⟨theory-expr⟩ in ⟨theory-expr⟩
                | ⟨procedure-name⟩(⟨theory-expr⟩[⟨signature-change⟩], . . . ,
                        ⟨theory-expr⟩[⟨signature-change⟩])

The fact that a theory name can be a theory expression is analogous to a variable being a term. The expressions of the form theory . . . endth convert enrichments into theories. The theory building binary operator '+' combines its two operand theory expressions into a single one, but without duplicating any shared subtheories; see also Example 12.8.

The theory building operator enrich extends a specification with additional sorts, operators and equations. By contrast, derive enables the derivation of new theories from those already defined by hiding or renaming sorts and operators. The enrichment that follows the keyword derive may consist of new sorts and operators. The source theory is indicated by the keyword from. Any subtheories in the source theory specified by the keyword using are to be retained in the result. The signature change appearing after by provides a map for translating the sorts and operators in the source theory to those in the newly derived theory. Any operator not mentioned there is to be 'forgotten'.

A clause of the form 'let *Temp* = . . . in . . . ' allows the definition of a local theory named *Temp* to be used in the theory following the keyword in. Obviously, *Temp* itself can be arbitrarily complex and can have enrichments as well as other local definitions.

The use of constructs involving procedures is explained in Section 12.3.4.

12.3.4 Parameterised Theories

In Section 12.3.2 we came across the notion of *loose theory* that deals with structures such as sequences, partially ordered sets, etc., that can consist of all kinds of objects. The characteristics of these structures do not depend on their content and, therefore, they can in effect be described independently.

This is done using *parameterised theories*. They are also referred to as *theory procedures*, since they produce theories once their formal parameters are instantiated with particular structures as actual parameters.

The syntax of a theory procedure definition has the form

proc ⟨procedure-name⟩(⟨theory-name⟩ : ⟨theory-expr⟩, . . . ,
⟨theory-name⟩ : ⟨theory-expr⟩) =
⟨theory-expr⟩ ⟨spec⟩

Within the parantheses of the above are the formal parameters of the parameterised theory and on the right hand side of the equality sign is the body of the theory. As shown in Section 12.3.2, an application of a theory procedure takes the form

⟨procedure-name⟩(⟨theory-expr⟩[⟨signature-change⟩], . . . ,
⟨theory-expr⟩[⟨signature-change⟩]])

Note that [. . .] in the above indicates optional signature changes.

EXAMPLE 12.6 Let *List*(X : *Item*) be a theory of lists of an arbitrary sort *item* defined by the theory *Item* and *item* be equipped with an ordering relation $\preceq$. Assume that *Sort* is the definition of a theory procedure

$Sort(x : List) = \ldots \ldots$

that can sort any list of items by $\preceq$. Suppose that *Nat* is a specification of numbers, with *nat* as its carrier and $\leqslant$ as its ordering relation. Obviously, *Sort* can be used to sort a list of numbers. This new theory for sorting lists of numbers is given by

$Sort(Nat[item$ is $nat, \preceq$ is $\leqslant$])

12.3.5 Meta Theories

Meta theories are used to specify the requirements that must be satisfied by the actual parameters to parameterised specifications.

EXAMPLE 12.7 Referring to Example 12.6, this example illustrates how to specify the requirements on *Item* – the formal parameter of *List*(X : *Item*). These requirements concern the ordering relation $\preceq$, used to sort a list of elements drawn from *item* defined in the theory *Item* by *Sort*. This kind of requirement can be specified as meta *Item* = enrich *Bool-opn by*

    opns $\preccurlyeq : item, item \rightarrow bool$

        $\doteq : item, item \rightarrow bool$

  eqns all $x, y, z : sort$.

      $x \preccurlyeq x = true$

      $(x \preccurlyeq y \ and \ y \preccurlyeq x \Rightarrow x \doteq y) = true$

      $(x \preccurlyeq y \ and \ y \preccurlyeq z \Rightarrow x \preccurlyeq z) = true$

      $(x \preccurlyeq y \ or \ y \preccurlyeq x) = true$

        $\vdots$

  enden

where it is assumed that the theory *Bool-opn* includes the definition of the usual Boolean operators *not*, *and*, *or* and $\Rightarrow$ on *bool*, and that the sort *bool* consists of the truth values *true* and *false*. Note that symbols $\preccurlyeq$ and $\doteq$ denote binary infix operators. Although undefined above, symbol $\doteq$ plays the role of the identity operator $==$ mentioned on page 245; see the note below. According to the above, $\preccurlyeq$ is a total ordering on *item*.

NOTE: The definition of *Item* given above lacks a data constraint; this explains the need for the definition of an identity operator. A definition of $\doteq$ may be found in the theory *Object* given in Section 12.4.2.   ♡

12.3.6 Base Theories

When used in conjunction with specification building operations discussed in Section 12.3.3, the concept of parameterised theory as discussed so far can be problematic. This is because it can give rise to name clashes between sorts and operators belonging to different theories playing the role of actual parameters. In order to disambiguate any confusion, the semantics of CLEAR uses the notion of *tagging* in order to tag sorts and operators by the name of their theories of origin. This is achieved by having the concept of a *base* of theories; the tags of which are fixed once and for all by their respective names. The theories not belonging to this base, usually the theories used as formal parameters to parameterised theories, are tagged with fresh names each time a formal parameter is instantiated with an actual parameter, that is, when a parameterised specification is applied to appropriate arguments. The theories in this base are named using the syntax 'const *TN* = *expr*', but with the restriction that *TN* is a unique name and that *expr* does not contain *TN*. Obviously, the theory concerned can be referred to (retrieved) in any other theory by its name *TN*.

EXAMPLE 12.8 Continuing with Examples 12.6 and 12.7, let us assume that *List*(X : *Item*) is defined as

proc $List(X : Item) =$
  enrich X by
    sorts $list$
    opns $empty : \rightarrow list$
        $unit : item \rightarrow list$
        $\frown\; : list, list \rightarrow list$
    eqns all $x, y, z : list$ •
        $empty \frown x = x$
        $x \frown empty = x$
        $x \frown (y \frown z) = (x \frown y) \frown z$ enden

Relying on *Bool* and *Bool-opn* as outlined in previous examples, but not on *Nat*, consider also the following enrichments to *Bool*:

const $Nat =$ enrich $Bool\text{-}opn$
  data sorts nat
  opns $zero : \rightarrow nat$
     $succ : nat \rightarrow nat$
     $\leqslant\; : nat, nat \rightarrow bool$
  eqns all $l, m, n : nat$ •
     $n \leqslant n = true$
     $n \leqslant succ(n) = true$
     $l \leqslant m \;and\; m \leqslant n \Rightarrow l \leqslant n = true$ enden

and

const $Bool\text{-}ordered =$ enrich $Bool\text{-}opn$
  data opns $\trianglelefteq\; : bool, bool \rightarrow bool$
  eqns $true \trianglelefteq true = true$
    $true \trianglelefteq false = false$
    $false \trianglelefteq true = true$
    $false \trianglelefteq true = true$ enden

Thus, $\leqslant$ is an ordering on *nat* and $\trianglelefteq$ on *bool*. Now consider the following instantiations of *List*:

$List(Nat[item$ is $nat, \preccurlyeq$ is $\leqslant\,])$

and

$List(Bool\text{-}ordered[item$ is $bool, \preccurlyeq$ is $\trianglelefteq\,])$

According to the tagging convention adopted, sorts and operators of the two instantiations are tagged as follows:

$List(Nat[item$ is $nat, \preccurlyeq$ is $\leqslant$ $]) =$

    sorts $bool_{Bool}, nat_{Nat}, list_{tag_1}$

    opns $empty_{tag_1} : \rightarrow list_{tag_1}$

        $unit_{tag_1} : nat_{Nat} \rightarrow list_{tag_1}$

        $\overset{tag_1}{\frown} : list_{tag_1}, list_{tag_1} \rightarrow list_{tag_1}$

    eqns all $x_{tag_1}, y_{tag_1}, z_{tag_1} : list_{tag_1}$ •

        $(empty_{tag_1}) \overset{tag_1}{\frown} x_{tag_1} = x_{tag_1}$

        $x_{tag_1} \overset{tag_1}{\frown} (empty_{tag_1}) = x_{tag_1}$

        $x_{tag_1} \overset{tag_1}{\frown} (y_{tag_1} \overset{tag_1}{\frown} z_{tag_1}) = (x_{tag_1} \overset{tag_1}{\frown} y_{tag_1}) \overset{tag_1}{\frown} z_{tag_1}$

        $\vdots$

$List(Bool\text{-}ordered[item$ is $bool, \preccurlyeq$ is $\lhd$ $]) =$

    sorts $bool_{Bool}, list_{tag_2}$

    opns $empty_{tag_2} : \rightarrow list_{tag_2}$

        $unit_{tag_2} : bool_{Bool} \rightarrow list_{tag_2}$

        $\overset{tag_2}{\frown} : list_{tag_2}, list_{tag_2} \rightarrow list_{tag_2}$

    eqns all $x_{tag_2}, y_{tag_2}, z_{tag_2} : list_{tag_2}$ •

        $(empty_{tag_2}) \overset{tag_2}{\frown} x_{tag_2} = x_{tag_2}$

        $x_{tag_2} \overset{tag_2}{\frown} (empty_{tag_2}) = x_{tag_2}$

        $x_{tag_2} \overset{tag_2}{\frown} (y_{tag_2} \overset{tag_2}{\frown} z_{tag_2}) = (x_{tag_2} \overset{tag_2}{\frown} y_{tag_2}) \overset{tag_2}{\frown} z_{tag_2}$

        $\vdots$

NOTE: The notation used above gives the tag as a subscript or, as in the case of the infix operator $\frown$, as a 'stack' of the operator symbol and the tag.

The advantage gained by the above tagging convention in const theories can be seen in the following merger (union) of the above two applications of parameterised specifications:

$List(Nat[item$ is $nat, \preccurlyeq$ is $\leqslant$ $]) +$

    $List(Bool\text{-}ordered[item$ is $bool, \preccurlyeq$ is $\lhd$ $]) =$

        sorts $bool_{Bool}, nat_{Nat}, list_{tag_1}, list_{tag_2}$

        opns $empty_{tag_1} : \rightarrow list_{tag_1}$

            $empty_{tag_2} : \rightarrow list_{tag_2}$

            $unit_{tag_1} : nat_{Nat} \rightarrow list_{tag_1}$

            $unit_{tag_2} : bool_{Bool} \rightarrow list_{tag_2}$

            $\overset{tag_1}{\frown} : list_{tag_1}, list_{tag_1} \rightarrow list_{tag_1}$

$$\overset{tag_2}{\frown} : list_{tag_2}, list_{tag_2} \to list_{tag_2}$$

$$\text{eqns all } x_{tag_1}, y_{tag_1}, z_{tag_1} : list_{tag_1}, x_{tag_2}, y_{tag_2}, z_{tag_2} : list_{tag_2} \bullet$$

$$(empty_{tag_1}) \overset{tag_1}{\frown} x_{tag_1} = x_{tag_1}$$

$$(empty_{tag_2}) \overset{tag_1}{\frown} x_{tag_2} = x_{tag_2}$$

$$\vdots$$

Note how the sorts such as *nat* and *bool* defined by const theories are not duplicated in the process of the merger and how the sort *list* and the operators *empty*, *unit* and $\frown$ involving *list* have been tagged differently so that each version with a common tag serves either *Nat* or *Bool-ordered*.   ♡

12.3.7 Specifications

Sections 12.3.4–12.3.6 have outlined the kind of specification permitted by CLEAR. These three forms of specification are summarised in the following syntax definition:

⟨spec⟩ ::=   const ⟨theory-name⟩ = ⟨theory-expr⟩ ⟨spec⟩
      | meta ⟨theory-name⟩ = ⟨theory-expr⟩ ⟨spec⟩
      | proc ⟨procedure-name⟩(⟨theory-name⟩ : ⟨theory-expr⟩, . . . ,
            ⟨theory-name⟩ : ⟨theory-expr⟩) = ⟨theory-expr⟩ ⟨spec⟩

12.4 A Case Study: A Filing System

The following is a case study illustrating the algebraic approach to specification. It concerns a filing system consisting of both sequential and indexed files. As a part of a case study in VDM in Section 10.5, an informal description of requirements of indexed files may be found in Section 10.5.1. In sequential files, data are accessed or written in an orderly manner relative to the current position.

12.4.1 Some Basic Specifications

This section introduces some of the basic specifications. First, *Bool* and *Bool-opn* for dealing with Boolean values and operators with the obvious meanings.

1.1 const *Bool* = theory

 .2   data sorts *bool*

 .3   opns *true, false* : *bool*

 .4   *not* : *bool* → *bool*

.5   eqns $not(true) = false$
.6 $not(false) = true$ endth

2.1   const $Bool\text{-}opn$ = enrich $Bool$ by
.2   opns $and, or, \Rightarrow: bool, bool \rightarrow bool$
.3   eqns all $p, q : bool$ •
.4 $p\ and\ true = p$
.5 $p\ or\ true = true$
.6 $p\ and\ false = false$
.7 $p\ or\ false = p$
.8 $p \Rightarrow q = not(p\ and\ not(q))$ enden

Another specification required is a theory of natural numbers. Below is an outline specification.

3.1 const $Nat =$
.2   enrich $Bool$ by data
.3   sorts nat
.4   opns $0\ :\ \rightarrow nat$
.5 $succ, pred\ :\ nat \rightarrow nat$
.6 $\_ + \_, \_ - \_, \_ \leqslant \_\ :\ nat, nat \rightarrow nat$
.7   err-opns $error\ :\ \rightarrow nat$
.8   eqns all $m, n : nat$ •
.9 $pred(succ(n)) = n$
.10 $pred(0) = error$

$$\vdots$$

        enden

Note the error operator in line 3.7; it is intended produce a distinguished 'error' value in the event of an inappropriate argument to any of the operators listed under opns as, for example, in line 3.10.

12.4.2 A General Specification for Various Kinds of Object

Below is meta specification $Object$ used elsewhere in this case study. As was mentioned in the note on page 249, because of the absence of a data constraint the specification requires the inclusion of an identity operator, denoted here by $\doteq$ and defined as an equivalence relation.

4.1 meta $Object =$
.2   enrich $Bool\text{-}opn$ by

.3   sorts *element*

.4   opns $\_ \doteq \_ :$ *element, element* $\rightarrow$ *element*

.5   eqns all $m, n, p :$ *element* .

.6 $(m \doteq m) = true$

.7 $(m \doteq n) = (n \doteq m)$

.8 $((m \doteq n) and (n \doteq p) \Rightarrow (m \doteq p)) = true$ enden endth

12.4.3 Maps

The theory of 'maps' introduced here is intended for use in the specification of indexed files. With this specific use in mind, let us first derive two other specifications from *Object*, namely, *Record* and *Index*, to be used respectively as abstract representations of records of data and keys used for accessing records in indexed files. By continuing to treat them as meta theories, the specification deliberately avoids dealing with any specific form of their representation.

5.1   meta *Record* =

.2   derive sorts *record*

.3   opns $\doteq:$ *record, record* $\rightarrow$ *bool*

.4   using *Bool*

.5   from *Object*

.6   by *record* is *element*, $\doteq$ is $\doteq$ endde

6.1   meta *Index* = theory

.2   derive sorts *key*

.3   opns $\doteq:$ *key, key* $\rightarrow$ *bool*

.4   using *Bool*

.5   from *Object*

.6   by *key* is *element*, $\doteq$ is $\doteq$ endde

Maps are essentially mathematical functions from one set to another. Since these sets can be arbitrary, as given in line 7.1, maps are parameterised here with respect to theories *Key* and *Record*. According to our representation, maps require several specific operators for their manipulation, namely, those listed in lines 7.5–7.8. Lines 7.5 and 7.9 present as operators two distinguished values: the former for the empty map and the latter as an error value.

7.1   proc $Map(Id : Key, Rec : Record) =$ theory

.2   enrich $Id + Rec + Bool\text{-}opn$ by data

.3   sorts *map*

.4   opns $new : \to map$

.5 $retrieve : key, map \to record$

.6 $insert : key, record, map \to map$

.7 $remove : key, map \to map$

.8 $is\text{-}empty : map \to bool$

.9   err-opns $error : \to map$

.10   eqns all $i, i_1, i_2 : key;\ j, j_1, j_2 : record;\ m : map$ •

.11 $is\text{-}empty(new) = true$

.12 $is\text{-}empty(insert(i, j, m)) = false$

.13 $retrieve(i, insert(i, j, m)) = j$

.14 $retrieve(i, new) = error$

.15 $not(i_1 \doteq i_2) \Rightarrow (insert(i_1, j_1, insert(i_2, j_2, m)) \doteq$
                $insert(i_2, j_2, insert(i_1, j_1, m))) = true$

.16 $insert(i, j_1, insert(i, j_2, m)) = error$

.17 $remove(i, insert(i, j, m)) = m$

.18 $not(i_1 \doteq i_2) \Rightarrow (remove(i_1, remove(i_2, m)) \doteq$
                $remove(i_2, remove(i_1, m))) = true$

.19 $not(i_1 \doteq i_2) \Rightarrow (remove(i_1, insert(i_2, j, m)) \doteq$
                $insert(i_2, j, remove(i_1, m))) = true$

.20 $remove(i, remove(i, j, m)) = error$

.21 $remove(i, new) = error$

.22   enden endth

The notion of a map being empty is captured by the equations in lines 7.11 and 7.12. According to lines 7.15 and 7.18, the operators *insert* and *remove* are in effect associative, provided that, as pointed out by the Boolean term $not(i_1 \doteq i_2)$, the keys concerned are distinct. In other words, the order of insertion, or removal, of records against different keys is immaterial. Note the use of the phrase 'in effect being associative' because of the use of an identity relation, instead of an equation directly to that effect.

According to line 7.19, the order is immaterial even for any mix of insertion and removal operations affecting different keys. However, the same does not apply when the two operations concern the same key: according to line 7.17 the removal of a previously inserted record should have no effect on the map, whereas, in the absence of an equation to that effect, an interchange of the order of the two operations may not necessarily result in the same.

Dealing with error cases, according to line 7.14, any attempt to retrieve a record from an empty map results in an error. According to line 7.16, no insertions are permitted against any key in a map containing a record.

According to lines 7.20 and 7.21, no removals can be against non–existing keys.

12.4.4 Sequences

Sequences are not different from lists, considered in Example 12.8. Therefore, here is another version of the definition given there but with a difference in sort names.

8.1 proc $Seq(X : Object) =$

.2   enrich X by

.3   sorts seq

.4   opns $empty : \rightarrow seq$

.5 $unit : element \rightarrow seq$

.6 $\_\frown\_ : seq, seq \rightarrow seq$

.7   eqns all $s, t, u : seq$ •

.8 $empty\frown s = s$

.9 $s\frown empty = s$

.10 $s \frown (t\frown u) = (s\frown t)\frown u$

.11   enden

However, it is convenient to have some additional operators for manipulating sequences, especially since we intend to use them as a representation for sequential files. Most of these operators are intended for traversing a given sequence, with or without modifying it.

9.1 proc $Seq\text{-}extended(X : Object) =$

.2   enrich $(X + Nat + Bool\text{-}opn)$ by

.3   opns $length : seq \rightarrow nat$

.4 $special : \rightarrow element$

.5 $extend : nat, seq \rightarrow seq$

.6 $drop, take, e\text{-}drop, e\text{-}take : nat, seq \rightarrow seq$

.7   err-opns $error : \rightarrow seq$

.8   eqns all $s : seq;\ a : element;\ n : nat$ •

.9 $length(empty) = 0$

.10 $length(unit(a)\frown s) = 1 + length(s)$

.11 $extend(0, s) = s$

.12 $extend(n, s) = extend(n - 1, s\frown unit(special))$

.13 $drop(0, s) = s$

.14 $not(n == 0) \Rightarrow (drop(n, unit(a)\frown s) \doteq drop(n - 1, s)) = true$

.15 $not(n == 0) \Rightarrow (drop(n, empty) \doteq empty) = true$

.16 $take(0, s) = empty$

.17 $not(n == 0) \Rightarrow (take(n, unit(a)^\frown s) \doteq$
$$unit(a)^\frown(take(n - 1, s))) = true$$

.18 $not(n == 0) \Rightarrow (take(n, empty) \doteq extend(n, empty)) = true$

.19 $e\text{-}drop(0, s) = s$

.20 $not(n == 0) \Rightarrow (e\text{-}drop(n, unit(a)^\frown s) \doteq e\text{-}drop(n - 1, s)) = true$

.21 $not(n == 0) \Rightarrow (e\text{-}drop(n, empty) \doteq error) = true$

.22 $e\text{-}take(0, s) = empty$

.23 $not(n == 0) \Rightarrow (e\text{-}take(n, unit(a)^\frown s) \doteq$
$$unit(a)^\frown(e\text{-}take(n - 1, s))) = true$$

.24 $not(n == 0) \Rightarrow (e\text{-}take(n, empty) \doteq error) = true$

.25   enden

The recursive definition of *length* in lines 9.9 and 9.10 gives the length of a given sequence. Given a number n, the operator $extends(n, s)$, defined in lines 9.11 and 9.12, extends the sequence s with n instances of the element *special*.

Given a number n, the operator $drop(n, s)$, defined in lines 9.13–9.15, allows n elements to be dropped from the 'head' of the sequence s if its length is greater than or equal to n, otherwise as many elements as possible without resulting in an error. Note the use of the standard identity operator '$==$' in the case of *nat*, thanks to the presence of a data constraint in *Nat*, and the specially introduced identity operator '$\doteq$' in the case of *element*, because of the absence of a data constraint in *Object* and its subsequent enrichments considered so far. The operator *e-drop* in lines 9.19–9.21 has the same functionality as its counterpart *drop*, except that the former produces an error when the length of the sequence happens to be less than n.

Given a number n, the operator $take(n, s)$, defined in lines 9.16–9.18, allows n elements to be skipped from the 'head' of the sequence s if its length is less than or equal to n, otherwise it extends the sequence with as many instances of the element *special* as necessary without any error. Its counterpart *e-take* in lines 9.22–9.24 has the same functionality, except that it results in an error when the length of the sequence happens to be less than n.

12.4.5 Indexed Files

With the above definitions in place, it is possible to define what files are. First, the concept of an indexed file.

As mentioned in Section 12.4.3, maps are a suitable representation for indexed files. Therefore, the specification begins in line 10.2 with a local definition F for a map from Id to Rec, which are the formal parameters of the theory procedure $IndFile$. F is used to define another local definition G, which derives the operators required for manipulating indexed files.

10.1	proc $IndFile(Id : Key, Rec : Record) =$ theory
.2	let $F = Map(Id, Rec)$ in
.3	let $G =$ derive
.4	using $Bool\text{-}opn$
.5	from F
.6	by key is key, $record$ is $item$, $ind\text{-}file$ is map, $\doteq$ is $\doteq$
.7	$init$ is new, $read$ is $retrieve$, add is $insert$, $delete$ is $remove$
.8	endde in
.9	enrich G by
.10	opns $write$: $key, record, ind\text{-}file \rightarrow ind\text{-}file$
.11	eqns all $i, i_1, i_2 : key$; $j, j_1, j_2 : record, f : ind\text{-}file$ $\bullet$
.12	$write(i, j_1, add(i, j_2, f)) = add(i, j_1, delete(i, f))$
.13	$(not(i_1 \doteq i_2)) \Rightarrow (write(i_1, j_1, add(i_2, j_2, f)) \doteq$
	$add(i_2, j_2, write(i_1, j_1, f))) = true$
.14	$write(i, j, init) = error$
.15	enden endth

As given in lines 10.6 and 10.7, most of these operators can be obtained by a simple renaming of map operators, with new file operators $init$, $read$, add and $delete$ for new, $retrieve$, $insert$ and $remove$ respectively. The only other required file handing operation is $write$, for overwriting a record against an existing key. Thus, the enrichment beginning with line 10.9 introduces its syntax in line 10.10 and its definition in lines 10.12–10.14.

12.4.6 Sequential Files

Since we are dealing here with sequential character files, let us settle on a specific character set, as given by

11.1	const $Char =$ theory
.2	data sorts $char$
.3	opns $none$: $\rightarrow char$
.4	$'a', 'b', \cdots$etc. : $\rightarrow char$
.5	endth

Note that $none$ in line 11.3 is a distinguished character to be used as a 'null' value in empty records. Other required characters are to be specified as indicated in line 11.3.

Our intention is to use sequences for the representation of sequential files. Therefore, the specification is developed from *Seq-extended* in several stages. First, it defines in line 12.2 a local theory F by applying the parameterised theory *Seq-extended* to the constant theory *Char*. In lines 12.3–12.7, F is then used to define another local theory G by deriving from F all except the operator *extend* but, at the same time, renaming several other sorts and operators to suit file handling purposes. In lines 12.8–12.17, G is in turn used to define another local theory H by enriching G with three operators: *read*, *write* and *delete*; their syntax being given in lines 12.9–12.11.

12.1   proc *SeqFile* = theory

.2   let $F = $ *Seq-extended*(*Char*[*char* is *element*, *none* is *special*,
                                    $==$ is $\doteq$]) in

.3   let $G = $ derive

.4   using *Nat*, *Bool-opn*

.5   from F

.6   by *seq-file* is *seq*, *init* is *empty*, *error* is *error*, *drop* is *drop*,
                      take is *take*, *e-drop* is *e-drop*, *e-take* is *e-take*, *length* is *length*

.7   endde in

.8   let $= H$ enrich G by

.9   opns *read* : *nat*, *nat*, *seq-file* → *seq-file*

.10   *write* : *nat*, *seq-file*, *seq-file* → *seq-file*

.11   *delete* : *nat*, *nat*, *seq-file* → *seq-file*

.12   eqns all s, f : *seq-file*; *offset*, *len* : *nat* .

.13 $not(f == init) \Rightarrow (read(offset, len, f) ==$
                          $e\text{-}take(len, e\text{-}drop(offset, f))) = true$

.14 $(offset = 0\ or\ len = 0) \Rightarrow$
                          $(read(offset, len, init) == error) = true$

.15 $write(offset, s, f) =$
                          $(take(offset, f))^\frown s^\frown drop(offset + length(s), f))$

.16 $not(f == init) \Rightarrow (delete(offset, len, f) ==$
                          $(e\text{-}take(offset, f))^\frown drop(offset + len, f)) = true$

.17   enden

.18   in derive

.19   using *Nat*, *Bool-opn*

.20   from H

.21   by *seq-file* is *seq-*, *init* is *init*, *error* is *error*,
                    read is *read*, *write* is *write*, *delete* is *delete*,

.22   endde endth

In the equations given in lines 12.12–12.16, variable f is supposed to represent the file being manipulated, s is a sequence of characters (but identical in structure to a 'file') to be read from, or written to, f. Variable *offset* denotes the number of characters serving as an offset from where the operation concerned is affected and variable *len* the length of characters affected by the operation.

The operator *read*(*offset*, *len*, *f*) is intended to read *len* number of characters from a given file f starting at an offset *offset*. According to line 12.14, application of *read* to an empty file with a non-zero value for *offset*, or *len*, results in an error. According to line 12.13, an error could also result in other cases. This follows from the definition of *read* in terms of *e-take* and *e-drop*, both being potentially capable of generating an error, as defined in the theory *Seq-extended*.

The operator *write*, defined in line 12.15, is not error–prone, because it allows the writing of an input sequence of any length into any file, including the empty file, at an offset of zero or more characters. This flexibility is achieved by defining *write* in terms of error-resilient operators *drop* and *take* of the theory *Seq-extended*. The effect of *write*(*offset*, *s*, *f*) is such that it concatenates in the given order three character sequences: a sequence of length *offset* taken from the beginning of f, the input sequence s, and a sequence of length obtained by dropping from the beginning of f a sequence of length *offset* plus the length of s. Note that in the case of offset being greater than the length of the file, the operator inserts the distinguished character *none* at the end of the file up to the length *offset*.

The operator *delete*(*offset*, *len*, *f*), defined in line 12.16, is intended for deleting *len* characters from f beginning from an offset *offset*. It is error–prone, since the operation is not applicable to an empty file with a non–zero offset. The operator is defined in terms of the error-resilient operator *drop* and the error–prone operator *take*, both of the theory *Seq-extended*.

12.4.7 File System

Let us also derive from *Object*, given in Section 12.4.2, a specification *Name* to be used as an abstract representation for file names, again deliberately avoiding the details of its representation.

13.1 meta *Name* =

.2   derive sorts *name*

.3   opns $\doteq$: *name*, *name* $\to$ *bool*

.4   using *Bool*

.5   from *Object*

.6   by *name* is *element*, $\doteq$ is $\doteq$ endde endth

The definition *FileSys* given below is an outline specification of the file system as whole, consisting of both indexed and sequential files. It is parameterised with respect to *Name, Key* and *Record*.

14.1   proc *FileSys*($nm : Name, Id : Key, Rec : Record$) = theory
.2   let *File* = enrich ($IndFile(Id : Key, Rec : Record) + SeqFile$) by
.3   sorts *file, access-args, output*
.4   opns *inj-ind-file* : *ind-file* → *file*
.5   *inj-seq-file* : *seq-file* → *file*
.6   *inj-key* : *key* → *access-args*
.7   *inj-key-rec* : *key, record* → *access-args*
.8   *inj-nat-seq-file* : *nat, seq-file* → *access-args*
.9   *inj-nat-pair* : *nat, nat* → *access-args*
.10   *inj-seq-file* : *seq-file* → *output*
.11   *inj-rec* : *record* → *output* enden in
.12   let $F = Map(Name, X : File)$ in
.13   let G = derive
.14   using F
.15   from F
.16   by *name* is *key, file* is *record, file-sys* is *map*, $\doteq$ is $\doteq$
.17   *init-file-sys* is *new, open* is *retrieve, close* is *insert,*
.18   *destroy* is *remove* endde in
.19   enrich G by data
.20   opns *create-ind-file* : *name, file-sys* → *file-sys*
.21   *create-seq-file* : *name, file-sys* → *file-sys*
.22   *read* : *access-args, file* → *output*
.23   *add, delete, write* : *access-args, file* → *file*
.24   err-opns *error* : → *file-sys*
.25   eqns all n : *name, fs* : *file-sys, k* : *key, r* : *record, i, j* : *nat,*
                f : *ind-file, g* : *seq-file* .
.26 $create\text{-}ind\text{-}file(n, fs) = close(n, inj\text{-}ind\text{-}file(init_{IndFile}), fs)$
.27 $create\text{-}seq\text{-}file(n, fs) = close(n, inj\text{-}seq\text{-}file(init_{SeqFile}), fs)$
.28 $read(inj\text{-}key(k), inj\text{-}ind\text{-}file(f)) = read_{IndFile}(k, f)$
.29 $read(inj\text{-}nat\text{-}pair(i, j), inj\text{-}seq\text{-}file(g)) = read_{SeqFile}(i, j, g)$
.30 $add(inj\text{-}key\text{-}rec(k, r), inj\text{-}ind\text{-}file(f)) = add_{IndFile}(k, r, f)$
.31 $write(inj\text{-}key\text{-}rec(k, r), inj\text{-}ind\text{-}file(f)) = write_{IndFile}(k, r, f)$
.32 $write(inj\text{-}nat\text{-}seq\text{-}file(i, s), inj\text{-}seq\text{-}file(g)) =$

$$write_{SeqFile}(i, s, g)$$

.33 $delete(inj\text{-}key(i), inj\text{-}ind\text{-}file(f)) = delete_{IndFile}(i, f)$

.34 $delete(inj\text{-}nat\text{-}pair(i, j), inj\text{-}seq\text{-}file(g)) =$
$$delete_{SeqFile}(i, j, g)$$

$\cdots$ (the rest, including error equations, is omitted) $\cdots$

enden endth

The operations defined in lines 14.4–14.11 are for internal use only. For example, the operations *inj-ind-file* and *inj-seq-file* enable the treatment of files of the two types, that is, indexed and sequential files, as just files, belonging to the sort *file*. Likewise, the operations *inj-key-rec* and *inj-nat-pair* enable the arguments required in individual file operations, such as keys, offsets, etc., to be treated in a uniform manner as 'access arguments', that is, as elements of the sort *access-args*. Since these operations are for internal use, they can be hidden by using a derive clause in a complete version of the above specification.

The operation *init-file-sys*, defined in line 14.17, is a system level operation for creating a file system. The operations *open*, *close* and *destroy* in lines 14.17 and 14.18 are system level file access operations, intended respectively for opening, closing and deleting a given file.

The operations *create-ind-file* and *create-seq-file*, defined in lines 14.20 and 14.21, are intended respectively for creating an indexed, or a sequential, file. The operations *read*, *add*, *write* and *delete* lines 14.22 and 14.23 are system level operations for performing individual file operations, obviously, for reading, adding, writing and deleting records or text. These have been specified in a manner independent of the file type so that they can be invoked in an 'object oriented' manner in terms of operations that specialise on different file types.

Obviously, the above approach relies on the availability of two 'internal' versions for each of these operations. This is in line with our discussion in Section 12.3.6 on different tags used for referring to operators belonging to non–base theories. For example, based on this tagging convention, $read_{FileSys}$ could result in either $read_{IndFile}$ or $read_{SeqFile}$, depending on whether the file to be manipulated is an indexed file or a sequential file.

Consider, for example, $create\text{-}ind\text{-}file(n, fs)$ in line 14.26. Its effect is expressed on the right hand side as $close(n, inj\text{-}ind\text{-}file(init_{IndFile}), fs))$, which amounts to, in terms of *IndFile*, an 'insertion' of a newly 'initialised' indexed file in *fs* at 'key' position n. Likewise, $read(inj\text{-}nat\text{-}pair(i, j), inj\text{-}seq\text{-}file(g))$, in line 14.29, with an access argument $inj\text{-}nat\text{-}pair(i, j)$ and a sequential file $inj\text{-}seq\text{-}file(g)$ in the file system as arguments, is the same as $read_{SeqFile}(i, j, g)$, which amounts to, in terms of *SeqFile*, reading j characters from the sequential file g starting from the offset i.

Also note that the operations *create-ind-file*, *create-seq-file*, *read*, *write* and *delete* are error–prone; incorrect argument types could lead to an error value, eventually resulting in a system level error as represented by *error*, but these have not been formally specified here for brevity.

12.5 Bibliographical Notes

The material in this chapter is based primarily on Burstall and Goguen [12] and Sannella [50].

Exercises

12.1 Specify in an algebraic style sets, bags and relations, with operations as understood in Z.

12.2 Specify in an algebraic style the board game snakes and ladders covered in Section 4.3.

A. Exercises on Reading Formal Specifications

This appendix proposes three case studies for improving skills in reading and interpreting specifications. The case studies in Sections A.1 and A.2 only contain the bare mathematics with cursory explanations about any non-standard notations. As exercises, provide a narrative for each in English, explaining:

(i) Your understanding of the requirements.
(ii) The use of mathematics and the schema language of Z in expressing these requirements.

With respect to (ii), pay particular attention to various specification constructs, namely type introductions, signature declarations, predicates, schemas defining states, state transformations, preconditions, etc.

A.1 Exercise - A Simple Text Editor

The case study is inspired by that of Sufrin [58]. The mathematical definition given below is just a part of the specification on a simple text editor.

$[Char]$

$$prefixes : \text{seq } Char \leftrightarrow \text{seq } Char$$

$$\forall s_1, s_2 : \text{seq } Char \bullet$$

$$s_1 \ prefixes \ s_2 \Leftrightarrow s_1 = ((1..\#s_1) \lhd s_2)$$

$Report ::=' At\ top\ of\ the\ file!'\ |'\ At\ bottom\ of\ the\ file'\ |$
$\quad\quad 'String\ not\ found!'\ |'\ Empty\ string!'$

___Document___
$$text, left, right : \text{seq } Char$$
$$text = left \frown right$$

$CreateDoc \mathrel{\widehat{=}} Document' \mid text' = \varnothing$

$BeginEdit \mathrel{\widehat{=}} Document' \mid left' = \varnothing$

$MoveLeft_0$ _____

$\Delta Document$

$left \neq \varnothing$

$left' = front\ left$

$right' = \langle(last\ left)\rangle \frown right$

$MoveRight_0$ _____

$\Delta Document$

$right \neq \varnothing$

$left' = left \frown \langle(head\ right)\rangle$

$right' = tail\ right$

$Delete_0$ _____

$\Delta Document$

$left \neq \varnothing$

$left' = front\ left$

$right' = right$

$FindAny$ _____

$\Delta Document$

$string? : seq\ Char$

$string?\ prefixes\ right'$

$left' = (1..(\#text - \#right')) \triangleleft text$

$text' = text$

$FindOnRight$ _____

$FindAny$

$\neg\ \exists\, Document'' \mid text'' = text \bullet$

$\quad \#right \geqslant \#right'' > \#right' \wedge$

$\quad string?\ prefixes\ right''$

$\#right > \#right'$

```
┌─ FindFromTop ─────────────────────────────────────────
│ FindAny
│ ─────────────────────────
│ ¬ ∃ Document″ | text″ = text •
│
│     #text ⩾ #right″ > #right′ ∧
│
│     string? prefixes right″
│
│ #right ⩽ #right′
└───────────────────────────────────────────────────────
```

```
┌─ AtTopOfFile ─────────────────────────────────────────
│ Ξ Document
│
│ rep! : Report
│ ─────────────────────────
│ left = ∅
│
│ rep! =′ At top of the file!′
└───────────────────────────────────────────────────────
```

```
┌─ AtBottomOfFile ──────────────────────────────────────
│ Ξ Document
│
│ rep! : Report
│ ─────────────────────────
│ right = ∅
│
│ rep! =′ At bottom of the file!′
└───────────────────────────────────────────────────────
```

```
┌─ NotFound ────────────────────────────────────────────
│ Ξ Document
│
│ string? : seq Char
│
│ rep! : Report
│ ─────────────────────────
│ ¬ ∃ Document″ | text″ = text •
│
│     string? prefixes right″
│
│ string? ≠ ∅
│
│ rep! =′ String not found!′
└───────────────────────────────────────────────────────
```

```
┌─ EmptyString ─────────────────────────────────────
│ Ξ Document
│
│ string? : seq Char
│
│ rep! : Report
│ ──────────────────────────────
│ string? = ∅
│
│ rep! =' Empty string!'
└────────────────────────────────────────────────────
```

```
┌─ Insert ──────────────────────────────────────────
│ Δ Document
│
│ ch? : Char
│ ──────────────────────────────
│ left' = left ⌢ ⟨ch?⟩
│
│ right' = right
└────────────────────────────────────────────────────
```

$MoveLeft \mathrel{\widehat{=}} MoveLeft_0 \lor AtTopOfFile$

$MoveRight \mathrel{\widehat{=}} MoveRight_0 \lor AtBottomOfFile$

$Delete \mathrel{\widehat{=}} Delete_0 \lor AtTopOfFile$

$FindString \mathrel{\widehat{=}} (FindFromTop \oplus FindOnRight) \lor NotFound \lor$
$\qquad\qquad\qquad EmptyString$

where the schema overriding operator $\oplus$ defined as:

$A \oplus B \mathrel{\widehat{=}} (A \land \neg \text{ pre } B) \lor B$

A.2 Let's Play A Game of Cards

The aim of this exercise is to see whether the reader can work out the rules of the game from the given mathematical specification. If you are interested, play it. Have a pack of cards handy. For obvious reasons, the definition contains only the rules of the game, and the reader has to gradually learn the best way of playing it, i.e. the heuristics.

Let us first enumerate the elements of two types,

$Suit ::= \heartsuit \mid \diamondsuit \mid \clubsuit \mid \spadesuit$

$Rank ::= 2 \mid 3 \mid 4 \mid 5 \mid 6 \mid 7 \mid 8 \mid Q \mid K \mid 10 \mid A \mid 9 \mid J$

which form the foundation of the rest of this specification.

$Pack \;\widehat{=}\; Suit \times Rank$

$Symbol : Pack \to Suit$

$Ranking : Pack \to Rank$

$\forall\, s : Suit;\; r : Rank \bullet$

$\quad Symbol(s, r) = s$

$\quad Ranking(s, r) = r$

$\_\, Dominates \,\_\; : Rank \leftrightarrow Rank$

$Dominates = \{(3,2), (4,3), (5,4), (6,5), (7,6), (8,7),$

$\quad (Q,8), (K,Q), (10,K), (A,10), (9,A), (J,9)\}^{+}$

Note that the superscript '+' in the set definition of $Dominates$ given above stands for the irreflexive transitive closure.

$FaceValue : Pack \to \mathbb{N}$

$FaceValue = Ranking \,\fatsemi\, \{(2,0), (3,0), (4,0), (5,0), (6,0), (7,0), (8,0),$

$\quad (Q,2), (K,3), (10,10), (A,11), (9,20), (J,30)\}$

$CardStatus ::= \mathsf{open} \mid \mathsf{close}$

$Biddable : \mathbb{F}\, \mathbb{N}_1$

$Count : \mathbb{P}\, Pack \to \mathbb{N}$

$Biddable = 1 \mathinner{\ldotp\ldotp} (Count\ Pack)$

$\forall\, p : \mathbb{P}\, Pack \mid p \neq \varnothing \ \bullet$

$\qquad Count\ \varnothing = 0$

$\qquad Count\ p\ =\ FaceValue\ x + Count(p - \{x\})$

where $x = \mu\ p$, (i.e. an arbitrary choice from the set p)

$Shuffle : \mathrm{seq}\ Pack \leftrightarrow \mathrm{seq}\ Pack$

$Shuffle = \{p, q : \mathrm{seq}\ Pack \mid p \neq q \wedge \mathrm{dom}\ p = \mathrm{dom}\ q = 1 \mathinner{\ldotp\ldotp} \#Pack \wedge$

$\qquad\qquad \mathrm{ran}\ p = \mathrm{ran}\ q = Pack \bullet (p, q)\}$

Whenever the card pack is shuffled, we should end up with a different order of cards on different occasions even if the initial order of the pack happens to be the same. For this purpose, we introduce a new operator called μ_{random} for the arbitrary random selection of an element from a set. The difference between this and μ is subtle. Though the latter makes an arbitrary choice, it makes the same choice for any given instance of a set. For a set S, we use the newly introduced notation in the manner:

$\mu_{random}\ S$

and require

$x = \mu_{random}\ S \Rightarrow x \in S$

Let *Positions* denote the permitted player positions:

$Positions : \mathbb{P}\, \mathbb{N}$

$Positions = \{0, 1, 2, 3\}$

Let us define $\oplus_4$, the operator for addition modulo 4, as,

$\_ \oplus_4 \_ : \mathbb{N} \times \mathbb{N} \to \mathbb{N}$

$\forall\, m, n : \mathbb{N} \mid m, n < 4 \bullet m \oplus_4 n = (m + n)\ \mathrm{mod}\ 4$

Some examples are:

$0 \oplus_4 1 = 1 \qquad\qquad 0 \oplus_4 2 = 2 \quad$ etc.

$1 \oplus_4 1 = 2 \qquad\qquad 1 \oplus_4 2 = 3$

$2 \oplus_4 1 = 3 \qquad\qquad 2 \oplus_4 2 = 0$

$3 \oplus_4 1 = 0 \qquad\qquad 3 \oplus_4 2 = 1$

Given a set of bids made by players, the function *Highest* returns the highest bid among them and the function *TopChallenger* returns the highest bidder:

$Highest : (\mathbb{N} \nrightarrow Biddable) \nrightarrow Biddable$

$TopChallenger : (\mathbb{N} \nrightarrow Biddable) \nrightarrow \mathbb{N}$

$\forall s : \mathbb{N} \nrightarrow Biddable;\ i \in Positions;\ n : Biddable\ |$

    $\#s > 1 \wedge \mathrm{dom}\, s \subseteq Positions \bullet$

        $Highest\{(i, n)\} = n$

        $Highest\ s = n,\ \text{if}\ n \in \mathrm{ran}\, s \wedge n > Highest(s \rhd \{n\})$

        $TopChallenger\{(i, n)\} = i$

        $TopChallenger\ s\ = i,\quad \text{if}\ (i, n) \in s \wedge n > Highest(s \rhd \{n\})$

$Beater : (\mathbb{N} \rightarrowtail Rank) \nrightarrow \mathbb{N}$

$\forall s : \mathbb{N} \rightarrowtail Rank, i \in Positions;\ r : Rank\ |$

    $\#s > 1 \wedge \mathrm{dom}\, s \subseteq Positions \bullet$

        $Beater\{(i, r)\} = i$

        $Beater\ s = i,\ \text{if}\ (i, r) \in s \wedge \forall t \in \mathrm{ran}\, s \mid r \neq t \bullet r\ Dominates\ t$

__ *Player* _____

$hand, winnings : \mathbb{P}\, Pack$

$\#hand \leqslant \#Pack\ \mathbf{div}\ (\#Positions)$

$hand \cap winnings = \varnothing$

__ *PlaceCard* _____

$\Delta Player$

$card? : Pack$

$status? : CardStatus$

$card? \in hand$

$hand \neq \varnothing$

$hand' = hand - \{card?\}$

$winnings' = winnings$

WonTheRound

$\Delta Player$

$cards? : \mathbb{P}\, Pack$

$\#cards? = \#Positions$

$cards? \cap (hand \cup winnings) = \varnothing$

$hand' = hand$

$winnings' = winnings \cup cards?$

CardTable

$players : \mathbb{N} \nrightarrow Player$

$cardsOnTable : \mathbb{F}(\mathbb{N} \times Pack \times CardStatus)$

$startingPosition, nextPlayer : \mathbb{N}$

$\mathrm{dom}\, players = Positions$

$\{startingPosition, nextPlayer\} \subseteq Positions$

$\{(p, q, r) \in cardsOnTable \bullet p\} \subseteq Positions$

$\forall\, q : Pack;\ r : CardStatus \bullet$

$\quad ((startingPosition, q, r) \in cardsOnTable \Rightarrow r = \mathsf{open})\ \wedge$

$\quad ((startingPosition, q, r) \notin cardsOnTable \Rightarrow cardsOnTable = \varnothing)$

$\forall\, p \in Positions;\ q_1, q_2 \in Pack;\ r_1, r_2 \in CardStatus \bullet$

$\quad \{(p, q_1, r_1), (p, q_2, r_2)\} \subseteq cardsOnTable \Rightarrow q_1 = q_2 \wedge r_1 = r_2$

$\exists\, lot : \mathbb{F}(\mathbb{F}\, Pack) \mid lot = \{p \in \mathrm{ran}\, players \bullet p.hand\}\ \cup$

$\quad \{p \in \mathrm{ran}\, players \bullet p.winnings\}\ \cup\ \{(p, q, r) \in cardsOnTable \bullet q\} \bullet$

$\qquad \bigcup lot = Pack \wedge lot \in MutuallyDisjoint$

---

where *MutuallyDisjoint* stands for the set of all mutually disjoint subsets of *Pack*.

$\_\_$ *Trump* $_____$

$trumpCard : Pack$

$trumpStatus$: concealed | disclosed

$holdersPosition : \mathbb{N}$

$holder : Player$

$bid : Biddable$

$_____$

$holdersPosition \in Positions$

$\_\_$ *TrumpConcealed* $_____$
CardTable

Trump

$_____$

$trumpStatus =$ concealed

$holder = players\ holdersPosition$

$trumpCard \in holder.hand \otimes$

$\quad (holdersPosition, trumpCard, \text{close}) \in cardsOnTable$

$\forall\, p \in Positions;\ q_1, q_2 : Pack;\ r_1, r_2 : CardStatus \mid$

$\quad p \neq startingPosition \bullet r_1 = \text{open} \wedge$

$\quad\quad \{(startingPosition, q_1, r_1), (p, q_2, r_2)\} \subseteq cardsOnTable \Rightarrow$

$\quad\quad (Symbol\ q_1 \neq Symbol\ q_2 \Leftrightarrow r_2 = \text{close})$

where $\otimes$ stands here for 'exclusive or'.

$\_\_$ *TrumpDisclosed* $_____$
CardTable

Trump

$_____$

$trumpStatus =$ disclosed

$holder = players\ holdersPosition$

$\{(p, q, r) \in cardsOnTable \bullet r\} \subseteq \{\text{open}\}$

$\boxed{\begin{array}{l} \underline{\;Declare\;} \\ \Delta\,CardTable \\ \Delta\,Trump \\ \hline TrumpConcealed \\ TrumpDisclosed' \\ trumpCard' = trumpCard \\ holdersPosition' = holdersPosition \\ holder' = holder \\ bid' = bid \\ startingPosition' = startingPosition \end{array}}$

$\boxed{\begin{array}{l} \underline{\;TrumpHoldersTurn\;} \\ \Delta\,CardTable \\ \Delta\,Trump \\ card? : Pack \\ \hline startingPosition = nextPlayer = holdersPosition \\ Symbol\ card? = Symbol\ trumpCard \Rightarrow card? = trumpCard \end{array}}$

$Disclose \;\widehat{=}\; TrumpHoldersTurn \wedge Declare$

$\boxed{\begin{array}{l} \underline{\;Deal\text{-}Aux\;} \\ CardTable' \\ dealer? : \mathbb{N} \\ inPack?, outPack : \text{seq } Pack \\ \hline \text{ran } inPack? = Pack \\ (inPack?, outPack) = \mu_{random}\ Shuffle \\ dealer? \in Positions \\ \forall (i, p) \in players' \bullet p.hand = (outPack \circ \\ \qquad \{(k, c) \in outPack \bullet (k \bmod (\#Positions), k)\} \circ \\ \qquad \{j \in Positions \bullet (dealer? \oplus_4 j, j)\})\,(\!|\ \{i\}\ |\!) \\ startingPosition' = nextPlayer' = dealer? \oplus_4 1 \end{array}}$

where $\circ$ denotes a composition operator such that: $R \circ S \mathrel{\widehat{=}} S \mathrel{\raise.5ex\hbox{$_\S$}} R$.

$Deal \mathrel{\widehat{=}} Deal\text{-}Aux \setminus outPack$

<hr>

Bid

$\Xi\, CardTable$

$bids! : \mathbb{N} \nrightarrow Biddable$

$\varnothing \subset \operatorname{dom} bids! \subseteq Positions$

<hr>

Settle Trump

$\Xi\, CardTable$

$Trump\,Concealed'$

$bids? : \mathbb{N} \nrightarrow Biddable$

$\varnothing \subset \operatorname{dom}\ bids? \subseteq Positions$

$trumpCard' \in holder.hand$

$holdersPosition' = TopChallenger\ bids?$

$bid' = Highest\ bids?$

<hr>

$BeginPlay \mathrel{\widehat{=}} Deal \mathrel{\raise.5ex\hbox{$_\S$}} Bid[bids'/bids!] \mathrel{\raise.5ex\hbox{$_\S$}} SettleTrump[bids/bids?]$

<hr>

PutCards-Aux

$\Delta\, CardTable$

$\Delta\, Trump$

$PlaceCard$

$\#cardsOnTable < \#players$

$\theta\,Player = players\ nextPlayer$

$players' = players \oplus \{(nextPlayer, \theta\,Player')\}$

$cardsOnTable' = cardsOnTable \cup \{(nextPlayer, card?, status?)\}$

$nextPlayer' = nextPlayer \oplus_4 1$

$startingPosition' = startingPosition$

$\Xi\, Trump \otimes Disclose$

<hr>

$PutCards \cong PutCards\text{-}Aux \setminus (Player, Player', card?, status?)$

_ResolveRoundWinner _____

$\Delta CardTable$

$\Delta Trump$

$winner : \mathbb{N}$

$trumpChallengers,$

$otherChallengers : \mathbb{N} \nrightarrow Rank$

$\#cardsOnTable = \#players$

$trumpChallengers = \{(i, r, s) \in cardsOnTable \wedge$

$\qquad Symbol\ r = Symbol\ trumpCard \bullet (i, Ranking\ r)\}$

$otherChallengers = \{\{(i, r, \mathsf{open}), (startingPosition, p, \mathsf{open})\} \subseteq$

$\qquad cardsOnTable \wedge Symbol\ r = Symbol\ p \bullet (i, Ranking\ r)\}$

$trumpChallengers \neq \varnothing \Rightarrow (winner = Beater\ trumpChallengers \wedge$

$\qquad TrumpConcealed \Rightarrow Declare \wedge players' = players \wedge$

$\qquad nextPlayer' = nextPlayer \wedge startingPosition' = startingPosition)$

$trumpChallengers = \varnothing \Rightarrow (winner = Beater\ otherChallengers \wedge$

$\qquad \Xi Trump \wedge players' = players \wedge$

$\qquad nextPlayer' = nextPlayer \wedge startingPosition' = startingPosition)$

_RoundFinish-Aux _____

$\Delta CardTable$

$\Delta Trump$

$ResolveRoundWinner$

$WonTheRound$

$cards? = \{(i, r, s) \in cardsOnTable \bullet r\}$

$\theta Player = players\ winner$

$players' = players \oplus \{(winner, \theta Player')\}$

$cardsOnTable' = \varnothing$

$startingPosition' = nextPlayer' = winner$

$RoundFinish \mathrel{\widehat{=}} RoundFinish\text{-}Aux \setminus (Player, Player', cards?, winner,$
$\qquad\qquad trumpChallengers, otherChallengers)$

$PlayTheRound \mathrel{\widehat{=}} (\mathbin{\substack{\circ\\\circ}}^{\#\,Positions} PutCards) \mathbin{\substack{\circ\\\circ}} RoundFinsh$

where we use $\mathbin{\substack{\circ\\\circ}}^{\#\,Positions}$ for 'iterative schema composition' as many times as the size of $Positions$.

$\underline{\quad EndOfGame \quad\rule{8cm}{0pt}}$

$CardTable$

$Trump$

$trumpPartners, challengers, winners! : \mathbb{F}\,\mathbb{N}$

$trumpPartnersScore, challengersScore, score! : Biddable$

$\rule{8cm}{0.4pt}$

$cardsOnTable = \varnothing$

$\forall\, player \in \operatorname{ran} players \bullet player.hand = \varnothing$

$trumpPartners = \{holdersPosition, holdersPosition \oplus_4 2\}$

$challengers = Positions - trumpPartners$

$trumpPartnersScore = Count(\bigcup\{x \in trumpPartners \land$
$\qquad player = players\ x \bullet player.winnings\})$

$challengersScore = (Count\ Pack) - trumpPartnersScore$

$trumpPartnersScore \geqslant bid \Rightarrow$
$\qquad winners! = trumpPartners \land$
$\qquad score! = trumpPartnersScore$

$trumpPartnersScore < bid \Rightarrow$
$\qquad winners! = challengers \land$
$\qquad score! = challengersScore$

$CheersToWinners! \mathrel{\widehat{=}} EndOfGame \upharpoonright (CardTable, Trump, winners!, score!)$

$CarryOnPlaying \mathrel{\widehat{=}} PlayTheRound \otimes CheersToWinners!$

$Game \mathrel{\widehat{=}} BeginPlay \mathbin{\substack{\circ\\\circ}} (\mathbin{\substack{\circ\\\circ}}\, CarryOnPlaying)$

where the composition operator ' $\mathbin{\substack{\circ\\\circ}}$ ' when applied in prefix form means its 'distributed application' of the operation on its right hand side until termination, i.e. until an operation with no 'after state' is reached.

A.3 Unix Filing System

Read the case study *Specification of the UNIX filing system* by Morgan [39] and answer the following questions. It also appears in Hayes [23] with certain improvements but for the purpose of this exercise, the case study in [39] is preferred.

1. Give an example of a '*FILE*' which is not less than ten characters long. Using this, and some non–trivial values for '*offset?*', '*length?*' and '*data?*' illustrate the following in detail mathematically:
   (i) How the value of '*data!*' may be determined in '*readFILE*'
   (ii) How the state of the file may be determined after writing '*data?*' into the file. Choose here '*offset?*' and '*data?*' so that the file length after the operation is greater than its length before.

2. Annotate each signature declaration and predicate in '*readSS*', explaining its significance and your understanding of the writer's intention.

3. The schemas '*readSS*' and '*writeSS*' require the knowledge of '*offset?*' for performing the relevant operation. This is inconvenient if one is scanning a file sequentially, and in this connection, the specification provides a facility for sequential access of data. Discuss this facility in detail, including how it is constructed and incorporated into read and write operations on files.

4. Assuming a suitable list of names and file identifiers required by '*NS*', and with the help of an example, illustrate the effect of the operation '*lsNS*'.

5. Sections 4.3.12–4.3.15 of [23] (pp. 73–74) describe the complete filing system and some selected operations on it, namely '*read*' and '*open*'. Likewise, define the operation '*write*' on the complete filing system. Also, give its expanded version, and explain (annotate) the significance of its declarations and predicates.

6. Comment on the successes and drawbacks of the given specification.

NOTE: In answering the above questions, use sets, relations, functions and sequences. In the case of sequences, it is important to use the relational representation of sequences and the graphical representation (graphs) of relations. Once represented in this form, sequences may be manipulated by the common relational operations such as composition, iteration etc. and graphs. For example, an answer to (1) given in the style of the examples in the source references is less beneficial to our exercise. Note that the relational representation of the sequence $\langle a, b, f, s \rangle$ is $\{(1, a), (2, b), (3, f), (4, s)\}$.

B. Exercises on Writing Formal Specifications

This appendix provides a number of problems for specification in Z. Since a specification is supposed to describe only 'what a system does', rather than 'how to realise it' in practice, the reader should be on guard not to be drawn into implementation issues. On the other hand, the specification must be 'sufficiently complete', so that both the user of the software and the implementor know exactly what functionality is intended.

B.1 A Catalogue Shop

Imagine a system for maintaining stock and a catalogue of goods in the environment of a shop.

1. Using suitable types, suggest an abstract (mathematical) data structure for keeping a track of stock, and another for maintaining a catalogue of goods and their prices.
2. Using the λ notation or named functions, define functions for:
   (i) Giving the number in stock of a particular item
   (ii) Giving the goods with a stock level below a given threshold number
   (iii) Updating the stock with a new item
   (iv) Disposing of the complete stock of a given collection of goods
   (v) Accepting new stock of a certain item if the total does not exceed a given threshold number
   (vi) Saying whether a given item is in stock or not
   (vii) Giving the price of a requested item
   (viii) Giving the total price of a collection (a set) of items if they are in the catalogue
   (ix) Giving the total value (based on price) of goods kept in stock
   (x) Giving the total value of goods kept in stock below a given threshold price
   (xi) Whether a given item is in stock and its price within a given price bracket
3. Based on your answer to question (1), write a schema for a 'Shop' giving just what you think is realistic and necessary for our purpose (note that we are not concerned with all aspects of running a shop). Explain the

intention behind every mathematical expression in your schema and list, in a broad sense, the situations allowed and disallowed by your schema.

4. Enhance your answer to question (3) in order to satisfy the following additional requirements:
   (i) The stock of each item should not to exceed a predefined number for each item.
   (ii) The total value of stock not to exceed a predefined amount.

5. Using the schema given in the answer to question (3), and any functions defined in (2), give:
   (i) The set of goods available in a shop
   (ii) The set of goods unavailable but catalogued in a shop
   (iii) A relation 'price tags', giving the prices and the required number of price tags for use in current stock
   (iv) A set of shops, a) which normally sell electrical goods (defined as a set) among the goods sold, and b) having in stock all electrical goods usually sold by them

6. Based on your definition of 'Shop', define the following operations as state transformations:
   (i) Updating the catalogue
       (This must cater for the addition of items non-existent in the catalogue, as well as price changes.)
   (ii) Updating stock to account for incoming stock with all items existing in current stock
   (iii) Updating stock for incoming stock outside the existing stock, (Envisage the possibility that the new stock is not covered by the current catalogue)
   (iv) Disposing of the complete stock of a given collection of goods
   (v) Partial disposal of stock of a given collection of goods
   (vi) Using the above, construct more general operations for stock–taking and disposal. Make sure that these operations are defined in a secure manner with helpful messages notifying the user of the success or failure of the operation.

B.2 Know Your Place if You Succeed in Politics!

Imagine a scenario where the legislative voting process at the Houses of Parliament in the United Kingdom is to be computerised. With such a scenario in mind, describe mathematically the organisation of the legislative and the executive aspects of the system of government.

Alternatively, attempt a specification of the organisational structure of the legislature of your country, or that of a third country such as the United States of America, and the relationship of the legislature with the executive.

Note the word 'organisation' and that what is required is just how various individuals may fit into this organisation. Below is a brief description of the system in the United Kingdom. In case of any inaccuracies, the reader may rely on his/her own understanding of the Parliament.

Informal Description

The U.K. Parliament consists of the monarch and two legislative chambers, the appointed House of Lords and the elected House of Commons, each with varying powers and responsibilities. The House of Lords consists of Lords temporal (hereditary lords, life peers, and those there by virtue of title such as dukes, viscounts and earls) and Lords spiritual (bishops and arch-bishops). The House of Commons is elected from eligible candidates by popular vote. The members of the Commons must be at least 21 years of age. Certain public and judicial figures are ineligible, such as members of the armed forces, police officers and top civil servants. The members of the two chambers usually represent political parties, but there can also be independent members. Take the executive branch as consisting of just the cabinet headed by the Prime Minister. The membership of these bodies is quite clearly defined. For example, nobody may belong to more than one party or to more than one legislative chamber. However, the cabinet is open to members of more than one party (e.g. in coalition governments) and to both legislative chambers. The premier is normally from the Commons and is the leader of the party in Government, but technically the post is open to both chambers and to the leaders of minority parties. The leader of the opposition is the leader of the largest party outside the government.

NOTE: The reader may notice that various bodies in this structure consist of groups of people, each headed by one person (e.g. leader of the party, the Speaker of the House, etc.). So one may first define the following:

$[\ Person\ ]$

$$
\begin{array}{|l}
\hline
\_\ Group _____ \\
\quad leader\ :\ Person \\
\quad members\ :\ \mathbb{F}\ Person \\
\hline
\quad members\ \neq\ \varnothing \\
\quad leader\ \in\ members \\
\hline
\end{array}
$$

and re-use it as effectively and as often as possible in defining other specific bodies (e.g. by renaming components and by combining two or more bodies in defining new ones).

B.3 Traffic Lights

Give a mathematical specification for a set of traffic lights considering the following requirements.

Informal Description

The set of lights is for a junction of four (two intersecting) roads. Assume that the lights obey the mode of operation and the road safety measures as practised in your country. The lights may incorporate an optional filter to the right, or the left, if it does not obstruct the main traffic flow. The specification may take into account the actual positioning of lights on the supporting frame (i.e. the red light being at the top etc.).

NOTE: As a simplification, the timing aspects may be ignored and the problem may be treated purely within a state transformation framework.

B.4 A Vending Machine

Specify mathematically a vending machine. What is given below are the minimal requirements, but the reader is free to add any other facilities as desired.

Informal Description

The use of the machine is free. It must be able to serve tea or coffee, with or without sugar. Such crazy things as mixing coffee and tea together, or dispensing sugar on its own must not be allowed. The supplies of the ingredients are finite, and when they run out the relevant options must be withdrawn, but with some notification to that effect. When the operator of the machine chooses to refill the supplies, he/she fills the supplies of all ingredients up to the maximum capacity. The deliveries of drinks are made using predefined fixed amounts of ingredients. After each delivery the machine reverts to a neutral state, which always requires the users to make a choice out of the options available, and confirm the choice (say, by the press of a button). Obviously, the deliveries of drinks must agree with the requested options.

B.5 A Bank

Develop a specification for a simple bank operating only two types of current accounts: individual accounts and joint accounts. The features may include those found in ordinary banks. The specification should preferably be based on the alternative mathematical definitions for *Account* and *Bank* considered in Chapter 2.

Informal Description

Some suggested features are as follows. Student accounts may earn interest. The rate of interest is fixed and the amount of interest paid is based on the lowest balance over the six month period just prior to the interest payment date but subject to this balance being above a certain strictly positive fixed threshold. The accounts are credited bi-annually with any accumulated interest. Students are not allowed credit.

Non-student account holders may operate joint accounts. They are not eligible for interest payments and pay interest on any credit obtained during the above six month period based on the maximum overdraft.

B.6 A Flight Reservation Service for an Airline

Starting afresh, or by extending the case study 'flight booking service' carried out in Chapter 3, specify a more general flight reservation facility for an airline.

Informal Description

The aspects related to the flight route remain the same as in Chapter 3. That is:

- The airline operates flights on a number of different routes. A flight is understood to be an unbroken non-circular journey between two airports, visiting the scheduled international airports on its route only once.

According to the new system specification, each flight is to incorporate additionally:

- A flight schedule,
  This must give arrival and departure times of the flight for all airports on its route. Your definition must consider, among other things, that travel times become progressively longer with the length of the journey.
- A passenger list.
  The passenger list must contain the usual travel information on passengers, namely, some form of passenger identification, and the origin and destination of journey.

The primary purpose of the system is to support the recording, retrieval and updating of both passenger and flight details. The aspects related to passenger travel should cover seat reservation, cancellation, and other travel details of individual passengers. Queries related to flight accommodation in general concern the seat availability on board of any flight.

The aspects relating to flight details must cover updates of the flight state with the progress of the flight, modifications to the flight route (e.g. addition/withdrawal of airports to/from the route) and retrieval of flight information. Queries about flights may cover the information on the flight schedule and the current state of the flight.

The reader is free to assume the relevant details as appropriate in the airline business. Also, if you disagree with the requirements indicated here, you may adopt alternative requirements if you state your reasons and assumptions.

NOTE: The reader may find it easier to introduce a type called '*Time*', without considering the detailed structure of time involving hours and minutes etc. Also, assume that '*Time*' is totally ordered (i.e. any two time values are comparable) by relations such as $\leq$ and $\geq$, and that the operations '+' and '-' on '*Time*' are given for the addition and subtraction of time.

In order to avoid the complexity of concurrent updates (of the flight reservation data base), the reader may assume that this has been somehow or other guaranteed not to occur in the given case.

B.7 A Hospital Register

Specify mathematically a software system for maintaining a hospital register of patients. Given below are some basic requirements, but the reader is free to consider additional functionality if desired.

Informal Description

The patients registered at the hospital may be either in–patients (i.e. those temporarily resident in hospital wards) or out–patients (i.e. those resident outside). Any patient may only reside in one ward. Some wards specialise in certain categories of patient care (e.g. maternity, pediatrics, infectious diseases, etc.), while others cater for more general purpose patient care. In–patients must be automatically transferred to the out–patients register when they are discharged from the wards. All out–patients must have a date for the next appointment. The system must allow its user(s) to admit new patients, discharge patients from wards and out–patient care, and query the system on dates of admission and the whereabouts of in–patients.

C. The Mathematical Notation

This is a summary of the mathematical notation appearing in the book. It is limited essentially to Z and the reader should consult Spivey [57] for a full definition of the Z notation.

General:

$x : X$ A typical type declaration (to be read as 'x has the type X')

$\widehat{=}$ and $\overset{def}{=}$ Syntactic equality of objects such as sets

$\overset{def}{\Leftrightarrow}$ Syntactic equivalence of propositions and predicates

On Logic:

$\neg$	Negation
$\wedge$	Conjunction
$\vee$	Disjunction
$\Rightarrow$	Material implication
$\Leftrightarrow$	Material equivalence
$\Rrightarrow$	Logical implication
$\Lleftrightarrow$,	Logical equivalence
$\bullet$	Delimiter between declarations and an associated predicate (see below)
$\mid$	Delimiter between declarations and a constraint (see below)
$\forall$	Universal quantifier.

$$\forall\, x : X \mid p(x) \bullet q(x) \overset{def}{\Leftrightarrow} \forall\, x : X \bullet p(x) \Rightarrow q(x)$$

$\exists$ Existential quantifier

$$\exists\, x : X \mid p(x) \bullet q(x) \overset{def}{\Leftrightarrow} \exists\, x : X \bullet p(x) \wedge q(x)$$

$\exists_1\, x \bullet \cdots$ Existential quantifier quantifying a unique occurrence of x.

On Sets:

$\{..\}$ Set definition

Applicable to set comprehension as shown below:
$$\{x : X \mid p(x) \bullet t(x)\}$$
          – the set of elements as defined by term $t(x)$ with x of type X satisfying the predicate $p(x)$

$\{a, b, ..\}$	Set enumeration
$\varnothing$	Empty set
$\#S$	Cardinality (size) of set S
$\cup$	Set union
$\cap$	Set intersection
$-$	Set difference ($S - T$ - the difference between the set S and the set T)
S'	Complement of the set S (i.e. set difference between the universal set and the set S)
$\times$	Cartesian product
$\mathbb{P}$	Power set (set of all subsets of its operand set; e.g. $\mathbb{P}\,S$ for the power set of the set S)
$\mathbb{F}$	Set of finite subsets of its operand set (e.g. $\mathbb{F}\,S$)
μ	Choice operator for choosing an element arbitrarily from a set

On Numbers:

$\mathbb{N}$	Set of natural numbers including zero
$\mathbb{N}_1$	Set of natural numbers excluding zero
$m \mathrel{..} n$	Set of natural numbers from m to n inclusively
$\mathbb{Z}$	Set of integers
$\mathbb{R}$	Set of real numbers
$\mathbb{Q}$	Set of rational numbers
$\mathbb{C}$	Set of complex numbers
div, mod	Operators of modular arithmetic

On Relations:

$\leftrightarrow$	Relational type (in type declarations)
dom	Domain of a relation
ran	Range of a relation
id	Identity relation
$(\!| \ |\!)$	Relational image ($R(\!|\ S\ |\!)$ - the image of the relation R thorough the set S)
$\circ$	Relational (function) composition (the standard mathematical notation)
$\overset{\circ}{\underset{9}{}}$	Forward relational (function) composition (an alternative for the above in Z) (Note that $R \mathbin{\overset{\circ}{\underset{9}{}}} S \mathbin{\widehat{=}} S \circ R$)
$\lhd$	Restriction of the domain of a relation (the right operand) to a set (the left operand)
$\rhd$	Restriction of the range of a relation (the left operand) to a set (the right operand)
$\mathbin{\lhd\!\!\!-}$	Co-restriction of the domain of a relation (the right operand) to a set (the left operand); also known as domain subtraction

$\rhd$	Co-restriction of the range of a relation (the left operand) to a set the right operand); also known as range subtraction
$S^{\sim}$ and S^{-1}	Inverse of the relation S
$\oplus$	Relational overriding, $(S \oplus R \overset{def}{=} (\mathrm{dom}\,R \lhd S) \cup R)$
/	Quotient operator (A/R - the quotient of A induced by R and R being a relation on A)
R^n	n-th Iteration of relation R defined on a set
R^*	Reflexive transitive closure of relation R
R^+	Irreflexive transitive closure of relation R

On Functions:

$f(x)$, $f\,x$	Function application (of the function f to argument x).
$\rightarrow$	Total functions (in type declarations)
$\nrightarrow$	Partial functions (in type declarations)
$\rightarrowtail\!\!\!\!\!\rightarrow$	Partial injective (one-to-one) functions (in type declarations)
$\rightarrowtail$	Total injective (one-to-one) functions (in type declarations)
$\twoheadrightarrow\!\!\!\!\!\!$	Partial surjective (onto) functions (in type declarations)
$\twoheadrightarrow$	Total surjective (onto) functions (in type declarations)
λ	Prefix indicating anonymous functions (Lambda function notation)

On Sequences: Given that s and t are sequences,

seq	Sequences (in type declarations)
$\langle a,\ b,\ \cdots \rangle$	shows a sequence containing the elements a, b, etc.
$s(i)$	i-th element of sequence s (since sequences are mathematical functions)
head	Function returning the first element (head) of a given sequence
tail	Function returning the tail end of a sequence (without its first element)
last	Function returning the last element of a given sequence
front	Function returning the front end of a sequence (without its last element)
$s^\frown t$	Concatenation of the sequences s and t.
$\restriction$	Filtering ($U \restriction s$ denotes the sequence obtained by retaining the elements occurring in s and given in the set U but in the order they appear in s.)
squash	Function compacting any mapping f from $\mathbb{N}_1$ to an arbitrary type X into a sequence s of elements of X such that: (1) for each pair in f there is an exactly one corresponding pair in s and vice versa, and (2) the indices of the corresponding pairs in f and s are in the same relative order.

$\#s$	Length of the sequence s (since sequences are also sets)
in	Subsequence relation (s in t if, and only if, s is a contiguous subsequence anywhere in t. Given that s is singleton sequence of the form $s = \langle a \rangle$, we may write a in t instead of $\langle a \rangle$ in t.)
ran s	The elements in the sequence s as a set (since sequences are also relations)

On Bags

bag	Bags (in type declarations)
$[\![\ ]\!]$	Definition of elements in a bag
$[\![\ a, b, c, ..]\!]$	Enumeration of elements a, b, .. etc in a bag
$count$	Function returning multiplicity of an element in a bag (e.g. '$count$ a x' denoting the number of occurrences of the element a in the bag x)
$\sharp$	Bag multiplicity; $b\sharp x = count\ b\ x$
$\in$	Bag membership; $x\in b$ holds if, and only if, the element x is in bag b
$\uplus$	Bag union
$\uminus$	Bag difference
$\sqsubseteq$	Sub-bag Relation; $b \sqsubseteq c$ holds if, and only if, bag b is a sub-bag of bag c

References

1. Schumann & pitt approach. In S. Stepney and D. Barden, R. Cooper, editors, *Object Orientation in Z*. Springer-Verlag, 1992.
2. A. J. Alencar and J. A. Goguen. OOZE. In S. Stepney and D. Barden, R. Cooper, editors, *Object Orientation in Z*. Springer-Verlag, 1992.
3. J. F. Allen. Towards a general theory of action and time. *Artificial Intelligence*, 23, 1984.
4. D. Andrews and D. Ince. *Practical Formal Methods with VDM*. McGraw-Hill, 1991.
5. G. Barthelot and R. Terrat. Petri nets theory for correctness of protocols. *IEEE Trans. on Communications*, 30(12), December 1982.
6. A. T. Bertizz and S. Thatte. Specification and implementation of data types. *Advances in Computers*, 22, 1983.
7. R. Bird. *Introduction to Functional Programming using Haskell*. Prentice Hall Europe, 1998.
8. G. Birkhoff and J. D. Lipson. Heterogeneous algebras. *Journal of Combinatorial Theory*, 8:115–133, 1970.
9. G. V. Bochmann. A general transition model for protocols and communication services. *IEEE Trans. on Communications*, 28(4), April 1980.
10. G. V. Bochmann, E. Cerny, M. Gagne, C. Jard, A. Leville, et al. Experience with formal specifications using an extended state transition model. *IEEE Trans. on Communications*, 30(12), December 1982.
11. G. V. Bochmann and C. A. Sunshine. Formal methods in communication protocol design. *IEEE Trans. on Communications*, 28(4), April 1980.
12. R. M. Burstall and J. A. Goguen. An informal introduction to specifications using CLEAR. In R. S. Boyer and J. S. Moore, editors, *The Correctness Problem in Computer Science*. Academic Press, 1981.
13. G. F. Coulouris and J. Dollimore. *Distributed Systems*. Addison-Wesley, 1994.
14. A. S. Danthine. Protocol representation with finite–state models. *IEEE Trans. on Communications*, 28(4), April 1980.
15. J.A. Goguen. Parametrized programming. *IEEE Trans. on Software Engineering*, 10(5), September 1984.
16. J.A. Goguen, J. W. Thatcher, and E. G. Wagner. An initial algebra approach to the specification, correctness and implementation of data types. In R. T. Yeh, editor, *Data Structuring*, volume IV of *Current Trends in Programming Methodology*. Prentice-Hall, 1977.
17. A. Goldberg and D. Robson. *Smalltalk–80, The Language*. Addison–Wesley, 1989.
18. D. Gries. *The Science of Programming*. Springer-Verlag, 1983.
19. V. Griffiths. State based refinement of concurrent processes (M.Sc. dissertation). Technical report, Programming Research Group, Oxford University Computing Laboratory, 1988.

20. J. Guttag. Notes on type abstraction. In N. Gehani et al., editors, *Software Specification Techniques*. Addison-Wesley, 1986.
21. J. V. Guttag and J. J. Horning. The algebraic specification of data types. *Acta Informatica*, 10:27–52, 1978.
22. F. Halsall. *Data Communications, Computer Networks and OSI*. Addison-Wesley.
23. I. Hayes. *Specification Case Studies*. Prentice Hall, 1993.
24. C. A. R. Hoare. *Communicating Sequential Processes*. Prentice Hall, 1985.
25. I. Van Horebeek and J. Lewi. *Algebraic Specifications in Software Engineering*. Springer-Verlag, 1989.
26. He Jifeng. Process refinement. In J. McDermid, editor, *The Theory and Practice of Refinement*. Butterworths, 1989.
27. C.B. Jones. *Systematic Software Development Using VDM*. Prentice Hall, 1986.
28. C.B. Jones and R. C. Shaw. *Case Studies in Systematic Software Development*. Prentice Hall, 1990.
29. P. W. King. Formalisation of protocol engineering concepts. *IEEE Trans. on Computers*, 40(4), April 1991.
30. K. Lano and H. Haughton. A comparative description of object-oriented specification languages. In K. Lano and H. Haughton, editors, *Object-Oriented Specification Case Studies*. Prentice Hall, 1993.
31. K. Lano and H. Haughton. Object-oriented specification languages in the software life cycle. In K. Lano and H. Haughton, editors, *Object-Oriented Specification Case Studies*. Prentice Hall, 1993.
32. K. C. Lano. Z^{++}. In S. Stepney and D. Barden, R. Cooper, editors, *Object Orientation in Z*. Springer-Verlag, 1992.
33. B. Liskov and S. Zilles. An introduction to formal specifications of data abstractions. In R. T. Yeh, editor, *Software Specification and Design*, volume I of *Current Trends in Programming Methodology*. Prentice-Hall, 1977.
34. J. Loeckx, H-D. Ehrich, and M.. Wolf. *Specification of Abstract Data Types*. Wiley-Teubner, 1996.
35. J. J. Martin. *Data Types and Data Structures*. Prentice Hall, 1986.
36. J. Meseguer and J.A. Goguen. Initiality, induction, and computability. In J. C. Reynolds, editor, *Algebraic Methods in Semantics*. Cambridge University Press, 1985.
37. B. Meyer. *Object–oriented Software Construction*. Prentice Hall, 1988.
38. R. Milner. *Communications and Concurrency*. Prentice Hall, 1989.
39. C. Morgan. Specification of the UNIX filing system. *IEEE Trans. on Software Engineering*, 10(2), 1984.
40. C. Morgan. *Programming from Specifications*. Prentice Hall, 1994.
41. N Nissanke. *Realtime Systems*. Prentice Hall Series in Computer Science by Tony Hoare and Richard Bird. Prentice Hall, 1997.
42. N. Nissanke. Safety specification in deontic logic. In *Proceedings*, 2nd IMA Conference on the Mathematics of Dependable Systems, York, England, pages 113–133. Oxford University Press, 1997.
43. N Nissanke. *Introductory Logic and Sets for Computer Scientists*. Addison Wesley Longman, 1999.
44. N. Nissanke and N. Robinson. Formal methods in safety analysis. In V. Maggioli, editor, *SAFECOMP'94*, International Conference on Computer Safety, Reliability and Security, pages 239–248, Anaheim, California, 1994. Instrument Society of America.
45. B. Potter, J. Sinclair, and D. Till. *An Introduction to Formal Specification and Z*. Prentice Hall, 1996.

46. G. Rose. Object–Z. In S. Stepney and D. Barden, R. Cooper, editors, *Object Orientation in Z*. Springer-Verlag, 1992.
47. G. Rose and R. Duke. An object–Z specification of a mobile phone system. In K. Lano and H. Haughton, editors, *Object-Oriented Specification Case Studies*. Prentice Hall, 1993.
48. K. Sabnani. An algorithmic technique for protocol verification. *IEEE Trans. on Communications*, 36(8), August 1988.
49. D. Sannella and A. Tarlecki. Some thoughts on algebraic specification. Technical Report ECS–LFCS–8–21, University of Edinburgh, 1986.
50. D. T. Sannella. A set theoretic semantics of clear. *Acta Informatica*, 21:443–472, 1984.
51. S. A. Schumann and D. H. Pitt. Object–oriented subsystem specification. In L. G. L. T. Meertens, editor, *Program Specification and Transformation*. Elsevier Science Publishers B. V. (North-Holland), 1987.
52. S. A. Schumann, D. H. Pitt, and Byers P. J. Object–oriented process specification. 1988.
53. R. L. Schwartz and P. Melliar-Smith. From finite machines to temporal logic: Specification methods for protocol standards. *IEEE Trans. on Communications*, 30(12), December 1982.
54. R. Sharp. Principles of protocol design. Technical Report ID-U: 87-20, ISSN 0902-283x, Department of Computer Science, Technical University of Denmark, 1988.
55. R. Sisto, L. Ciminiera, and A. Valenzano. Protocol for multirendezvous of LOTOS processes. *IEEE Trans. on Computers*, 40(4), April 1991.
56. J.M. Spivey. *Understanding Z*. Cambridge University Press, 1988.
57. M. Spivey. *The Z Notation*. Prentice Hall, 1992.
58. B. Sufrin. Formal specification of a display–oriented text editor. *Science of Computer Programming*, (1):157–202, 1982.
59. A. S. Tanenbaum. *Computer Networks*. Prentice-Hall, 1996.
60. K. Tarnay. *Protocol Specification and Testing*. Plenum Press, 1991.
61. S. Thompson. *Miranda – The Craft of Functional Programming*. Addison-Wesley, 1995.
62. K. Turner. *Using Formal Description Techniques*. Wiley, 1993.
63. S. Veloudis and N. Nissanke. Duration calculus in the specification of safety requirements. In *Formal Techniques in Real–Time and Fault–Tolerant Systems*, LNCS 1486, pages 103–112. Springer–Verlag, September 1998.
64. R. Welhelm. *The Pocket I Ching – The Richard Welhelm Translation*. Arkana, London, 1984.
65. R. Wilensky. *Common LISPcraft*. W. W. Norton and Company, 1986.
66. J. Woodcock and J. Davies. *Using Z – Specification, Refinement and Proof*. Prentice Hall, 1996.
67. J. C. P. Woodcock and C. Morgan. Refinement of state based concurrent systems. Technical report, Programming Research Group, Oxford University Computing Laboratory, 1989.
68. S. Zilles. An introduction to data algebras. In D. Bjorner, editor, *Abstract Software Specification*, volume 86 of *LNCS*. Springer-Verlag, 1980.

Index